GRAMMAR FOR LANGUAGE LEARNING

ELEMENTS
of SUCCESS

ANNE M. EDIGER

LINDA LEE

2A

OXFORD
UNIVERSITY PRESS

SHAPING learning TOGETHER

We would like to thank the following classes for piloting *Elements of Success*:

University of Delaware English Language Institute
Teacher: Kathleen Vodvarka
Students: Ahmad Alenzi, Bandar Manei Algahmdi, Fadi Mohammed Alhazmi, Abdel Rahman Atallah, Anna Kuzmina, Muhanna Sayer Aljuaid, Coulibaly Sita

ABC Adult School, Cerritos, CA
Teacher: Jenni Santamaria
Students: Gabriela A. Marquez Aguilar, Yijung Chen, Laura Gomez, Terry Hahn, EunKyung Lee, Subin Lee, Sunmin Lee, Jane Leelachat, Lilia Nunezuribe, Gina Olivar, Young Park, Seol Hee Seok, Kwang Mi Song

During the development of *Elements of Success*, we spoke with teachers and professionals who are passionate about teaching grammar. Their feedback led us to create *Elements of Success: Grammar for Language Learning*, a course that solves teaching challenges by presenting grammar clearly, simply, and completely. We would like to acknowledge the advice of teachers from

**USA • BRAZIL • CANADA • COSTA RICA • GUATEMALA • IRAN • JAPAN • MEXICO • OMAN • RUSSIA
SAUDI ARABIA • SOUTH KOREA • TUNISIA • TURKEY • UKRAINE • THE UNITED ARAB EMIRATES**

Mehmet Abi, Mentese Anatolian High School, Turkey; **Anna-Marie Aldaz**, Doña Ana Community College, NM; **Diana Allen**, Oakton Community College, IL; **Marjorie Allen**, Harper College, IL; **Mark Alves**, Montgomery College, Rockville, MD; **Kelly Arce**, College of Lake County, IL; **Irma Arencibia**, Union City Adult Learning Center, NJ; **Arlys Arnold**, University of Minnesota, MN; **Marcia Arthur**, Renton Technical College, WA; **Alexander Astor**, Hostos Community College, NY; **Chris Atkins**, CHICLE Language Institute, NC; **Karin Avila-John**, University of Dayton, OH; **Ümmet Aydan**, Karabuk University, Iran; **Fabiana Azurmendi**; **John Baker**, Wayne State University, MI; **Sepehr Bamdadnia**; **Terry Barakat**, Missouri State University, MO; **Marie Bareille**, Borough of Manhattan Community College, NY; **Eileen Barlow**, SUNY Albany, NY; **Denise Barnes**, Madison English as a Second Language School, WI; **Kitty Barrera**, University of Houston, TX; **Denise Barsotti**, EID Training Solutions, FL; **Maria Bauer**, El Camino College; **Christine Bauer-Ramazani**, Saint Michael's College, VT; **Jamie Beaton**, Boston University, MA; **Gena Bennett**, Cornerstone University, NE; **Linda Berendsen**, Oakton Community College, IL; **Carol Berteotti**; **Grace Bishop**, Houston Community College, TX; **Perrin Blackman**, University of Kansas, KS; **Mara Blake-Ward**, Drexel University English Language Center, PA; **Melissa Bloom**, ELS; **Alexander Bochkov**, ELS, WA; **Marcel Bolintiam**, University of Colorado, CO; **Nancy Boyer**, Golden West College, CA; **T. Bredl**, The New School, NY; **Rosemarie Brefeld**, University of Missouri, MO; **Leticia Brereton**, Kingsborough Community College, NY; **Deborah Brooks**, Laney College, CA; **Kevin Brown**, Irvine Community College, CA; **Rachel Brown**, Center for Literacy, NY; **Tracey Brown**, Parkland College, IL; **Crystal Brunelli**, Tokyo Jogakkan Middle and High School, Japan; **Tom Burger**, Harris County Department of Education, TX; **Thom Burns**, Tokyo English Specialists College, Japan; **Caralyn Bushey**, Maryland English Institute, MD; **Gül Büyü**, Ankara University, Turkey; **Scott Callaway**, Community Family Centers, TX; **Adele Camus**, George Mason University, VA; **Nigel Caplan**, University of Delaware, DE; **Nathan Carr**, California State University, CA; **Christina Cavage**, Savannah College of Art and Design,

GA; **Neslihan Çelik**, Özdemir Sabancı Emirgan Anatolian High School, Turkey; **Shelley Cetin**, Kansas City Kansas Community College, KS; **Hoi Yuen Chan**, University of Wyoming, WY; **Esther Chase**, Berwyn Public Library, IL; **Suzidilara Çınar**, Yıldırım Beyazıt University, Turkey; **Diane Cirino**, SUNY Suffolk, NY; **Cara Codney**, Emporia State University, KS; **Catherine Coleman**, Irvine Valley College, CA; **Jenelle Collins**, Washington High School, AZ; **Greg Conner**, Orange Coast Community College, CA; **Ewelina Cope**, The Language Company, PA; **Jorge Cordon**, Colegio Montessori, Guatemala; **Kathy Cornman**, University of Michigan, MI; **Barry Costa**, Castro Valley Adult and Career Education, CA; **Cathy Costa**, Edmonds Community College, WA; **Julia Cote**, Houston Community College NE, TX; **Eileen Cotter**, Montgomery College, MD; **Winnie Cragg**, Mukogawa Fort Wright Institute, WA; **Douglas Craig**, Diplomatic Language Services, VA; **Elizabeth Craig**, Savannah College of Art and Design, GA; **Ann Telfair Cramer**, Florida State College at Jacksonville, FL; **R. M. Crocker**, Plano Independent School District, TX; **Virginia Cu**, Queens Adult Learning Center, CT; **Marc L. Cummings**, Jefferson Community and Technical College, KY; **Roberta Cummings**, Trinidad Correctional Facility, CO; **David Dahnke**, Lone Star College-North Harris, TX; **Debra Daise**, University of Denver, CO; **L. Dalgish**, Concordia College, NY; **Kristen Danek**, North Carolina State University, NC; **April Darnell**, University of Dayton, OH; **Heather Davis**, OISE Boston, MA; **Megan Davis**, Embassy English, NY; **Jeanne de Simon**, University of West Florida, FL; **Renee Delatizky**, Boston University, MA; **Sonia Delgadillo**, Sierra Community College, NY; **Gözde Burcu Demirkul**, Orkunoglu College, Turkey; **Stella L. Dennis**, Longfellow Middle School, NY; **Mary Diamond**, Auburn University, AL; **Emily Dibala**, Bucks County Community College, PA; **Cynthia Dieckmann**, West Chester East High School, PA; **Michelle DiGiorno**, Richland College, TX; **Luciana Diniz**, Portland Community College, OR; **Özgür Dirik**, Yıldız Technical University, Turkey; **Marta O. Dmytrenko-Arab**, Wayne State University, MI; **Margie Domingo**, Intergenerational Learning Community, CO; **Kellie Draheim**, Hongik University, South Korea; **Ilke Buyuk Duman**, Sehir University, Turkey; **Jennifer Eick-Magan**, Prairie State College, IL;

Juliet Emanuel, Borough of Manhattan Community College, NY; **David Emery**, Kaplan International Center, CA; **Patricia Emery**, Jefferson County Literacy Council, WI; **Eva Engelhard**, Kaplan International Center, WA; **Nancey Epperson**, Harry S. Truman College, IL; **Ken Estep**, Mentor Language Institute, CA; **Cindy Etter**, University of Washington, WA; **Rhoda Fagerland**, St. Cloud State University, MN; **Anrisa Fannin**, Diablo Valley College, CA; **Marie Farnsworth**, Union Public Schools, OK; **Jim Fenton**, Bluegrass Community Technical College, KY; **Lynn Filazzola**, Nassau BOCES Adult Learning Center, NY; **Christine Finck**, Stennis Language Lab; **Mary Fischer**, Texas Intensive English Program, TX; **Mark Fisher**, Lone Star College, TX; **Celeste Flowers**, University of Central Arkansas, AR; **Elizabeth Foss**, Washtenaw Community College, MI; **Jacqueline Fredericks**, West Contra Costa Adult Education, CA; **Patricia Gairaud**, San Jose City College, CA; **Patricia Gallo**, Delaware Technical Community College, DE; **Beverly Gandall**, Coastline Community College, CA; **Alberto Garrido**, The Community College of Baltimore County, MD; **Debbie Garza**, Park University, MO; **Karen Gelender**, Castro Valley Adult and Career Education, CA; **Ronald Gentry**, Suenos Compartidos, Mexico; **Kathie Madden Gerecke**, North Shore Community College, MA; **Jeanne Gibson**, Colorado State University, CO; **A. Elizabeth Gilfillan**, Houston Community College, TX; **Melanie Gobert**, The Higher Colleges of Technology, UAE; **Ellen Goldman**, West Valley College, CA; **Jo Golub**, Houston Community College, TX; **Maria Renata Gonzalez**, Colegio Montessori, Guatemala; **Elisabeth Goodwin**, Pima Community College, AZ; **John Graney**, Santa Fe College, FL; **Karina Greene**, CUNY in the Heights, NY; **Katherine Gregorio**, CASA de Maryland, MD; **Claudia Gronsbell**, La Escuelita, NY; **Yvonne Groseil**, Hunter College, NY; **Alejandra Gutierrez**, Hartnell College, CA; **Eugene Guza**, North Orange County Community College District, CA; **Mary Beth Haan**, El Paso Community College, TX; **Elizabeth Haga**, State College of Florida, FL; **Saeede Haghi**, Ozyegin University, Turkey; **Laura Halvorson**, Lorain County Community College, OH; **Nancy Hamadou**, Pima Community College, AZ; **Kerri Hamberg**, Brookline Community and Adult Education, MA;

ii

Contents

3 | Nouns and Articles

4 | Pronouns and Determiners

5 | Future Forms

6 | Modals

7 | Gerunds and _To-_ Infinitives

GO ONLINE For the Class Audio tracks and scripts, go to the Online Practice.

OXFORD
UNIVERSITY PRESS

198 Madison Avenue
New York, NY 10016 USA

Great Clarendon Street, Oxford, OX2 6DP, United Kingdom

Oxford University Press is a department of the University of Oxford.
It furthers the University's objective of excellence in research, scholarship,
and education by publishing worldwide. Oxford is a registered trade
mark of Oxford University Press in the UK and in certain other countries.

© Oxford University Press 2014

The moral rights of the author have been asserted.

First published in 2014
2018 2017 2016 2015 2014
10 9 8 7 6 5 4 3 2 1

Director, ELT New York: Laura Pearson
Head of Adult, ELT New York: Stephanie Karras
Publisher: Sharon Sargent
Senior Development Editor: Andrew Gitzy
Senior Development Editor: Rebecca Mostov
Development Editor: Eric Zuarino
Executive Art and Design Manager: Maj-Britt Hagsted
Content Production Manager: Julie Armstrong
Image Manager: Trisha Masterson
Image Editor: Liaht Pashayan
Production Artists: Elissa Santos, Julie Sussman-Perez
Production Coordinator: Brad Tucker

Special thanks to Electra Jablons and Rima Ibrahim for assistance with
language data research.

ISBN: 978 0 19 402824 0 Student Book 2A with Online Practice Pack
ISBN: 978 0 19 402843 1 Student Book 2A as pack component
ISBN: 978 0 19 402879 0 Online Practice website

Printed in China

This book is printed on paper from certified and well-managed sources.

ACKNOWLEDGEMENTS
*Although every effort has been made to trace and contact copyright holders before publication,
this has not been possible in some cases. We apologize for any apparent infringement of
copyright and if notified, the publisher will be pleased to rectify any errors or omissions at the
earliest opportunity.*

*The authors and publisher are grateful to those who have given permission to reproduce the
following extracts and adaptations of copyright material:* p. 31 definitions reproduced
by permission of Oxford University Press from *Oxford Basic American Dictionary*
© Oxford University Press 2011; p. 35 "Advice on Writing from the Poet Gwendolyn
Brooks" from "Gwendolyn Brooks," as appeared in *The Place My Words Are Looking For:
What Poets Say About and Through Their Work* by Paul B. Janeczko. Reprinted by Consent
of Brooks Permissions; p. 38 reprinted with the permission of Simon & Schuster
Publishing Group from *The Book of Answers* by Barbara Berliner with Melinda Corey
and George Ochoa. Copyright © 1990 by The New York Public Library and The
Stonesong Press, Inc. All rights reserved; p. 59 "How to Make an Origami Whale,"
The World Almanac for Kids, 2000, Elaine Israel, editor. Copyright © 1999 by PRIMEDIA
Reference Inc. Reprinted by permission of Infobase Publishing; p. 64 reproduced
by permission of Oxford University Press from *IE Transitions Student Book Level 2* by
Linda Lee © Oxford University Press 1999; p. 311 and p. 333 definitions reproduced
by permission of Oxford University Press from *Oxford Basic American Dictionary*
© Oxford University Press 2011.

Illustrations by: 5W Infographics: p. 55, 66, 74, 177, 221, 252, 256, 285. Mark Duffin:
p. 312 (top, 4 cars), 313. Dermot Flynn/Dutch Uncle: p. 73, 113, 335, 336, 469.
Jerome Mireault: p. 208. Kevin Rechin/Mendola: p. 116. Tablet Infographics: p. 22,
90, 114, 158. Joe Taylor/Mendola: p. 136, 226, 301, 353, 370, 415, 419, 467.

We would also like to thank the following for permission to reproduce the following photographs:
Cover: blinkblink/shutterstock; back cover: lvcandy/Getty Images; global: Rodin
Anton/shutterstock; p. 2 Giorgio Fochesato/istockphoto; p. 5 OUP/pdesign, OUP/
Graphi-Ogre; p. 6 Newton Daly/Getty Images, Simon Jarratt/Corbis, Gene Chutka/
istockphoto, Blend Images/SuperStock, Andres Rodriguez/Alamy, Image Source/
Alamy, Clerkenwell/Getty Images; p. 8 Paul Simcock/Blend Images/Corbis; p. 19
Brasil2/istockphoto, Bettmann/Corbis; p. 22 Blend Images/Alamy; p. 32 AP Photo/
Phil Klein, Dave M. Benett/Getty Images, Walter McBride/Corbis; p. 35 AP Photo/

p. 39 Archer Street/Delux/Lion's Gate/Pathe/The Kobal Collection/BUITENDIJK, JAAP,
Tiger Moth/Miramax/The Kobal Collection; p. 42 Blend_Images/istockphoto;
p. 44 Visions of America/SuperStock; p. 46 Reuters/Corbis; p. 51 Gabriel Bouys/
AFP/Getty Images; p. 57 The Francis Frith Collection/Corbis, Caro/Alamy; p. 61
Prisma Archivo/Alamy; p. 62 Lordprice Collection/Alamy; p. 63 Grant Dixon/
Hedgehog House/Minden Pictures/Corbis; p. 64 Hulton Archive/Getty Images;
p. 66 kreego/shutterstock; p. 72 RW Photographic/Masterfile, Lei Wang; p. 76
Angela Waye/shutterstock; p. 78 Jiri Hera/Alamy, Hans Laubel/istockphoto,
Bombaert Patrick/shutterstock, Karl Weatherly/Corbis, Hanka Steidle/shutterstock,
Worldgraphics/shutterstock; p. 79 Clint Hughes/Getty Images; p. 84 Atlaspix/
shutterstock, Pedro Ladeira/AFP/Getty Images; p. 96 ClassicStock/Masterfile; p. 105
Lauri Patterson/istockphoto; p. 118 Actionplus/AGE fotostock; p. 121 PhotoAlto/
Alamy, jump fotoagentur Susanne Treubel/Alamy; p. 127 OUP/Fuse; p. 139 OUP/
Photodisc, valzan/shutterstock; p. 143 Rich Wheater/All Canada Photos/SuperStock;
p. 156 Donato Sardella/WireImage/Getty Images; p. 157 Jurgen Frank/Corbis; p. 160
Paul Raftery/VIEW/Corbis; p. 164 Troy Wayrynen/NewSport/Corbis, Shannon Fagan/
Getty Images, David H. Lewis/istockphoto, Henrik Sorensen/Getty Images, Masterfile,
MM Productions/Corbis; p. 168 Jerry Dohnal/Getty Images; p. 170 Bettmann/Corbis,
Javier Pierini/Getty Images; p. 172 John Lund/Getty Images; p. 178 Aspen Photo/
Shutterstock.com; p. 184 Christopher Futcher/istockphoto; p. 188 KidStock/Blend
Images/Corbis; p. 191 BlueLela/shutterstock; p. 192 Cultura RM/Masterfile; p. 195
Phil Schermeister/Corbis; p. 198 Massimo Merlini/Getty Images; p. 200 Lucenet
Patrice/Oredia Eurl/SuperStock; p. 201 Mika/Corbis; p. 202 svetikd/Getty Images;
p. 206 Steve Debenport/Getty Images; p. 207 Kevin P. Casey/WireImage/Getty Images;
p. 212 Monalyn Gracia/Corbis; p. 216 ClarkandCompany/istockphoto, ThinkDeep/
istockphoto; p. 217 Kelvin Murray/Getty Images; p. 219 Russell Shively/shutterstock;
p. 223 Westend61/Getty Images; p. 226 AP Photo/NASA, Radharc Images/Alamy; p. 228
Ann Cutting/Getty Images; p. 231 Neustockimages/istockphoto; p. 232 Gelpi JM/
Shutterstock; p. 237 luciaserra/Shutterstock; p. 239 Jose Luis Pelaez, Inc./Blend
Images/Corbis; p. 240 Jerzyworks/Masterfile; p. 242 frytka/istockphoto; p. 243 Blaz
Kure/Shutterstock, Jochen Tack/imagebrok/AGE fotostock; p. 245 Aurora Photos/
Masterfile; p. 247 JGI/Getty Images, Klaus Tiedge/Getty Images, PhotosIndia/AGE
fotostock; p. 248 imagebroker.net/SuperStock, Stan Honda/AFP/Getty Images; p. 250
Panoramic Images/Getty Images; p. 253 STOCK4B-RF/Getty Images, Sollina Images/
Blend Images/Corbis; p. 254 MBI/Alamy, Blend Images/Alamy; p. 260 Eric Isselée/
istockphoto; p. 262 Gabe Palmer/Corbis; p. 264 PCN Photography/Alamy; p. 265
Jewel Samad/AFP/Getty Images, IOC Olympic Museum/Allsport/Getty Images; p. 266
Colin McPherson/Corbis; p. 268 AGE fotostock/SuperStock; p. 270 Niday Picture
Library/Alamy; p. 273 Hulton Archive/Getty Images; p. 274 Marc Brasz/Corbis; p. 278
khoa vu/Getty Images; p. 281 rusm/istockphoto, Leksele/shutterstock, hnijjar007/
istockphoto; p. 283 arek_malang/shutterstock; p. 287 Jose Luis Pelaez, Inc./Blend
Images/Corbis; p. 288 OUP/Jon Arnold Images, Ekkapon/shutterstock, Dimedrol68/
shutterstock; p. 289 GlobalStock/istockphoto; p. 291 Paul Prescott/shutterstock,
Andreas Rodriguez/istockphoto, Randy Faris/Corbis, Aping Vision/STS/Getty Images,
Andersen Ross/Blend Images/Corbis, Andrew Rich/Getty Images; p. 294 Annie Engel/
Corbis, LAURENT/GAELLE/BSIP/SuperStock; p. 297 AlaskaStock/Masterfile; p. 301
prochasson frederic/shutterstock; p. 305 JGI/Jamie Grill/AGE fotostock; p. 307
fotoVoyager/Getty Images, catwalker/Shutterstock.com; p. 308 Vanni Archive/
Corbis, Ellen Rooney/Robert Harding World Imagery/Corbis, Frank Fennema/
shutterstock, David Samuel Robbins/Corbis; p. 310 epicurean/istockphoto; p. 311
ZUMA Press, Inc./Alamy, Eye Ubiquitous/Alamy, Beverly Armstrong/Getty Images,
OUP/Ellen McKnight311, Ocean/Corbis, Eric Nguyen/Science Photo Library; p. 312
MS Bretherton/Alamy, Ralph Lauer/ZUMA Press/Corbis, CB2/ZOB WENN Photos/
Newscom, Alvey & Towers Picture Library/Alamy, Lisa S./shutterstock, XiXinXing/
Getty Images, Car Culture/Getty Images, Road & Track Magazine/Guy Spange/
Transtock/Corbis; p. 319 OUP/Photodisc; p. 322 Craig Joiner Photography/Alamy;
p. 325 Scott E Read/shutterstock, KidStock/Blend Images/Corbis, stockstudioX/
Getty Images, Anne-Marie Palmer/Alamy; p. 327 Minden Pictures/Masterfile; p. 330
Norbert Wu/Science Faction/SuperStock; p. 331 OUP/Digital Vision; p. 332 Doug
Pearson/AGE fotostock, Sylvain Sonnet/Getty Images, Alan Schein Photography/
Corbis, Barry Lewis/Alamy, SeanPavonePhoto/Shutterstock.com, View Stock Stock
Connection USA/Newscom, PjrTravel/Alamy, Iain Masterton/AGE fotostock; p. 333
Robert Eastman/shutterstock, Mikhail Melnikov/shutterstock, OUP/David Cook/
blueshiftstudios, Sirikorn Techatraibhop/shutterstock, Anan Kaewkhammul/
shutterstock, Lingbeek/istockphoto, ConstantinosZ/shutterstock, OUP/D. Hurst,
f9photos/shutterstock, wikanda/shutterstock, Gunnar Pippel/shutterstock, JM-Design/
shutterstock; p. 338 Armando Gallo/Retna Ltd./Corbis; p. 342 Charles Gullung/Getty
Images; p. 346 SGranitz/WireImage/Getty Images; p. 349 OUP/BLOOMimage; p. 351
Jon Hicks/Corbis; p. 358 Mark Poprocki/shutterstock; p. 365 Tetra Images/Corbis,
Martin Diebel/Getty Images; p. 368 Radius Images/Corbis; p. 371 OUP/BlueMoon
Stock; p. 372 Andrea Pattaro/AFP/Getty Images; p. 377 olaser/Getty Images, pdesign/
shutterstock, Artgraphixel.com/shutterstock; p. 378 OUP/Graphi-Ogre, Globe
Turner/shutterstock, Jessica Peterson/Tetra Images/Corbis; p. 379 wavebreakmedia/
shutterstock; p. 382 Lindsay & Gavin Fries, silentwings/shutterstock; p. 386
Lex Rayton/AGE fotostock; p. 388 Abel Mitja Varela/Getty Images; p. 393 Alija/
istockphoto; p. 398 pictafolio/istockphoto; p. 400 Jeffrey Coolidge/Getty Images;
p. 402 OJO Images Ltd/Alamy; p. 406 OUP/David Cook/www.blueshiftstudios.co.uk,
OUP/Dennis Kitchen Studio, Inc, anafcsousa/istockphoto; p. 407 VI_K/Alamy,
karamysh/shutterstock; p. 410 Jo Ann Snover/shutterstock; p. 412 Blend Images/
Alamy; p. 417 B Calkins/shutterstock; p. 420 mathom/shutterstock, Mary Nguyen
NG/shutterstock; p. 424 James Morris/Axiom Photographic/Design Pics/SuperStock;
p. 426 BlueOrange Studio/shutterstock; p. 427 John Lund/Marc Romanelli/Getty
Images; p. 431 Zoonar GmbH/Alamy; p. 432 tarasov/shutterstock; p. 433 Junko
Chiba/Getty Images, Proehl Studios/Corbis, OUP/BananaStock, Wouter van Caspel/
Getty Images, Seokyong Lee/Bloomberg via Getty Images; p. 436 Album/Raga/Prisma/
Newscom, REUTERS/Tomas Bravo; p. 438 Chris Crisman/Corbis; p. 441 Keystone
Pictures USA/Alamy; p. 442 Tsuji/istockphoto; p. 444 Rich Legg/istockphoto; p. 446
Roy Ooms/Masterfile; p. 448 Sherrie Nickol/Citizen Stock/Corbis; p. 449 Sigurgeir
Jonasson/Getty Images; p. 452 Bettmann/Corbis, Peter Yates/Corbis; p. 458 Richmatts/
istockphoto; p. 459 Corbis; p. 460 picturepartners/shutterstock, Denys Kurbatov/
shutterstock; p. 461 Naypong/shutterstock; p. 462 Ruy Barbosa Pinto/Getty Images,
Photo Researchers/Alamy; p. 464 Johner Images/Johnér Images/Corbis; p. 465
Jonathan Blair/Corbis; p. 468 Aspen Photo/Shutterstock.com, PhotoStock10/
Shutterstock.com, esting/Shutterstock.com, Justin Horrocks/istockphoto.

Simple Present and Present Progressive

If we don't change, we don't grow. If we don't grow, we aren't really living.

—GAIL SHEEHY, JOURNALIST, LECTURER, AND AUTHOR (1937–)

Talk about It Do you agree or disagree with the quotation above? Why?

WARM-UP

A | Read these sentences and check (✓) *True* or *False*. Then compare answers with your classmates. What was the most common answer for each question?

Speaking English

	TRUE	FALSE
1. I **am taking** an English course this year.	☐	☐
2. My teacher only **uses** English in the classroom.	☐	☐
3. I **study** hard.	☐	☐
4. I **like** to talk in class.	☐	☐
5. My English **is getting** better.	☐	☐
6. Many jobs **require** knowledge of another language.	☐	☐
7. One out of six people in the world **speaks** English.	☐	☐
8. Other languages **are** now **borrowing** many words from English.	☐	☐

B | Answer these questions about the verbs in the sentences above.

1. The verbs in **blue** are simple present verbs. Some end in *-s* and some do not. Why is that?

2. The verbs in green are present progressive verbs. How are they different from the simple present verbs?

C | Look back at the quotation on page 2. Identify any present verb forms.

1.1 Using the Simple Present

A	**TIMELESS TRUTHS AND GENERAL STATEMENTS** **1** Most Canadians **speak** English. **2** The earth **moves** around the sun. **3** New York City **is** truly a unique place. **4** There **are** about 7 billion people in the world.	We use the **simple present** for timeless truths and general statements, as in **1 – 4**.
B	**HABITS AND ROUTINES** **5** My brother **works** five days a week. **6** My sister never **gets** home before 7:00. **7** The bank **opens** at 8:00 on Saturday.	We also use the simple present to describe habits and routines—things that take place regularly, as in **5 – 7**.

C	**HOW SOMEONE OR SOMETHING IS (STATES)**
	8 A: How's your back?
	   B: It **feels** worse today.
	9 A: Is Jenn OK?
	   B: Yeah, she **seems** fine now.
	10 A: I **like** this movie a lot.
	    B: Really? I **think** it's kind of strange.
		We can also use the simple present with non-action verbs to describe how someone or something is now, as in **8 – 10**. Some common non-action verbs are:
		
		be · have · look · remember
		believe · hear · love · seem
		contain · know · need · think
		feel · like · own · want
		
		GRAMMAR TERM: Non–action verbs are also called **stative verbs** because they describe states instead of actions. For a list of non-action verbs, see the Resources, page R-2.

1 | Noticing the Simple Present in General Statements Underline the simple present verbs. Then complete each sentence with an idea from the box. **1.1 A**

PROVERBS

1. Age and time <u>do not wait</u> _for people_____.
2. An apple a day keeps _____.
3. Two heads are _____.
4. Bad news travels _____.
5. A picture paints _____.
6. A good companion shortens _____.
7. The customer is _____.
8. Actions speak _____.
9. The bad worker always blames[1] _____.
10. Practice makes _____.

a thousand words
always right
better than one
fast
for people
his tools
louder than words
perfect
the doctor away
the longest road

Think about It We call the sentences above "proverbs." Why do you think we use the simple present form of verbs with proverbs?

Talk about It Take turns reading the proverbs above aloud with a partner. What do you think each proverb means? Do you agree or disagree?

[1] **blame:** to say that something else is the cause of a problem

2 | Noticing the Simple Present Underline the simple present verbs in these statements. Which country do the sentences describe? Choose from the list. (You will not use all the countries.) `1.1 A`

Descriptions of Countries

COUNTRY 1 _____

    a. It <u>is</u> the second largest country in the world.

    b. It borders the United States.

    c. The three biggest cities are Toronto, Montreal, and Vancouver.

COUNTRY 2 _____

    d. People in this country speak Arabic.

    e. The capital city of this country is Muscat.

    f. This country produces oil.

COUNTRY 3 _____

    g. This country shares borders with Belgium, Germany, Luxembourg, Switzerland, Spain, and Italy.

    h. The island of Corsica belongs to this country.

    i. A flight from this country to New York takes about six hours.

COUNTRY 4 _____

    j. This country has the longest river in South America.

    k. It produces 80 percent of the world's orange juice.

    l. The largest cities are São Paulo, Rio de Janeiro, and Salvador.

Brazil

Japan

Oman

Canada

France

Kenya

Write about It Write three facts about another country. Read your facts to your classmates, and ask them to guess the country.

3 | Describing Habits and Routines Underline the simple present verbs in these statements. Then check (✓) the statements that describe you. `1.1 B`

EATING HABITS

☐ 1. I <u>eat</u> a lot of fruit.

☐ 2. I drink a lot of coffee.

☐ 3. I eat breakfast every morning.

☐ 4. I eat slowly.

☐ 5. I avoid junk food.

☐ 6. I often skip meals².

☐ 7. I often eat late at night.

☐ 8. I drink a lot of water during the day.

SLEEPING HABITS

☐ 9. I sleep fewer than seven hours a night.

☐ 10. I get up at the same time every day.

☐ 11. I almost always go to bed late.

☐ 12. I sometimes fall asleep in front of the television.

PHYSICAL HABITS

☐ 13. I sit for many hours during the day.

☐ 14. I take a long walk almost every day.

☐ 15. I play a sport regularly.

²**skip meals:** to not eat meals

Think about It Circle the time expressions in the sentences in Activity 3. Which time expressions come before the verb? Which come after? Write each time expression in the chart below.

Time expressions before the verb	Time expressions after the verb
often	*every morning*

Talk about It Look at the sentences you checked in Activity 3. Which are healthy habits, and which are unhealthy habits? Tell a partner. Then think of three more healthy and unhealthy habits.

"My healthy habits are: I eat a lot of fruit...."   *"My unhealthy habits are: I drink a lot of coffee...."*

4 | Identifying Non-Action Verbs Underline the seven non-action verbs in these comments. Then match the sentences with non-action verbs to the pictures below. 1.1 C

COMMENTS

1. "She <u>feels</u> cold."
2. "He needs a haircut."
3. "He's tired."
4. "She has a headache."
5. "They dance very well."

6. "They look alike."
7. "She knows the answer."
8. "He drives a big car."
9. "They like ice cream."
10. "She usually wears black."

a. _6_

b. ____

c. ____

d. ____

e. ____

f. ____

g. ____

Write about It Think of another comment for each picture above. Ask your classmates to identify the action and non-action verbs in your comments. (Look at Chart 1.1 for a list of non-action verbs you can use.)

They have red shirts. They seem friendly.

1.2 Simple Present Statements

A

The simplest form of a verb is the **base form**. We use the base form for the simple present of most verbs, as in **1 – 3** and **5**. We add **-s** or **-es** when the subject is *he, she, it,* or a singular noun, as in **4**.

FIRST PERSON

base form

| 1 | I | **live** | there. |

| 2 | Dan and I / We | **live** | there. |

SECOND PERSON

base form

| 3 | You | **live** | there. |

THIRD PERSON

base form + -s / -es

| 4 | He/She/It / My friend | **lives** | there. |

base form

| 5 | They / My parents | **live** | there. |

For spelling rules of third-person singular verbs, see Activity 6, page 8.
For the simple present of the verb *be*, see Chart 1.4, page 16.

B

For negative statements, we use *do not / does not* + the **base form of a main verb**, as in **6 – 10**.
When we use the verb **do** in this way, we call it a **helping verb**.

do + not / base form

| 6 | I | **do not / don't** | **like** | it. |
| 7 | We | **do not / don't** | **like** | it. |

do + not / base form

| 8 | You | **do not / don't** | **like** | it. |

does + not / base form

| 9 | He/She/It | **does not / doesn't** | **like** | it. |

do + not

| 10 | They | **do not / don't** | **like** | it. |

We often use the contractions *don't* or *doesn't* instead of *do not* or *does not*, especially in conversation.

C

11 My sister **doesn't work** here.
12 I **do** the dishes, and my kids **do** the laundry.
13 I **don't do** anything on Saturdays.

The verb *do* is special. We can use the verb *do* as:
• a **helping verb**, as in **11**
• a **main verb**, as in **12**

It's even possible to use the helping verb *do* with the main verb *do*, as in **13**.

D

CORRECT THE COMMON ERRORS (See page R-13.)

14 ✗ She don't have time for this.
15 ✗ He email his family a lot.
16 ✗ She is a housewife and have three children.
17 ✗ It make me happy.

GO ONLINE

5 | Using the Correct Form
Complete these sentences with the correct form of the verb in parentheses.
Then check (✓) *True* or *False*. **1.2 A**

DESCRIBING PEOPLE IN YOUR CLASS

	TRUE	FALSE
1. My classmates and I _____*talk*_____ a lot in class. (talk/talks)	☐	☐
2. My teacher _____ glasses. (wear/wears)	☐	☐
3. My classmates _____ the same music I _____ . (like/likes)	☐	☐
4. Nobody _____ a musical instrument. (play/plays)	☐	☐
5. One person _____ in a hospital. (work/works)	☐	☐
6. I _____ pretty good today. (feel/feels)	☐	☐
7. Two people _____ to class every day. (drive/drives)	☐	☐
8. I _____ to class on Tuesdays and Thursdays. (come/comes)	☐	☐

	TRUE	FALSE
9. In class, we _____ in chairs in a circle. (sit/sits)	☐	☐
10. A few of my classmates _____ Chinese. (speak/speaks)	☐	☐
11. Everybody _____ a lot of words in English. (know/knows)	☐	☐
12. Everyone _____ more than one language. (speak/speaks)	☐	☐

Think about It Which statements in Activity 5 describe a habit or routine?

Sentence 1 describes a habit or routine.

> **FYI**
>
> Indefinite pronouns such as *everybody*, *somebody*, and *nobody* are always singular.
>
> **Everybody** in my class speaks English.

6 | Spelling Note: Third-Person Singular Verbs Read the note. Then do Activity 7.

To form the third-person singular (*he/she/it*) for the simple present:

1 Add *-es* to verbs that end in *-sh*, *-ch*, *-ss*, *-s*, *-x*, or *-z*.

| finish | finishes | touch | touches | pass | passes | relax | relaxes |

2 For verbs ending in a consonant + *-y*, change the *-y* to *-i* and add *-es*.

| study | studies | worry | worries | deny | denies | fly | flies |

3 Three verbs have a special spelling:

| go | goes | do | does | have | has |

4 For all other verbs, add *-s*.

| like | likes | buy | buys | see | sees | speak | speaks |

7 | Forming Third-Person Singular Verbs Complete these statements with the correct form of the bold verb. `1.2 A`

HOW ARE YOU AND YOUR SPOUSE DIFFERENT?

1. I **watch** a lot of movies on TV, and my husband ___*watches*___ a lot of news programs.

2. I **belong** to a basketball team, and he _____ to a soccer team.

3. I **wash** the dishes, and he _____ the clothes.

4. I **do** karate for exercise, and he _____ weight-lifting.

5. I **worry** about money, and he _____ about the future.

6. I **go** to work by subway, and he _____ by bus.

7. I **get up** early on weekends, but my wife _____ late.

8. I **have** a lot of books, and she _____ a lot of videos.

9. I **fly** to Los Angeles once a month, and she _____ to New York every other week.

10. I **finish** work at 6:00, and she _____ at 5:00.

11. I **buy** a lot of clothes, and my wife _____ a lot of jewelry.

12. I always **carry** a briefcase with me, and she always _____ a purse.

Write about It Think of a friend or family member. How are you different? Write three sentences like the ones in Activity 7.

I have short hair, and my sister has long hair.

🔊 8 | Pronunciation Note: Third-Person Singular Verbs Listen to the note. Then do Activity 9.

We usually pronounce the -s or -es ending on a verb as a /s/ or /z/ sound. Notice that in a sentence, it's often difficult to hear the difference between the two sounds.

1 He eat**s** here every day.

2 She make**s** a lot of money.

3 He always leave**s** before me.

4 She worrie**s** too much.

We pronounce the -es ending as /əz/ with an extra syllable when the base form of the verb ends in a hissing or buzzing sound. (These words are often spelled with a final -ce, -ge, -se, -ze, -ch, -sh, and -ss).

5 She really miss**es** him.

6 He choos**es** his own clothes.

7 The company publish**es** good books.

8 She arrang**es** all of our meetings.

9 He teach**es** math.

🔊 9 | Pronouncing Third-Person Singular Verbs How do you pronounce the -s or -es ending on these **bold** verbs? Check (✓) your ideas. Then listen and confirm your answers. `1.2 A`

	/s/ OR /z/	AN EXTRA SYLLABLE /əz/
1. She **watches** a lot of TV.	☐	☑
2. He always **relaxes** on the weekend.	☐	☐
3. She usually **takes** a nap around 3:00.	☐	☐
4. He **hopes** to finish soon.	☐	☐
5. She **expresses** herself well.	☐	☐
6. He always **shares** his lunch with me.	☐	☐
7. He never **raises** his hand in class.	☐	☐
8. She **notices** everything.	☐	☐
9. He **shakes** hands with everyone.	☐	☐
10. She **washes** her clothes by hand.	☐	☐
11. He never **finishes** on time.	☐	☐
12. Our boss **makes** us come in early on Fridays.	☐	☐
13. He **manages** his money well.	☐	☐
14. My job **involves** a lot of travel.	☐	☐
15. Your dinner **includes** soup and a salad.	☐	☐
16. Canada **produces** a lot of oil.	☐	☐

10 | Using *Don't or Doesn't* Complete these descriptions with the negative form of the verb in parentheses. 1.2 B

TYPES OF PEOPLE

1. Vegetarians _____*don't eat*_____ meat. (eat)

2. A couch potato _____ anything all day. (do)

3. A technophobe _____ to use computers or technology. (like)

4. A conformist _____ to be different from other people. (want)

5. A night owl _____ at night. (sleep)

6. A pacifist _____ in war. (believe)

7. Pessimists _____ the positive in things. They only see the negative. (see)

8. Homebodies _____ to go out or travel. They prefer to stay home. (like)

9. Early birds _____ in bed in the morning. They get up early. (stay)

10. Optimists _____ when things go wrong. They believe that everything will be OK. (worry)

Talk about It Do any of the words above describe you? Why? Tell a partner.

"I'm a night owl because I like to stay up late."

11 | Making Negative Statements Rewrite these sentences to describe a bad job. Use the negative form of the verb. 1.2 B

Characteristics of a good job	Characteristics of a bad job
1. You get a lot of vacation time.	1. *You don't get a lot of vacation time.*
2. You have a long time for lunch.	2. _____
3. The company provides good health insurance.	3. _____
4. The office has good lighting.	4. _____
5. The company pays overtime[3].	5. _____
6. The company lets people work flexible hours.	6. _____
7. You get a big bonus at the end of the year.	7. _____
8. The office has its own gym.	8. _____
9. You get out early on Friday.	9. _____
10. You enjoy the work.	10. _____
11. Your co-workers do their work on time.	11. _____

Write about It Write two other characteristics of a good job and a bad job.

[3] **overtime:** extra hours worked

12 | Helping Verb or Main Verb? Is the **bold** verb a helping verb or a main verb? Check (✓) your answers. `1.2 C`

PERSONAL HABITS	HELPING VERB	MAIN VERB
1. I don't usually **do** my homework.	☐	☑
2. I don't **do** anything on the weekend.	☐	☐
3. I **don't** have a lot of close friends.	☐	☐
4. I **do** most of the cooking at home.	☐	☐
5. I **do** a lot for other people.	☐	☐
6. I **don't** cause trouble at school.	☐	☐
7. I don't always **do** the right thing.	☐	☐
8. I **don't** talk a lot in class.	☐	☐
9. I rarely **do** the dishes at home.	☐	☐
10. I always **do** my best on tests.	☐	☐
11. I **don't** drink a lot of coffee.	☐	☐
12. I **do** the laundry at home.	☐	☐
13. I **do** my shopping online.	☐	☐
14. I **don't** exercise every day.	☐	☐

Think about It Why does *do* appear twice in three of the sentences above?

Talk about It Which sentences above describe you? Tell a partner.

13 | Error Correction Correct any errors in these sentences. (Some sentences may not have any errors.)

FAMILY MEMBERS

1. My mother is get up early every day and cook breakfast for everyone.

   My mother gets up early every day and cooks breakfast for everyone.

2. My father works hard and help all of his neighbors. I am very much respect him.
3. My mother help me in many ways, but I don't rely on her for everything.
4. My brother is not eat meat. He's a vegetarian.
5. My older brother work every day. At home, he take care of his baby daughter.
6. My parents are my security. They accepts my ideas or at least they doesn't show their disagreement.
7. My father is also my good friend. He and I do a lot of things together and we talk a lot.
8. My father is a helpful person, and he give me lots of advice. For example, he often talk to me about my future. He ask me lots of questions and listen carefully.
9. My grandmother tell great stories, and she always make me laugh. She also make great cookies and cakes. I am sad every time I leave her.
10. My brother is a nurse. He works very hard, but he still find time to visit our parents almost every week. He is a good son, unlike his younger brother (me). I live far away, so I only visits my parents once a year.
11. One of my favorite people is my aunt. We talk on the phone almost every day. My aunt don't like to fly, so I don't get to see her often. In fact, I only see her on holidays when I fly home. Unfortunately, that don't happen very often.

1.3 Questions with the Simple Present

We use the helping verb *do* to ask questions with the simple present.

For *yes/no* questions, we use *do / does* and the **base form of a main verb**, as in **1 – 3**. We can give short answers to *yes/no* questions with *do / does*, as in **4 – 9**. In negative short answers, we often use contractions, as in **7 – 9**.

A

YES/NO QUESTIONS

	do / does	subject	base form
1	Do	I / you	work?
2	Does	he / she / it	work?
3	Do	we / you / they	work?

SHORT ANSWERS

		do / does	
4	Yes,	you / I	do.
5	Yes,	he / she / it	does.
6	Yes,	you / we / they	do.

		do / does + not	
7	No,	you / I	don't.
8	No,	he / she / it	doesn't.
9	No,	you / we / they	don't.

B

For *wh-* questions, we use a **wh- word** + *do / does* and the **base form of a main verb**, as in **10 – 21**.

WH- QUESTIONS

	wh- word	do	subject	base form
10	What		you	want?
11	Where		they	live?
12	When	do	the stores	open?
13	Why		we	exercise?
14	Who		you	know?
15	How		I	begin?

	wh- word	does	subject	base form
16	What		he	want?
17	Where		Sarah	live?
18	When	does	it	open?
19	Why		Tom	exercise?
20	Who		she	know?
21	How		the movie	begin?

When the **wh- word** is the subject, don't use *do* or *does*. Use the base form + **-s** or **-es**, as in **22 – 23**.

WH- QUESTIONS ABOUT THE SUBJECT

	subject	base form + -s / -es	
22	Who	lives	there?
23	What	happens	in the morning?

For information about forming questions with the verb *be*, see Chart 1.4, page 16.

GO ONLINE

14 | Choosing *Do* or *Does* Complete the questions with *Do* or *Does*. Then say where you might hear each question. Check (✓) one or more places. `1.3 A`

PERSONAL HABITS	RESTAURANT	CLOTHING STORE	AIRPORT
1. ___*Do*___ you have this in size 12?	☐	☐	☐
2. _____ the chicken come with a salad?	☐	☐	☐
3. _____ you take credit cards?	☐	☐	☐
4. _____ we need a reservation?	☐	☐	☐
5. _____ this shirt come in other colors?	☐	☐	☐
6. _____ you have your ticket?	☐	☐	☐

	RESTAURANT	CLOTHING STORE	AIRPORT
7. _____ you want a table near the window?	☐	☐	☐
8. _____ you sell shoes?	☐	☐	☐
9. _____ soup come with this?	☐	☐	☐
10. _____ you have any luggage?	☐	☐	☐

Think about It What is the main verb in each question in Activity 14? Circle it.

Talk about It Work with a partner. Choose one of the questions in Activity 14 and use it to create a short conversation. Present your conversation to the class.

A: Do you have this in size 12?
B: No, I'm sorry, we don't. Do you want to try size 10 or size 14?
A: Sure.

15 | Forming *Yes/No* Questions with *Do* or *Does* Choose verbs from the boxes to complete these conversations. Use the correct form. Then practice with a partner. [1.3 A]

1. A: _____*Do*_____ you _____*know*_____ Philip Winski?

   B: No, I don't. _____ he _____ here?

   A: Yes, he _____ the mail room.

   | know |
   | manage |
   | work |

2. A: What's the matter with the printer?

   B: I _____ _____ .

   A: _____ it _____ paper?

   B: Yes, I _____ so.

   | have |
   | not/know |
   | think |

3. A: _____ you _____ Anne's number?

   B: No, I don't, but I _____ it on my phone.

   _____ you _____ me to get it?

   A: Please.

   | have |
   | remember |
   | want |

4. A: _____ Jen _____ Mexican food?

   B: I think so. Why?

   A: Because tomorrow's her birthday, and Ben and I _____ to take her out.

   B: _____ you _____ a good Mexican restaurant?

   A: Yeah. People say Café Central _____ good Mexican food.

   | know |
   | like |
   | serve |
   | want |

5. A: How's the new baby girl?

   B: Great, but Dan and I are both pretty tired.

   A: _____ she _____ through the night yet?

   B: No, but she's healthy, and she _____ happy.

   A: That's good.

   | seem |
   | sleep |

Think about It Which verbs above describe a state (how someone or something is) rather than an action?

16 | Asking *Wh*-Questions Complete these quiz questions with a *wh*- word (*when, who, where, what, how long,* or *how often*). Then circle your answers. `1.3 B`

The Olympic Games Quiz

1. _____How often_____ do the Olympic Games take place?
   a. every year
   b. every two years
   c. every ten years

2. _____ do the Games last?
   a. about one week
   b. about two weeks
   c. about four weeks

3. _____ does the host country[4] do?
   a. It organizes the Games.
   b. It chooses the winners of the events.
   c. It selects the athletes.

4. _____ marches in the opening parade?
   a. one athlete from each country
   b. only the athletes from the host country
   c. athletes from all countries

5. _____ does the winner of an event get?
   a. a medal
   b. some money
   c. a new uniform

6. _____ leads the opening parade?
   a. athletes from Afghanistan
   b. athletes from Greece
   c. athletes from the host country

7. _____ do the athletes live during the Games?
   a. in the Olympic Village
   b. in nearby cities
   c. in private hotels

8. _____ chooses the athletes?
   a. the Olympic Committee
   b. each country
   c. the host country

9. _____ do the Olympic Games take place?
   a. in Greece
   b. in Asia
   c. in a different country each time

10. _____ do the skiing events take place?
   a. in the Winter Games
   b. in the Summer Games
   c. in the Winter Games and Summer Games

Answers: 1. b; 2. b; 3. a; 4. c; 5. a; 6. b; 7. a; 8. b; 9. c; 10. a

Think about It What is the main verb in each question above? Underline it.

17 | Pronunciation Note: Question Intonation Listen to the note. Then do Activities 18 and 19.

Yes/No questions usually end with rising intonation.

1 Do you work?   **2** Do you play soccer?   **3** Does she need some money?

Wh- questions usually end with falling intonation.

4 What do you do?   **5** Where do you live?   **6** Where does he go to school?

[4]**host country:** the country where the Games take place

18 | Listening for Question Intonation Listen to each question. Circle ↗ (rising intonation) or ↘ (falling intonation). Then listen again and repeat the questions. **1.3 A–B**

1. (↗) ↘	4. ↗ ↘	7. ↗ ↘	10. ↗ ↘	13. ↗ ↘
2. ↗ ↘	5. ↗ ↘	8. ↗ ↘	11. ↗ ↘	14. ↗ ↘
3. ↗ ↘	6. ↗ ↘	9. ↗ ↘	12. ↗ ↘	15. ↗ ↘

19 | Using Question Intonation Read these questions and mark them ↗ (for rising intonation) or ↘ (for falling intonation). Then listen and repeat the questions. **1.3 A–B**

TWELVE COMMON QUESTIONS IN CONVERSATION

1. Do I make myself clear? ↗
2. Do you mind? ____
3. How do you like this weather? ____
4. Does anyone know? ____
5. How do you do? ____
6. What does that prove? ____

7. Who do you want to talk to? ____
8. What does it matter? ____
9. Does it work for you? ____
10. Who do you think you are? ____
11. Do you understand? ____
12. What do you mean? ____

> **RESEARCH SAYS...**
>
> We often use these verbs in the simple present form:
>
> doubt   mind
> know   suppose
> matter   think
> mean
>
> CORPUS

Think about It In what situations do people use the questions above? Share ideas with your classmates.

20 | Pronunciation Note: Reduced Words Listen to the note. Then do Activity 21.

We usually pronounce *Do you* as "Duh yuh" or "D'yuh" except in very formal speech.

1 Do you like this?	*sounds like*	"D'yuh like this?"
2 Do you have a minute?	*sounds like*	"Duh yuh have a minute?"

We also pronounce *wh-* questions with "Duh yuh" or "D'yuh" except in very formal speech.

3 What do you need?	*sounds like*	"What-d'yuh need?"
4 Where do you live?	*sounds like*	"Where duh yuh live?"
5 Why do you ask?	*sounds like*	"Why duh yuh ask?"

21 | Listening for Reduced Words Listen and repeat. Then ask a partner the questions. **1.3 A–B**

QUESTIONS FROM PERSONALITY TESTS

1. Do you talk a lot?
2. Do you get angry easily?
3. Do you make friends easily?
4. Do you like animals?
5. Do you work hard?
6. Do you usually show your feelings?

7. How much time do you spend on the Internet?
8. What do you do for fun?
9. How do you handle a disagreement?
10. How do you handle stress?
11. Where do you like to go on vacation?
12. Where do you go for advice?

A: Do you talk a lot?
B: I do! I love to sit in a café and talk for hours.

1.4 Simple Present of the Verb *Be*

The simple present of *be* has three forms: *am*, *is*, and *are*, as in **1 – 5**.

A

FIRST PERSON

		be	
1	I	am / 'm	fine.
2	We	are / 're	ready.

SECOND PERSON

		be	
3	You	are / 're	alone.

THIRD PERSON

		be	
4	He/She/It	is / 's	right.
5	They	are / 're	good.

B

We add **not** after *am* / *is* / *are* for negative statements, as in **6 – 10**.

		be + not	
6	I	am not / 'm not	sure.
7	We	are not / 're not / aren't	certain.

		be + not	
8	You	are not / 're not / aren't	careful.

		be + not	
9	He/She/It	is not / 's not / isn't	ready.
10	They	are not / 're not / aren't	alone.

C

We put *am* / *is* / *are* before the subject to ask *yes/no* questions, as in **11 – 12**.
We can give short answers to *yes/no* questions, as in **13 – 16**.
In negative short answers, we often use contractions, as in **15 – 16**.

YES/NO QUESTIONS

	be	subject	
11	Am	I	late?
	Are	you	
	Is	he / she / it	

	be	subject	
12	Are	we / you / they	OK?

SHORT ANSWERS

			be
13	Yes,	you	are.
		I	am.
		he / she / it	is.

			be
14	Yes,	you / we / they	are.

			be + not
15	No,	you	're not. / aren't.
		I	'm not.
		he / she / it	's not. / isn't.

			be + not
16	No,	you / we / they	're not. / aren't.

WARNING! We don't use contractions with short yes answers.
(NOT: ~~Yes, you're.~~)

D

For *wh-* questions, we use a **wh- word** + *am* / *is* / *are*, as in **17 – 22**.
In conversation, we often use a contraction, as in **23 – 28**.

WH- QUESTIONS

	wh- word	*be*	
17	What	is	his name?
18	Where		my computer?
19	When		your birthday?
20	Who		that?
21	Why	are	we here?
22	How		you?

CONTRACTIONS WITH WH- WORDS

	wh- word + *be*	
23	What's	his name?
24	Where's	my computer?
25	When's	your birthday?
26	Who's	that?
27	Why're	we here?
28	How're	you?

16

22 | Choosing *Is* or *Are* Describe some of your favorite things. Use *is* or *are* in your sentences. 1.4 A

FAVORITE THINGS

1. My favorite colors ___are___ _____ .
2. My favorite day of the week _____ _____ .
3. My favorite sports to watch on TV _____ _____ .
4. Two of my favorite movies _____ _____ .
5. My favorite website _____ _____ .
6. My favorite sport _____ _____ .
7. My favorite hot drinks _____ _____ .
8. My favorite school subject _____ _____ .
9. My favorite cities _____ _____ .
10. My favorite kind of music _____ _____ .

> **WARNING!**
> In English, every complete sentence needs a subject and a verb. We can't leave out the verb *be* as we can in some other languages.
>
> She is happy.
> (NOT: ~~She happy.~~)

Talk about It Compare the statements you wrote above with a partner. How many of your favorite things are the same?

23 | Using *Is/Isn't* and *Are/Aren't* Complete these facts with the correct form of the verb *be*. Use the negative form of the verb in the first sentence of each pair. (Use a contraction where possible.) 1.4 B

○ ○ ○ ○

Ten Facts about Geography

1. The earth ___isn't___ flat. It ___'s___ round.
2. The national language of Brazil _____ Spanish. It _____ Portuguese.
3. The Mississippi River _____ the longest river in the world. The Nile _____ .
4. The world's two highest mountains _____ in Europe. They _____ in Asia.
5. The Atlantic Ocean _____ the largest ocean in the world. The Pacific _____ .
6. Canada's official languages _____ English and Spanish. They _____ English and French.
7. Canada _____ the biggest country in the world. Russia _____ .
8. The world's two largest cities _____ in South America. They _____ in Asia.
9. The world's largest desert _____ the Sahara Desert. It _____ Antarctica.
10. Mars _____ the hottest planet in our solar system. Venus _____ .

Think about It Read each sentence above aloud two times. Use different negative contractions in each reading.

"The earth isn't flat. It's round."   *"The earth's not flat. It's round."*

Talk about It What other geography facts do you know? Share information with your classmates.

24 | Using *Be* in *Yes/No* Questions and Answers Complete these conversations with the positive or negative form of the verb *be*. (Use a contraction where possible.) Then practice with a partner. `1.4 C`

ON AN AIRPLANE

1. A: Excuse me, but I think you __'re__ in my seat.

   B: _____ you sure?

   A: Yes, I _____ pretty sure.

2. A: _____ the restroom in the back of the plane?

   B: No, it _____ in the front.

IN A STORE

3. A: _____ you open on Sundays?

   B: No, we _____. We _____ only open from Monday to Saturday.

4. A: _____ this shirt on sale?

   B: Yes, it _____. It _____ 50 percent off.

   A: Ooh! That _____ a good price.

5. A: Excuse me. _____ women's shoes on the first floor?

   B: No, they _____ on the second floor.

   A: Thanks.

AT AN AIRPORT

6. A: _____ Flight 245 on time?

   B: Yes, it _____.

7. A: _____ this your suitcase?

   B: Yes, it _____.

   A: I _____ sorry, but it _____ too big to carry on the plane.

ON THE TELEPHONE

8. A: _____ Amanda there?

   B: No, she _____ here right now.

9. A: _____ this David?

   B: Yes, it _____. _____ that you, Carlos?

   A: Yeah. Hi, David.

IN A RESTAURANT

10. A: _____ you ready to order?

    B: Yes, I think so.

11. A: _____ everything OK?

    B: Yes, the food _____ delicious.

---

25 | Understanding *Wh-* Questions Complete these questions with *is* or *are*. `1.4 D`

TWELVE COMMON WH- QUESTIONS WITH IS AND ARE

1. What _____ new?

2. How _____ you?

3. What _____ the matter?

4. Who _____ that guy?

5. What _____ the problem?

6. Where _____ you?

7. Where _____ my keys?

8. What _____ on your mind?

9. How _____ your food?

10. Who _____ your friend?

11. How _____ things with you?

12. How _____ the weather?

Talk about It Work with a partner. Choose one of the questions above and use it to create a short conversation. (Use a contraction where possible.) Present your conversation to the class.

A: What's new?
B: I have a new job. I really like it.
A: Great!
B: What about you?

26 | Usage Note: *How* Questions Read the note. Then do Activity 27.

We use the question word *how* in special ways. We can use:

1	*How* + an adjective	How **old** are you? How **serious** is it? How **important** is this test?
2	*How* + an adverb	How **often** does your class meet? How **well** does she speak English?
3	*How* + ***many*** + a plural count noun	How **many students** are here today? How **many times** a day do you eat?
4	*How* + ***much*** + a noncount noun	How **much money** is in the desk? How **much water** do you usually drink?

27 | Asking *Wh-* Questions with *Be* Complete the questions about each place. Use a *wh-* word from the box and *is* or *are*. (You will use some *wh-* words more than once.) **1.4 D**

how big	how far	how many	how old	what	where

BRASILIA

1. Question: *Where is*_____ Brasilia?

   Answer: It's in Brazil.

2. Question: _____ the population of Brasilia?

   Answer: About 1,750,000 people.

3. Question: _____ Brasilia from São Paulo?

   Answer: 544 miles or 875 kilometers.

4. Question: _____ the city?

   Answer: About 70 years old.

5. Question: _____ special about Brasilia?

   Answer: It's an example of modern architecture and urban planning.

Brazilian National Congress
building in Brasilia

CAVE PAINTINGS OF LASCAUX

6. Question: _____ the cave paintings?

   Answer: In southwestern France.

7. Question: _____ they?

   Answer: Up to 20,000 years old.

8. Question: _____ the animals in the paintings?

   Answer: Some are huge—10 to 15 feet long.

9. Question: _____ animals _____ in the pictures?

   Answer: Horses, deer, and bulls.

10. Question: _____ pictures _____ in the cave?

    Answer: About 2,000.

cave paintings of Lascaux

Write about It Write a *wh-* question about a place. Find the answer online and report to the class.

28 | Error Correction Correct any errors in these sentences. (Some sentences may not have any errors.)

1. She always late.
2. Is you OK?
3. I very proud of my parents.
4. Why we are here?
5. Sometimes she very strong, and sometimes she very weak.
6. My parents they are always very busy, but they always ready to help me.
7. It hard to raise a family.
8. My parents happy with their life? Yes, I think so.
9. The weather in Moscow colder than in Berlin.

1.5 Using Time Expressions with the Simple Present

A

ADVERBS OF FREQUENCY

always 100%	almost always	usually often frequently	sometimes occasionally	hardly ever rarely seldom	almost never	never 0%
				negative adverbs of frequency		

1 We **almost always** eat at home.

2 We **hardly ever** eat out.

3 It **almost never** rains here.

(NOT: It doesn't never rain here.)

Adverbs of frequency are one kind of time expression.

- We use adverbs of frequency with the simple present to say how often something happens, as in **1 – 3**.
- We don't use *not* with a negative adverb, as in **3**.

B

4	This room	is	**usually**	open.
5	Vacations	aren't	**always**	fun.

6	We	don't	**usually**	meet	on Friday.
7	She	doesn't	**always**	know	the answer.

8	The game	**almost never**	starts	on time.
9	She		**always**	does	her work.

10 Do you **ever** feel sleepy in class?

11 She **doesn't ever** call me.

Adverbs of frequency usually come:

- after the **main verb be**, as in **4 – 5**

- after a **helping verb** like *do*, as in **6 – 7**

- before other **main verbs**, as in **8 – 9**

We use *ever* most often in questions and negative statements, as in **10 – 11**.

ever = at any time	not **ever** = never

C

MULTI-WORD TIME EXPRESSIONS

12 Do you go there **every day**?

13 I get my hair cut **once a month**.

14 A: How often does the class meet?

B: **Two times a week**.

15 A: Are you open **on Saturdays**?

B: Yes, we're open **all day**.

We often use **multi-word time expressions** when we talk about current habits, as in **12 – 15**. Some common examples are:

every	+	morning/day/week/year/Sunday/time
once/twice a	+	day/week/month/year
two times a	+	day/week/month/year
on	+	weekdays/weekends/Mondays
all	+	day/week/the time

D

CORRECT THE COMMON ERRORS (See page R-13.)

16 ✗ He walks to school usually every morning.

17 ✗ They always are busy.

18 ✗ They always don't leave a tip.

19 ✗ John don't never visit us.

29 | Choosing Adverbs of Frequency Complete these statements with an adverb of frequency. (Make the statements true for you.) `1.5 A`

YOUR HABITS

1. I _____ get up before 7:00 in the morning.
2. In the evening, I _____ play games on the computer.
3. I am _____ sleepy during the day.
4. I _____ eat a big breakfast.
5. I am _____ ready for a test.
6. I _____ do all of my homework for class.
7. I am _____ late to class.
8. I _____ listen carefully in class.
9. I _____ keep my promises.
10. I _____ make bad decisions.
11. I _____ argue with other people.
12. I _____ pay my bills.
13. I am _____ calm in difficult situations.
14. I _____ feel angry.
15. I _____ forget to do things.

> **F Y I**
>
> For emphasis, we sometimes use the adverbs *usually, often, sometimes,* and *occasionally* at the beginning of a sentence.
>
> **Sometimes** he gets home really late.
>
> We can also use *often* and *sometimes* at the end of a sentence.
>
> We watch that program **sometimes**.

Talk about It Compare your statements above with a partner. How many of your statements are the same?

30 | Placement of Adverbs of Frequency Add the adverbs in parentheses to these statements. Then check (✓) *True* or *False* for your class. `1.5 B`

DESCRIBING YOUR CLASS	TRUE	FALSE
never		
1. Our teacher ⌃ gives tests. (never)	☐	☐
2. Our classroom is too hot. (frequently)	☐	☐
3. We watch movies in class. (rarely)	☐	☐
4. We listen to music in class. (often)	☐	☐
5. We don't have homework. (ever)	☐	☐
6. We study grammar in class. (sometimes)	☐	☐
7. It's quiet in my classroom. (almost never)	☐	☐
8. Some students are late to class. (almost always)	☐	☐
9. We don't speak in our first language. (usually)	☐	☐
10. Our teacher isn't tired. (ever)	☐	☐
11. A few students fall asleep in class. (occasionally)	☐	☐
12. Our teacher asks questions. (hardly ever)	☐	☐

Think about It Think of a way to restate the information in sentences 1, 5, 10, and 12 in Activity 30.

1. Our teacher doesn't ever give us tests.

Write about It Rewrite the false statements in Activity 30. Make them true for your class.

Our teacher often gives us tests.

31 | Using Adverbs of Frequency Underline the adverbs of frequency in these sentences. Then rewrite them. Replace the **bold** words with the words in parentheses, and use a different adverb of frequency.

`1.5 A–B`

COMPLAINTS AND CRITICISMS

1. It's <u>almost always</u> **rainy** here. (sunny)

   It's almost never sunny here.

2. It's usually **noisy** here at night. (quiet)
3. The weather is always **bad** on the weekend. (nice)
4. My friends are usually **late**. (early)
5. You always **criticize** me. (praise)
6. You hardly ever **remember** to do your homework. (forget)
7. The bus is almost never **on time**. (late)
8. It's lonely in this town. I never **go out**. (stay at home)
9. You rarely **understand** me. (misunderstand)
10. He seldom **tells the truth**. (lie)

32 | Using Multi-Word Time Expressions Use this calendar to write six sentences about Isabel's schedule. Use a multi-word time expression in each sentence. `1.5 C`

Isabel goes to class twice a week.

SUNDAY	MONDAY	TUESDAY	WEDNESDAY	THURSDAY	FRIDAY	SATURDAY
11:00 PM–6:00 AM	11:00 PM–6:00 AM	11:00 PM–6:00 AM	11:00 PM–6:00 AM	11:00 PM–6:00 AM	11:00 PM–6:00 AM	11:00 PM–6:00 AM
Sleep	Sleep	Sleep	Sleep	Sleep	Sleep	Sleep
12:30 PM	8:30 AM–12:30 PM	9:00–11:00AM	8:30 AM–12:30 PM	8:30 AM–12:30 PM	8:30 AM–12:30 PM	9:00–11:00 AM
Meet Mom	Work	Volunteer	Work	Work	Work	Volunteer
2:00–6:00 PM	2:00–4:00 PM		2:00–4:00 PM	2:00–6:00 PM	2:00–6:00 PM	
Volunteer	Volunteer		Volunteer	Volunteer	Volunteer	
	4:30–6:00 PM		4:30–6:00 PM	7:00–9:00 PM		
	Class		Class	Study		

Write about It Write three to four sentences about your weekly schedule.

33 | Error Correction Correct any errors in these sentences. (Some sentences may not have any errors.)

1. When I get presents, I always am happy.
2. I enjoy usually board games.
3. She don't have often time to read.
4. He all the time is tired.
5. We don't do ever anything.
6. My sister doesn't never have time to visit me.
7. I only have class once week.
8. She studies here all the day.

1.6 Present Progressive Statements

A

1 A: Hey, John. Your phone's **ringing**. B: Thanks. **2** A: How **are** you **feeling** today? B: A little better, thanks. **3** Engineers **are looking** for ways to build better cars.	We use the **present progressive** form of a verb to show that something is: • in progress now and • temporary, or lasting for a limited time Now can be exactly at this moment or more general (*today, this week, this year*, etc.) as in **1 – 3**.
CHANGING STATES OR SITUATIONS **4** We are all **getting** older. **5** The price of food **is increasing**. **6** I'm **getting** tired.	We also use the present progressive to describe changing states or situations, as in **4 – 6**. Common verbs we use this way are: become decrease get grow increase **GRAMMAR TERM:** The present progressive is also called the **present continuous**.

B

For the present progressive, we use *am / is / are* + (**not**) + the **-ing form of a main verb**, as in **7 – 11**. With the present progressive, *be* is a helping verb.

FIRST PERSON

		be (+ not)	verb + -ing
7	I	am 'm am not 'm not	working.
8	We	are 're are not 're not aren't	working.

SECOND PERSON

		be (+ not)	verb + -ing
9	You	are 're are not 're not aren't	working.

THIRD PERSON

		be (+ not)	verb + -ing
10	He She It	is 's is not 's not isn't	working.
11	We	are 're are not 're not aren't	working.

For a list of spelling rules for the *-ing* form of verbs, see Activity 35, page 24.

GRAMMAR TERM: The *-ing* form of a verb is sometimes called the **present participle**.

GO ONLINE

34 | Noticing Present Progressive Verbs Underline the present progressive verbs in these sentences. Then check (✓) *True* or *False*. 1.6 A

		TRUE	FALSE
1.	I'<u>m feeling</u> pretty good today.	☐	☐
2.	I'm just sitting at home right now.	☐	☐
3.	We're still studying verbs in class this week.	☐	☐
4.	My English is getting better and better.	☐	☐
5.	I'm making a lot of new friends these days.	☐	☐
6.	The weather is getting colder now.	☐	☐
7.	The price of gasoline is increasing again.	☐	☐
8.	The days⁵ are getting shorter now.	☐	☐
9.	My understanding of English is improving.	☐	☐
10.	I'm finding a lot of interesting things to do these days.	☐	☐
11.	I'm spending a lot of money this year.	☐	☐
12.	I'm taking an interesting course this semester.	☐	☐

> **F Y I**
>
> We sometimes use the adverbs *just* and *still* with present progressive verbs.
>
> He is **just** finishing his homework now.
> (just = at this moment)
>
> She is **still** eating dinner.
> (still = something continuing until now, often longer than expected)

Think about It Which verbs above describe a changing state or situation?

Think about It Circle the time expressions above that we use with the present progressive.

Write about It Rewrite the false statements above to make them true. Then compare ideas with your classmates.

I'm feeling pretty tired today.

35 | Spelling Note: *-ing* Verbs Read the note. Then do Activity 36.

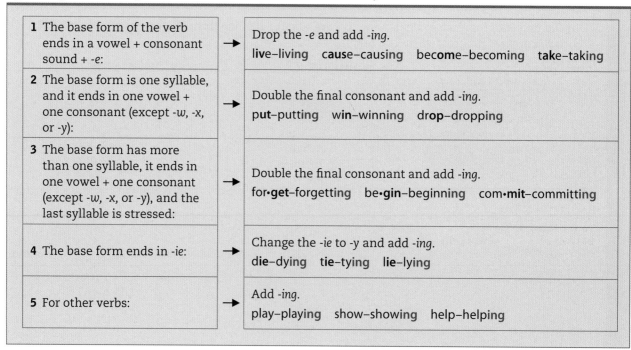

1 The base form of the verb ends in a vowel + consonant sound + *-e*:	→	Drop the *-e* and add *-ing*. live–living cause–causing become–becoming take–taking
2 The base form is one syllable, and it ends in one vowel + one consonant (except *-w, -x,* or *-y*):	→	Double the final consonant and add *-ing*. put–putting win–winning drop–dropping
3 The base form has more than one syllable, it ends in one vowel + one consonant (except *-w, -x,* or *-y*), and the last syllable is stressed:	→	Double the final consonant and add *-ing*. for·**get**–forgetting be·**gin**–beginning com·**mit**–committing
4 The base form ends in *-ie*:	→	Change the *-ie* to *-y* and add *-ing*. die–dying tie–tying lie–lying
5 For other verbs:	→	Add *-ing*. play–playing show–showing help–helping

⁵ **days:** the amount of daylight during the day

36 | Spelling -ing Verbs Write the -ing form of these verbs. `1.6 B`

Base form	-ing form	Base form	-ing form	Base form	-ing form
1. run	_____	11. leave	_____	21. increase	_____
2. shop	_____	12. wait	_____	22. decrease	_____
3. make	_____	13. sit	_____	23. get	_____
4. rain	_____	14. stand	_____	24. improve	_____
5. bring	_____	15. wear	_____	25. change	_____
6. buy	_____	16. hold	_____	26. look	_____
7. carry	_____	17. live	_____	27. watch	_____
8. come	_____	18. stay	_____	28. feel	_____
9. cry	_____	19. joke	_____	29. stare	_____
10. laugh	_____	20. talk	_____	30. refer	_____

37 | Using Present Progressive Verbs Write the present progressive form of the verb in parentheses. Use contractions. Then practice with a partner. `1.6 B`

1. A: Where's Matt Jacobs? I never see him anymore.
   B: He _'s living_ in Thailand this year. (live)

2. A: Are you OK?
   B: Yeah, I ____ just _____ a little tired. (feel)

3. A: Let's go. It _____ late. (get)
   B: But I _____ fun. (have)

4. A: What's the matter?
   B: Dad _____ dinner. (cook)
   A: Why?
   B: Because Mom _____ late. (work)

5. A: Why is it so quiet in here?
   B: Shhh. James and Toshi _____ chess. (play)
   A: Why does James look so unhappy?
   B: Because Toshi _____ . (win)

6. A: What's that noise?
   B: It's Anna. She _____ the piano. (play)

7. A: This is a great picnic.
   B: I'm glad you _____ yourself. (enjoy)

8. A: What's the problem?
   B: My phone _____ again. (not/work)
   A: Do you want to use mine?
   B: Thanks.

9. A: Where's your brother?
   B: He ____ still _____ dressed. (get)
   A: But it's already 8:00. We need to leave now.

10. A: Do you like your new boss?
    B: Yes, but he's about 200 years old.
    A: I think you _____ . (exaggerate)
    B: OK, so maybe he's 70.

38 | Describing Changing Things Write a sentence telling how each item in the box is changing. `1.6 A–B`

airplanes	computers	the Internet	the price of gasoline
cell phones	newspapers	the number of cars on the road	TV sets

TV sets are getting thinner and bigger.   OR   *The picture on a TV set is getting better.*

Talk about It Compare ideas from your sentences with your classmates.

1.7   Questions with the Present Progressive

To form present progressive *yes/no* questions, we put *am / is / are* before the subject and use the **-ing form** of a main verb, as in **1 – 2**. We can give short answers to *yes/no* questions with *am / is / are*, as in **3 – 6**.

A

YES/NO QUESTIONS

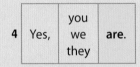

SHORT ANSWERS

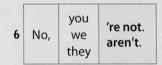

WARNING! We don't use contractions with short *yes* answers.

For *wh-* questions, we use a **wh- word** + *am / is / are* and the **-ing form of a main verb**, as in **7 – 18**. In **17 – 18**, the *wh-* word is the subject.

B

WH- QUESTIONS

	wh- word	be	subject	verb + -ing
7	Where	am	I	going?
8	How		I	doing?
9	Why		you	laughing?
10	Who	are	they	calling?
11	What		your kids	doing?

	wh- word	be	subject	verb + -ing
12	Where		Tom	going?
13	How		she	doing?
14	Why	is	he	laughing?
15	Who		Sarah	calling?
16	What		it	doing?

WH- QUESTIONS ABOUT THE SUBJECT

	subject	be	verb + -ing
17	What	is	happening?
18	Who		calling?

39 | Asking *Yes/No* Questions Use the words in parentheses to write short conversations. Use the present progressive form of the **bold** verb. Then practice with a partner. ▐ 1.7 A ▐

1. A: _Is it getting late?_ _____ (it/**get**/late?)

   B: _Yes, it is._ _____ (yes)

2. A: _____ (you/**listen**/to me?)

   B: _____ (yes)

3. A: _____ (I/**talk**/too loudly?)

   B: _____ (no)

4. A: _____

   _____ (anyone else in your family/**take**/an English class?)

   B: _____ (no)

5. A: _____ (I/**bother**/you?)

   B: _____ (no)

6. A: _____ (it/**rain**?)

   B: _____ (yes)

7. A: _____ (they/**pay**/attention/now?)

   B: _____ (yes)

8. A: _____ (you/**speak**/to me?)

   B: _____ (yes)

9. A: _____ (he/**wait**/for the bus?)

   B: _____ (yes)

10. A: _____ (you/**worry**/about the test?)

    B: _____ (no)

Think about It Underline the main verbs in the conversations above. Circle the helping verbs.

Talk about It Ask a partner the questions you wrote above. Use your own ideas to give answers.

🔊 **40 | Pronunciation Note: Contractions with *Wh-* Words** Listen to the note. Then do Activity 41.

> In conversation, we usually contract (or shorten) the verb *be* in *wh-* questions.
>
> | **Contracted, spoken form** | **Full, written form** |
> | --- | --- |
> | **1** What's she reading? | What is she reading? |
> | **2** Where're you living? | Where are you living? |
> | **3** Who's talking? | Who is talking? |

🔊 **41 | Listening for Contractions** Listen and repeat the questions. Then write the full, written form of each question. ▐ 1.7 B ▐

CONTRACTED, SPOKEN FORM	FULL, WRITTEN FORM
1. Why's she crying?	_Why is she crying?_
2. How're they doing?	_____

CONTRACTED, SPOKEN FORM	FULL, WRITTEN FORM
3. Who's calling me?	_____
4. What're they making?	_____
5. How's she feeling?	_____
6. Why're we leaving now?	_____
7. Why're you being so rude?	_____
8. What's he talking about?	_____
9. Who's singing?	_____
10. Why's she doing that?	_____
11. Who're you talking to?	_____
12. Where's his computer?	_____
13. What's making that noise?	_____
14. Who's cooking dinner?	_____

Talk about It **Work with a partner. Choose three of the questions in Activity 41 and create short conversations.**

A: *Why's she crying?*
B: *She failed the test!*

42 | Forming *Wh-* Questions **Complete these conversations with a *wh-* word and the present progressive form of the verb in parentheses. Then practice with a partner.** `1.7 B`

1. A: *What are you doing* _____? (do)

   B: I'm watching a movie. What about you?

2. A: _____? (cry)

   B: Because his stomach hurts.

3. A: _____ that noise? (make)

   B: It's Dad. He's building something outside.

4. A: _____ for a job? (look)

   B: Because she needs the money.

5. A: _____? (live)

   B: In an apartment with her mother.

6. A: _____ in school? (do)

   B: Great. I'm learning a lot.

7. A: _____ in school? (study)

   B: She's majoring in engineering.

8. A: _____ that away? (throw)

   B: Because I don't need it anymore.

9. A: _____ now? (work)

   B: At a bank. I really like it.

10. A: _____ my phone? (use)

    B: Not me. Maybe Rob has it.

> **RESEARCH SAYS...**
>
> The present progressive form of verbs is much more common in conversation than in writing.

43 | Error Correction Correct any errors in these sentences. (Some sentences may not have any errors.)

1. Where she going?

2. Who you talking to?

3. They leaving?

4. What he is doing?

5. What are you do with my computer?

6. Why is she leaving?

7. Are you talk to me?

8. What happening?

1.8 Comparing the Simple Present and Present Progressive

A

SIMPLE PRESENT

We use the **simple present** to describe things that are habitual or generally true, as in **1a – 4a**.

1a You **make** me nervous.
(= It's always true. You always make me nervous.)

2a He **cooks** dinner, not me.
(= It's habitual. He always cooks dinner.)

3a She's rude.
(= It's always true. She's always rude.)

4a The cost of living **increases** every year.
(= It's generally true. It increases.)

PRESENT PROGRESSIVE

We use the **present progressive** to describe temporary things in progress now, as in **1b – 3b**, or changing states or situations, as in **4b**.

1b You **are making** me nervous.
(= It's temporary. You are making me nervous now.)

2b He's **cooking** dinner.
(= It's in progress. He's cooking now.)

3b She's **being** rude.
(= It's temporary. She's being rude right now.)

4b The cost of living **is increasing**.
(= The cost of living is changing now.)

We use different **time expressions** with the simple present and present progressive, as in **5 – 6**.

B

Common time expressions used with the simple present include:

always	every day	once a day
never	every month	twice a day
usually	on Saturday	

5a My sister **usually drives** me to school.
6a I **work every day**.

Common time expressions used with the present progressive include:

now	this week	today
right now	this month	these days
at the moment	this year	nowadays

5b I'm **taking** the bus to school **today**.
6b I'm **working** every day **this week**.

C

CORRECT THE COMMON ERRORS (See page R-14.)

7 ✗ I'm usually going to school on Monday.

8 ✗ He cooks dinner right now.

9 ✗ You're always make fun of me.

10 ✗ They watching TV every evening.

GO ONLINE

44 | **Distinguishing the Simple Present and Present Progressive** Circle the simple present verbs in these paragraphs. Underline the present progressive verbs. `1.8 A`

THE TRADITIONAL ROLES OF FATHERS AND MOTHERS

1. I (think) that the traditional role of fathers <u>is changing</u>. It's not common yet, but more and more fathers are leaving their careers. They are staying home and taking care of the children while their wives go to work.

2. The traditional role of fathers is slowly changing. In many homes today, both parents work outside the home. This means that fathers need to do some of the work at home. For example, my father does the food shopping, and he usually washes the dishes; my mother cooks all the food.

3. In many countries, the traditional role of mothers is changing very little or not at all. In my country, many women prefer to stay at home. They don't want to work outside the home.

4. Many people think that mothers belong at home when they have young children. I don't agree with this. I have two young children, but I still work five days a week. My children go to a good daycare center every day.

Think about It Why does the writer use the simple present or present progressive above? Choose a reason from the chart below. Write the number of the reason over the verb. (More than one answer may be possible for each verb.)

Reasons for using the simple present	Reasons for using the present progressive
1. for habits and routines 2. for timeless truths and general statements 3. for states—how someone or something is (These are also a kind of general statement.)	4. for temporary actions in progress now 5. for changing states or situations

45 | **Usage Note: Verbs with Active and Non-Active Meanings** Read the note. Then do Activity 46.

Some verbs have both active and non-active meanings. We use the present progressive with the active meaning of these verbs to show that something is temporary.

Active meaning	**Non-active meaning**
He **is being** friendly.	He **is** friendly.
(= He is behaving in a friendly way right now.)	(= He is always friendly.)
I'm **thinking** about it. (= I am using my mind.)	I **think** you are right. (= In my opinion, you are right.)
We're **having** a lot of fun. (= We are experiencing fun.)	He **has** my book. (= He possesses my book.)

46 | Choosing the Correct Meaning Match the **bold** verbs with the dictionary definitions. Write the letter of the definition. (Some definitions can be used more than once.) `1.8 A`

<u>*a*</u> 1. A: Do you know how to use this computer?

    B: What do you mean?

    A: Well, it's turned on, but I**'m** not **seeing** anything on the screen.

____ 2. A: I don't want to go to that movie tonight.

    B: I **see**. Is there something else you want to do?

____ 3. A: I **see** you as a famous scientist someday.

    B: Me? Really?

    A: Yeah. You're really smart, and you work really hard.

____ 4. A: Do you **see** that big bird over there?

    B: Yeah. What is it?

____ 5. A: Please **see** that the children do their homework.

    B: No problem.

____ 6. A: What time is it?

    B: I **think** it's about 3:00.

____ 7. A: What **are** you **thinking** about?

    B: Nothing special. Just my work.

____ 8. A: What are you **thinking** of cooking for dinner?

    B: What about chicken?

    A: Sounds good.

____ 9. A: Do you **think** Jon is OK?

    B: Yeah, I **think** he's just tired.

____10. A: Do you **have** a cell phone?

    B: Yeah. Do you need it?

____11. A: Are you **having** fun?

    B: Yes. This is a great football game.

____12. A: What's the matter?

    B: Nothing, really. I just **have** a headache.

____13. A: Why is everybody here?

    B: Because we**'re having** a picnic.

---

see /si/ *verb* (**saw, seen, see·ing**)

  a. to notice something using your eyes

  b. to understand

  c. to imagine

  d. to make sure

---

think /θɪŋk/ *verb* (**thought, thought, think·ing**)

  a. to use your mind

  b. to believe; to have as an opinion

  c. to plan

---

have /hæv/ *verb* (**had, had, hav·ing**)

  a. to own; to possess

  b. to be sick with

  c. to experience something

  d. to hold or organize an event

---

47 | Present Progressive or Simple Present? Complete these conversations. Use the present progressive or simple present form of the verb in parentheses. Then practice with a partner. `1.8 A–B`

1. A: (*telephone rings*) Hello.

    B: Hi, Sam. It's me. Are you busy?

    A: Yeah, I <u>*'m making*</u> dinner. (make)

2. A: Why don't you like Mr. Jones?

    B: I don't know. He _____ me nervous. (make)

3. A: How do you get to work?

    B: I usually _____. (drive)

4. A: Who _____ me to school today? (drive)

    B: Ask your father.

5. A: How is the baby?

    B: Fine, but she still _____ through the night. (not/sleep)

6. A: Can I talk to Emma?

    B: She _____ right now. (sleep)

7. A: _____ you usually _____ a
   suit to work? (wear)

   B: No, thank goodness.

8. A: Why _____ you _____ a suit
   today? (wear)

   B: I have an important meeting.

9. A: What _____ you _____ ? (drink)

   B: It's just water.

10. A: Do you want some coffee?

    B: Thanks, but I _____ coffee.
    (not/drink)

11. A: _____ you _____ a lot?
    (travel)

    B: No, only a few times a year.

12. A: Where's Hassan?

    B: He _____ this week. (travel)

Think about It Circle the time expressions in the conversations in Activity 47.

48 | Choosing the Simple Present or Present Progressive Choose verbs from the boxes to
complete these paragraphs. Use the simple present or present progressive form. ` 1.8 A–B `

FAMOUS PEOPLE WHO HELP

1. The actor Leonardo DiCaprio _____*believes*_____ that
   the environment[6] is a very important issue. Right now he
   _____ a television series about a town in the U.S.
   The people in this community _____ their town
   to be environmentally healthy. DiCaprio _____
   this town is a good model for the rest of the world.

   | believe |
   | produce |
   | rebuild |
   | think |

2. The actors Gwyneth Paltrow and Cameron Diaz
   _____ to a group called the Union of Concerned
   Scientists. This group _____ environmental
   scientists, famous people, and regular people. These days, they
   _____ together on issues such as global warming
   and nuclear power.

   | belong |
   | include |
   | work |

3. Russell Simmons _____ to help children.
   He _____ art and education programs for
   children in New York City. Simmons is a famous rap music
   producer, and he _____ a lot about music and
   how it affects the lives of children. This year his organization
   _____ money to build a large arts education
   center.

   | know |
   | raise |
   | run |
   | want |

Think about It Underline each time expression above. Think of a different time expression you
could use.

[6] **the environment:** the air, water, land, animals, and plants around us

49 | Error Correction Correct any errors in these sentences. (Some sentences may not have any errors.)

1. We are going there every day.
2. You work too hard.
3. My mother is usually cooking dinner.
4. He is a vegetarian, so he is not eating any meat.
5. When I have a problem, I'm thinking of him.
6. The earth is dying because it's more and more trash building up.
7. When I feeling sad, she tell me a funny story and I laugh.
8. He is running his business well.
9. Every month she receive money and is sending it to her family at home.
10. I feel good every time I am answering an email.
11. The universities in my country are getting better.

1.9 Imperatives

A

1 **Stop** it!
2 **Turn** right at the corner.
3 **Remember** to call your father.
4 **Watch** out! There's glass on the floor.
5 **Get** home safely.

6 Please **help** me.
7 Please **stop** talking.

We can use the **base form of a verb** to:
- give commands, as in **1**
- give instructions, as in **2**
- give advice, as in **3**
- give a warning, as in **4**
- wish something, as in **5**

We call these sentences **imperatives**. The subject of an imperative statement is always *you*, but we don't say or write *you*.

We often use the word *please* to soften an imperative, as in **6 – 7**.

B

8 **Don't open** that.
9 **Don't forget** your sister's birthday.
10 **Don't worry** about it.
11 **Don't be** late.

We use **don't** + the **base form of a verb** for a negative imperative, as in **8 – 11**.

GO ONLINE

---

50 | Using Imperatives Write each imperative under the correct group in the chart below. (Some may fit in both groups.) **1.9 A**

Be a good girl.	Leave your sister alone.	Repeat after me.	Stop talking.
Eat your vegetables.	Please be quiet.	Say "please."	Take out your books.
Go to your room.	Please pass in your papers.	Sit up straight.	Turn to page 43.

Things teachers say to students	Things parents say to their children
Please be quiet.	*Please be quiet.*

Write about It Add three more imperative sentences to each group in Activity 50.

Think about It Which of the statements in Activity 50 are commands? Which are instructions?

51 | Understanding Informal Expressions Match each imperative to an informal expression with a similar meaning. `1.9 A–B`

IMPERATIVES

1. Please start eating. _e_
2. Have a good night's sleep. ____
3. Be careful. ____
4. Don't say anything. ____
5. Wait. Slow down. Be patient. ____
6. Go away. ____
7. Don't stop. ____
8. Stop doing that. ____
9. Stop complaining. ____
10. Relax. ____

INFORMAL EXPRESSIONS

a. Cut it out.
b. Get lost.
c. Sleep tight.
d. Chill out.
e. Dig in.
f. Watch your step.
g. Quit your moaning.
h. Hang in there.
i. Hold your horses.
j. Hold your tongue.

> **WARNING!**
> Be careful how you use informal expressions like the ones in Activity 51. Some of them may sound impolite if you use them in the wrong situation.

52 | Giving Advice Choose verbs from the boxes to complete the advice. (You will need to use *don't* in some of your answers.) `1.9 A–B`

USEFUL ADVICE

I don't sleep well at night. How can I get more sleep?

1. _____ _Don't drink_ _____ a lot of coffee.
2. _____ regularly.
3. _____ a nap during the day.
4. _____ to bed at the same time every night.
5. _____ a big meal just before you go to bed.

> drink
> eat
> exercise
> go
> take

What's the best way to learn a foreign language?

1. _____ interesting books and magazines.
2. _____ afraid to make mistakes.
3. _____ some people to practice with.
4. _____ in a country where people speak the language.
5. _____ about having an accent.

> be
> find
> live
> read
> worry

Write about It Write two other pieces of advice to answer each question above. Use imperatives.

53 | Giving Written Advice Complete the advice on page 35 with the verbs from the box. `1.9 A–B`

be	be	circle	imitate	talk	talk
be	buy	collect	read	talk	talk

34

Gwendolyn Brooks,
winner of the Pulitzer
Prize for Poetry, 1950

ADVICE ON WRITING FROM THE POET GWENDOLYN BROOKS

In your poems, _____talk_____ about what you know. _____
   1   2
about what you think. _____ about what you feel.
                            3
_____ about what you wonder. _____ words!
      4   5
_____ your own dictionary. _____ your dictionary
      6   7
every day. _____ exciting words. The more words you know, the
                  8
better you will be able to express yourself, your thoughts.

_____ yourself. Do not _____ other poets. You are
      9   10
as important as they are. Do not _____ afraid to say something
                                          11
new. In some of your poems, _____ a little mysterious. Surprise
                                        12
yourself and your reader.

1.10 Using the Present in Speaking

A

1 Nice shirt. (= That's a nice shirt.)

2 Ready to go? (= Are you ready to go?)

3 You see that guy? (= Do you see that guy?)

4 You doing anything? (= Are you doing anything?)

5 See that man? (= Do you see that man?)

6 Looking for something?
(= Are you looking for something?)

In everyday conversation, we often shorten statements and questions. We can sometimes leave out:
- the subject and main verb *be*, as in **1 – 2**
- a helping verb, like *do* or *be*, as in **3 – 4**
- a helping verb and the subject, as in **5 – 6**

B

7 A: Are you ready?
   B: **Uh-huh.**

8 A: Are you sleeping?
   B: **Nope.**

9 A: Do you have your cell phone?
   B: **I think so.**

In everyday conversation, we sometimes use these words to answer *yes/no* questions, as in **7 – 9**.

POSITIVE ANSWERS		NEGATIVE ANSWERS	
Yep.	Sure.	Nah.	I don't think so.
Yeah.	I think so.	Nope.	I doubt it.
Uh-huh.	Of course.	Uh-uh.	Of course not.

C

10 A: Are you watching this program?
   B: Yes, **it's really interesting.**

11 A: Are you calling Tina?
   B: No, **I'm calling Paul.**

12 A: Does your rent include heat and electricity?
   B: No, **I pay extra for them.**

In conversation, we often answer a *yes/no* question with *yes* or *no* and more information, as in **10 – 12**.

◄)) 54 | Understanding Shortened Sentences Listen and complete the shortened sentences. Then listen again and repeat the sentences. `1.10 A`

1. _____New_____ sweater?
2. _____ now?
3. _____ that?
4. _____ tired?
5. _____ OK?
6. _____ anything?
7. _____ for that job interview tomorrow?
8. _____ to know something?
9. _____ this?
10. _____ to see you.
11. _____ answer.
12. _____ car.

Think about It What words did the speaker leave out in each sentence above? Share ideas with your classmates. (More than one answer may be possible.)

1. _Is that a new sweater?_
2. _____
3. _____
4. _____
5. _____
6. _____
7. _____
8. _____
9. _____
10. _____
11. _____
12. _____

55 | Shortening Statements and Questions Complete the conversations by shortening the statements in parentheses. (More than one answer may be possible.) Then practice with a partner. `1.10 A`

1. A: This is my friend John.
   B: _Pleased to meet you._ _____ (I'm pleased to meet you.)

2. A: How's everything?
   B: _____ (Everything is fine.)

3. A: What smells so good?
   B: Spaghetti. _____ (Do you want some?)

4. A: Let's have sushi for dinner.
   B: _____ (That's an interesting choice.)

5. A: _____ (Do you want my dessert?)
   B: Sure. Thanks.

6. A: _____ (Are you listening to this?)
   B: No, turn it off.

7. A: _____ (Are you talking to me?)
   B: No, I'm talking to myself.

8. A: _____ (Is everybody here?)
   B: Yes, I think so.

9. A: _____ (Do you need some more paper?)
   B: No, I have plenty.

10. A: _____ (Is this your coat?)
    B: No, I think it's David's.

56 | Understanding Positive and Negative Answers Listen to these questions and answers. Does the speaker give a positive answer or a negative answer? Check (✓) your answers. 1.10 B

	Positive	Negative
1.	☐	✓
2.	☐	☐
3.	☐	☐
4.	☐	☐
5.	☐	☐
6.	☐	☐
7.	☐	☐
8.	☐	☐
9.	☐	☐
10.	☐	☐
11.	☐	☐
12.	☐	☐
13.	☐	☐
14.	☐	☐
15.	☐	☐

PRONUNCIATION

Uh-huh means "yes." It is pronounced with stress on the second syllable. *Uh-uh* means "no." It is pronounced with stress on the first syllable.

A: Are you ready?   A: Are you ready?
B: **Uh-HUH.** (= yes)   B: **UH-uh.** (= no)

57 | Answering *Yes/No* Questions Match the questions with the answers. Then practice with a partner. 1.10 C

QUESTIONS

1. Does your class meet every day? __e__
2. Are you listening to me? ____
3. Are you hungry? ____
4. Do you feel OK? ____
5. Are you studying? ____
6. Do you drink coffee? ____
7. Is your sister here? ____
8. Does it ever snow here in the winter? ____
9. Are stores here closed on Sunday? ____
10. Is anyone using this computer? ____

ANSWERS

a. Yes, but I think you're wrong.
b. Yes, I'm starving.
c. No, she's at home.
d. No, they're usually open.
e. No, only on Tuesday and Thursday.
f. No, it's all yours.
g. No, it's too warm here.
h. No, I prefer tea.
i. Yeah, I'm doing my math homework.
j. Yes, I'm fine.

Talk about It Think of two more ways to answer each question above.

Question: Does your class meet every day?
Answers: Yes, but I don't go on Saturday or Sunday./No, it doesn't meet on Friday.

A

WRITING DESCRIPTIONS

1 A pyramid **is** a shape with a flat bottom and three sides. The sides **come** to a point at the top.

2 A dictionary **explains** the meaning of words from A to Z. Nowadays, many people **use** online dictionaries.

3 An internist **is** a doctor of internal medicine. Internists **specialize** in treating adults. Many internists **get** more training in another specialty. For example, a cardiologist **is** an internist with extra training in diseases of the heart.

We often use the **simple present** when we write descriptions of people and things, as in **1 – 3**.

B

WRITING SUMMARIES

4 The book *Mama's Bank Account* by Kathryn Forbes **tells** the story of an immigrant Norwegian family in San Francisco in the early 1900s. In one episode, Mama's daughter and son **need** to bring food to school for their classmates. . . .

Writers often use the simple present to review or summarize the plot of a book or movie, as in **4**.

C

WRITING LISTS AND INSTRUCTIONS

5
- **buy** some milk
- **call** Ben
- **pay** bills

6 Jog with your shoulders back and your arms and hands relaxed. **Bend** your elbows at your waist, and **let** your arms swing naturally.

We use **imperatives** to make written lists of things to do, as in **5**. We also use imperatives to give written instructions, as in **6**.

58 | Using the Simple Present in Descriptions Read these descriptions and add the simple present form of the verb in parentheses. **1.11 A**

Descriptive Paragraphs

1. Accidents often _____*happen*_____ at home. The Consumer Product Safety Commission
   (happen)

   _____ that the five most dangerous things in the house _____: stairs, glass
   (report)   (be)

   doors, cutlery[7], glass bottles and jars, and home power tools.

2. A bistro _____ a type of restaurant. These small restaurants _____ good food
   (be)   (serve)

   in a friendly atmosphere. However, don't expect to get your meal quickly. Bistros _____ not
   (be)

   fast-food restaurants. Bistros _____ French in origin, but they _____ now more
   (be)   (be)

   popular in other countries as well.

[7]**cutlery:** tableware (knives, forks, etc.)

3. Every airplane _____ a black box or flight data recorder. The black box _____
   (carry)   (be / not)
   actually black—it _____ orange. Inside the box, a stainless-steel tape _____
                     (be)   (contain)
   information on the airplane's airspeed and altitude[8]. A second orange box _____ a tape of
                                                                               (have)
   the last half-hour of conversation between the pilots in the cockpit.

Write about It Write a short description of something that interests you.

59 | Using the Present in Summaries Read these movie summaries and underline the verbs. `1.11 B`

Movie Plots

The movie *Girl with a Pearl Earring* <u>takes place</u> in the seventeenth century in Holland. It tells the story of the famous painter Johannes Vermeer and a young woman, his servant. In the movie, Vermeer decides to paint the young woman's picture, and he asks her to wear a pair of pearl earrings for the painting. Unfortunately, the earrings belong to Vermeer's wife. She becomes very jealous, and she begins to make the young woman's life difficult. In the end . . .

The movie *The English Patient* takes place in Italy during World War II. At the beginning of the movie, Hana, a nurse from Canada, is taking care of a badly injured pilot. The pilot says he doesn't remember his name or anything else about himself. Because he has an English accent, the doctors and nurses call him "the English patient." Over time, Hana learns more about the patient, and in the end . . .

Write about It Complete each summary above in your own words. (If you haven't seen the movies, make up your own endings.)

Write about It Choose a movie or book. Write a short summary of it. Answer these questions.
1. Where does the story take place?
2. When does the story take place?
3. What important things happen in the story?

[8] **altitude:** elevation; height in the sky

Writing Lists List ten things you need to do this week. `1.11 C`

Things to Do This Week	
1.	6.
2.	7.
3.	8.
4.	9.
5.	10.

Talk about It Talk to different classmates. Look for people who have the same things on their list.

A: Do you have "Study for the test" on your list?
B: Yes, I do. Do you have "Get some exercise" on your list?

WRAP-UP Demonstrate Your Knowledge

A | SURVEY Ask your classmates questions to find the information below. When someone answers "Yes," write the person's name in the box.

A: Do you speak Spanish?
B: No, I speak Arabic and English.

A: Do you speak Spanish?
C: Yes, I do.

FIND SOMEONE WHO . . .

1. speaks Spanish Name: _____	4. lives near here Name: _____	7. feels good today Name: _____
2. usually drives to school Name: _____	5. likes sports Name: _____	8. has a sister Name: _____
3. never studies on the weekend Name: _____	6. is looking for a job Name: _____	9. is having a good time in class Name: _____

B | PRESENTATION Think of a famous person who is alive today. Write sentences describing this person but don't name the person. Read your description aloud and let your classmates ask you more questions about the person. Then ask your classmates to identify the person.

This person is a famous athlete. He lives in . . .

C | WRITING Think of something that you like to do. Then answer these questions in a short piece of writing.

QUESTIONS

1. What is one of your favorite fun activities?
2. How often do you do this activity?
3. Why do you like to do this activity? How does it make you feel?

I like to watch movies—especially comedies. I usually watch three or four movies every week. I do this because movies relax me and make me feel happy. I also like to watch movies because they help me improve my English.

SIMPLE PRESENT

STATEMENTS		
I		work.
You We They		do not work. don't work.
He She It		works. does not work. doesn't work.

YES/NO QUESTIONS			
	Do	I / you / we / they	work?
	Does	he / she / it	

WH- QUESTIONS			
Where	do	I / you / we / they	work?
	does	he / she / it	
Who	works	here?	

USES

We use the **simple present**:
- for timeless truths and general statements
- to describe current habits and routines

SIMPLE PRESENT OF THE VERB *BE*

STATEMENTS		
I	am am not 'm not	
You We They	are are not aren't 're not	here.
He She It	is is not isn't 's not	

YES/NO QUESTIONS		
Am	I	
Are	you / we / they	here?
Is	he / she / it	

WH- QUESTIONS		
	am	I?
Where	are	you / we / they?
	is	he / she / it?
Who	is	here?

USES

We use the simple present of the **verb *be*** to describe current states and conditions.

PRESENT PROGRESSIVE

STATEMENTS		
I	am am not 'm not	
You We They	are are not aren't 're not	working.
He She It	is is not isn't 's not	

YES/NO QUESTIONS		
Am	I	
Are	you / we / they	working?
Is	he / she / it	

WH- QUESTIONS		
	am	I
Where	are	you / we / they	working?
	is	he / she / it
Who	is working?	

USES

We use the **present progressive** to show that something is:
- in progress now
- temporary, or lasting for a limited time

Simple Past and Past Progressive

I was working on . . .
one of my poems all
morning and took out a
comma. In the afternoon,
I put it back again.

—OSCAR WILDE,
  WRITER AND POET
  (1854–1900)

Talk about It What do you think the quotation above means?

WARM-UP

A | **Match the beginnings of these descriptions with their endings. Which of these habits do you think is the most unusual?**

Work Habits of Famous People

1. The movie director Ingmar Bergman (1918–2007) **hated** lateness. ____

2. The playwright Arthur Miller (1915–2005) **had** a destructive[1] routine. He usually **wrote** for several hours in the morning. ____

3. The architect Le Corbusier (1887–1965) **stayed** late in the office when his work **was going** well. ____

4. The mathematician Paul Erdos (1913–1996) **got up** early and **worked** for 19 hours straight[2]. ____

5. The philosopher Immanuel Kant (1724–1804) **didn't like** to get up early in the morning. ____

a. Then he **tore up** everything.

b. While he **was working**, he **drank** cup after cup of coffee.

c. Rehearsals[3] **began** promptly at 10:30, lunch **was** at 12:45, and work **finished** at 3:30.

d. Despite this, he **got up** at 5:00 a.m. every day.

e. When his work **wasn't going** very well, he **left** the office early.

B | **Answer these questions about the sentences above.**

1. Do the sentences describe people in the present or past? How do you know?
2. The words in **blue** are simple past verbs. Which of these verbs end in *-ed*? Which do not?
3. Which simple past verb above has a negative form?
4. The words in **green** are past progressive verbs. What is similar about the form of these three verbs?
5. Which past progressive verb has a negative form?

C | **Look back at the quotation on page 42. Identify any past verb forms.**

[1] **destructive:** causing damage
[2] **straight:** without stopping
[3] **rehearsals:** times when you practice something before a public performance

2.1 Using the Simple Past

A

1 Last year I **decided** to move to a new city.

2 We **heard** the news a few days ago.

3 As children, my sister and I **played** together a lot.

4 We **lived** in Costa Rica for 12 years.

5 My father **told** us lots of stories.

6 We **went** to school six days a week.

We often use the **simple past** to talk about something that began and ended in the past. This could be something that:

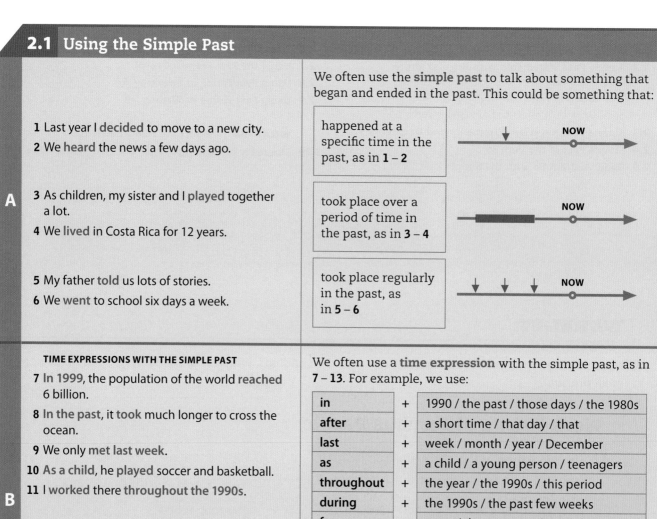

happened at a specific time in the past, as in **1 – 2**	NOW
took place over a period of time in the past, as in **3 – 4**	NOW
took place regularly in the past, as in **5 – 6**	NOW

B

TIME EXPRESSIONS WITH THE SIMPLE PAST

7 In 1999, the population of the world **reached** 6 billion.

8 **In the past**, it **took** much longer to cross the ocean.

9 We only **met** **last week**.

10 **As a child**, he **played** soccer and basketball.

11 I **worked** there **throughout the 1990s**.

12 She **started** playing tennis in April 2012. **A month later**, she **won** her first game.

13 They **got** married **a few years ago**.

We often use a **time expression** with the simple past, as in **7 – 13**. For example, we use:

in	+	1990 / the past / those days / the 1980s
after	+	a short time / that day / that
last	+	week / month / year / December
as	+	a child / a young person / teenagers
throughout	+	the year / the 1990s / this period
during	+	the 1990s / the past few weeks
for	+	years / the past year / several years
at	+	the age of four / that time / the end of the twentieth century

a day / a month / a year / soon	+	**after that**
a month / a year / several days	+	**later**
two days / a week / a few years	+	**ago**

ONLINE

1 | Noticing Simple Past Verbs

Underline the simple past verbs in these sentences. The number in parentheses shows the number of simple past verbs. **2.1 A**

INTERESTING FACTS ABOUT FAMOUS PEOPLE

1. For many years, the French writer Voltaire <u>drank</u> 30 cups of coffee a day. (1)

2. When Ludwig van Beethoven wrote his nine symphonies, he sometimes poured water over his head. That kept him awake. (3)

3. The French painter Paul Cézanne had a parrot[4]. He taught it to say, "Cézanne is a great painter!" (2)

4. When the Russian painter Marc Chagall bought things, he usually paid by check. Because he was very famous, people rarely cashed his checks[5], so he got a lot of things free. (5)

a painting by Marc Chagall

[4] **parrot:** a bird, often brightly colored, that can copy people's words

[5] **cash a check:** to get money for a check

5. The American writer Jack London did many adventurous[6] things while he was young. Later in life, however, he stayed in bed all day and wrote his books. (4)

6. When the British writer Anthony Burgess was 39, his doctors told him that he had only 1 more year to live. Burgess decided to write 10 novels in that year. During the year, Burgess wrote 5½ novels, and his illness disappeared. Burgess lived for 37 more years and wrote many more books. (8)

Think about It Look at the sentences in Activity 1. When did each action or event take place? Write each one under the correct group in the chart below. (More than one answer may be possible.)

Specific time in the past	Over a period of time in the past	Regularly in the past
		drank 30 cups of coffee a day

2 | Choosing Time Expressions Underline the simple past verbs and choose a time expression to complete each sentence. Check (✓) your answer. Then compare with a partner. 2.1 B

FAMOUS MOMENTS IN HISTORY

1. The first modern Olympic Games <u>took</u> place _____.
   - ☐ a. last year
   - ☐ b. during the 1950s
   - ☑ c. in 1896

2. Russians sent the first man into space _____.
   - ☐ a. during the 1950s
   - ☐ b. in the early 1960s
   - ☐ c. in 1971

3. The population of Earth reached 1 billion _____.
   - ☐ a. more than 200 years ago
   - ☐ b. during the 1980s
   - ☐ c. in 1900

4. Dinosaurs disappeared _____.
   - ☐ a. a few days ago
   - ☐ b. a very long time ago
   - ☐ c. in the 1200s

5. Teaching at Oxford University began _____.
   - ☐ a. in 1096
   - ☐ b. a short time ago
   - ☐ c. during the 1800s

6. Uruguay hosted the first World Cup games _____.
   - ☐ a. a few years ago
   - ☐ b. at the end of the nineteenth century
   - ☐ c. in 1930

7. The bicycle first became popular _____.
   - ☐ a. during the 1800s
   - ☐ b. 65 million years ago
   - ☐ c. in the twentieth century

8. Elizabeth I was queen of England _____.
   - ☐ a. throughout the late 1500s
   - ☐ b. in the 1800s
   - ☐ c. a few years ago

"I think the first modern Olympic Games took place in 1896. What do you think?"

[6] **adventurous:** enjoying exciting and dangerous things

3 | Identifying Time Expressions Read this text. Underline the time expressions with the simple past.

2.1 B

Working Together in Space

<u>In 1986,</u> the Russian space station *Mir* began to orbit Earth. During its lifetime, the space station was a temporary home to travelers from many different countries. In 1987, astronauts from Syria, Bulgaria, and Afghanistan spent time on *Mir*. Then, in 1990, a journalist from Japan, Toyohiro Akiyama, visited the space station and filed news reports from there. In 1991, Helen Sharman, a British chemist, traveled to the space station *Mir*. She was the winner of a contest with a prize of eight days on the *Mir* space station, and she became the first British astronaut. During her visit to *Mir*, Sharman did medical tests and other types of research. Throughout the 1990s, researchers and astronauts from different countries continued to visit and work on the Russian space station.

RESEARCH SAYS...

The most common time word used with the simple past is *then*. The most common time phrases use the prepositions *in*, *during*, *for*, and *throughout*.

CORP

Write about It Complete this timeline with information from the text above. Try to use your own words. Then compare with a partner. Were your timelines the same or different?

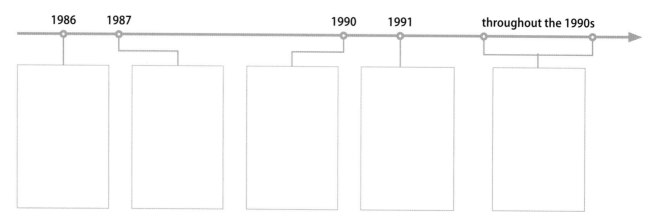

| 1986 | 1987 | 1990 | 1991 | throughout the 1990s |

Think about It Which time expressions from the text above can you also use with the simple present? Which ones cannot be used with the simple present?

2.2 Simple Past Statements with Regular and Irregular Verbs

There are two types of **simple past** verb forms: regular and irregular.

A

SIMPLE PAST WITH REGULAR VERBS

1 They **asked** me a lot of questions.

2 Somebody **called** late last night.

3 My sister **helped** me a lot.

For the simple past of regular verbs, we add *-d* or *-ed* to the base form, as in **1 – 3**.

REGULAR VERBS			
base form	simple past	base form	simple past
ask	ask**ed**	finish	finish**ed**
call	call**ed**	help	help**ed**
decide	decid**ed**	move	mov**ed**

4 We **studied** a number of surveys.

5 They **planned** everything carefully.

6 He **regretted** buying a used car.

A few regular verbs have a special spelling, as in **4 – 6**.

For a list of spelling rules, see Activity 9, page 50. For information on the pronunciation of *-ed* endings, see Activity 5, page 48.

B

SIMPLE PAST WITH IRREGULAR VERBS

7 She **sat** alone in the room.

8 I **forgot** my wallet.

9 Somebody **took** my lunch.

10 I needed to study, but I **went** out instead.

11 I **had** a great time.

About 200 verbs have an irregular past form, as in **7 – 11**. Some common irregular verbs are:

IRREGULAR VERBS			
base form	simple past	base form	simple past
get	**got**	say	**said**
go	**went**	see	**saw**
have	**had**	sit	**sat**
know	**knew**	take	**took**
make	**made**	think	**thought**

For a list of irregular verbs, see the Resources, page R-3.

C

CORRECT THE COMMON ERRORS (See page R-14.)

12 ✗ He attend, but he fail.

13 ✗ He teached me everything.

14 ✗ I sat and think for a while.

15 ✗ My grandfather dead five years ago.

GO ONLINE

4 | Using the Simple Past of Regular Verbs Complete these sentences with the simple past form of the **bold** verb. `2.2 A`

1. As a child, I _____*played*_____ a lot of football, but now I don't **play** anymore.

2. As children, my friends and I _____ the same things, and we still **enjoy** the same things.

3. My mother doesn't **help** me with my homework now, but she _____ me a lot in the past.

4. Ten years ago, I _____ a horse, but now I **want** a motorcycle.

5. As children, my brothers and I _____ a lot, and we still **laugh** a lot.

6. As a child, I _____ a lot of TV, but now I never **watch** TV.

7. I _____ hard in school when I was a child, but I don't **work** hard now.

8. As a child, I usually _____ to school, but now I never **walk** to school.

9. I don't often **stay up** late, but last night I _____ until two in the morning.

10. Our class **starts** at ten, but yesterday it _____ at eleven.

11. I usually **listen** to music in the morning, but yesterday I _____ to the news.

12. I don't usually **ask** questions in class, but yesterday I _____ several.

13. I don't typically **call** my husband at work, but yesterday I _____ him twice.

14. I usually **finish** my homework before class, but last week I _____ it in class.

Talk about It Are any of the statements in Activity 4 true for you? Tell a partner.

5 | Pronunciation Note: -ed Verb Endings Listen to the note. Then do Activities 6–8.

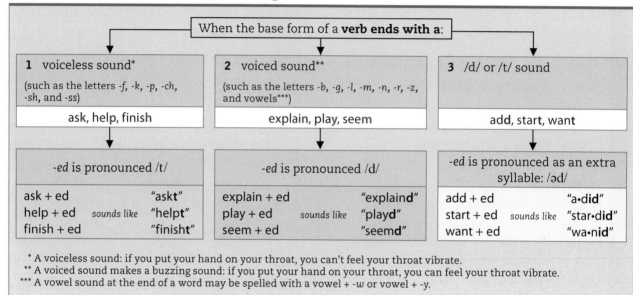

When the base form of a **verb ends with a**:		
1 voiceless sound* (such as the letters -f, -k, -p, -ch, -sh, and -ss)	**2** voiced sound** (such as the letters -b, -g, -l, -m, -n, -r, -z, and vowels***)	**3** /d/ or /t/ sound
ask, help, finish	explain, play, seem	add, start, want
-ed is pronounced /t/	-ed is pronounced /d/	-ed is pronounced as an extra syllable: /əd/
ask + ed "ask**t**" help + ed *sounds like* "help**t**" finish + ed "finish**t**"	explain + ed "explain**d**" play + ed *sounds like* "play**d**" seem + ed "seem**d**"	add + ed "a•**did**" start + ed *sounds like* "star•**did**" want + ed "wa•**nid**"

   * A voiceless sound: if you put your hand on your throat, you can't feel your throat vibrate.
  ** A voiced sound makes a buzzing sound: if you put your hand on your throat, you can feel your throat vibrate.
 *** A vowel sound at the end of a word may be spelled with a vowel + -w or vowel + -y.

6 | Pronouncing -ed Verb Endings Write each past verb under the correct group in the chart below. Then listen and confirm your answers. **2.2 A**

agreed	decided	listened	needed	showed	walked
believed	liked	looked	promised	suggested	watched

-ed ending sounds like /t/	**-ed** ending sounds like /d/	**-ed** ending sounds like /əd/
	agreed	

Think about It Listen and complete these sentences with the verbs above. Why are these verb endings difficult to hear in normal speech?

1. He ___*agreed*___ to go.
2. I _____ some help.
3. We _____ to the store.
4. They _____ to go.
5. He _____ it a lot.
6. I _____ a great movie.
7. She _____ me.
8. We _____ for a long time.
9. She _____ out the window.
10. He _____ to call.
11. She _____ her passport.
12. They _____ several good restaurants.

7 | Listening for the -ed Ending on Regular Verbs Listen for the simple past verb in each sentence. Check (✓) the ending you hear. `2.2 A`

	/t/ or /d/	/əd/		/t/ or /d/	/əd/
1. acted	☐	✓	10. encouraged	☐	☐
2. agreed	☐	☐	11. enjoyed	☐	☐
3. allowed	☐	☐	12. introduced	☐	☐
4. arranged	☐	☐	13. lasted	☐	☐
5. avoided	☐	☐	14. passed	☐	☐
6. burned	☐	☐	15. pointed	☐	☐
7. completed	☐	☐	16. separated	☐	☐
8. counted	☐	☐	17. talked	☐	☐
9. decided	☐	☐	18. waited	☐	☐

Talk about It Work with a partner. One person says the base form of a verb in the chart above. The other person says the simple past form.

A: *Complete.*
B: *Completed.*

8 | Present or Past? In normal speech, it is sometimes difficult to hear the difference between the simple present and simple past of regular verbs. Listen to the sentences and circle the verb you hear. `2.2 A`

1. She **works** / (**worked**) here.
2. They **like** / **liked** me.
3. She **agrees** / **agreed** with me.
4. He usually **arrives** / **arrived** at ten.
5. They **ask** / **asked** a lot of questions.
6. We **allow** / **allowed** everyone to go.
7. I always **enjoy** / **enjoyed** his company.
8. They always **finish** / **finished** before me.
9. We **discuss** / **discussed** lots of things.
10. She **calls** / **called** me every day.
11. We **move** / **moved** every year.
12. We never **talk** / **talked** about it.
13. I always **watch** / **watched** her games.
14. She **smiles** / **smiled** a lot.

> **F Y I**
>
> We can use some time expressions with more than one verb form. For example:
>
> **Simple Present**
> I **work** at home **every day**.
> I usually **study** at night.
>
> **Simple Past**
> I **worked** at home **every day**.
> I usually **studied at night**.

Talk about It Take turns reading the sentences above to a partner. Use either verb. Ask your partner to point to the verb you used.

A: *She works here.*
B: *[Points to "works."]*

9 | Spelling Note: Simple Past of Regular Verbs Read the note. Then do Activity 10.

	SPELLING RULES	base form	simple past
1	When the base form of a regular verb ends in -e, **add -d**.	close refuse	closed refused
2	When the base form ends in a consonant + **-y, change the -y to -i and add -ed**.	stud**y** worr**y** identif**y**	stud**ied** worr**ied** identif**ied**
3	When the base form has one syllable and ends in a **c**onsonant + **v**owel + consonant (CVC), **double the final consonant and add -ed**. (Warning! Do not double a final w, x, or y: play / played, wax / waxed, row / rowed.)	pla**n** jo**g** dro**p**	plan**ned** jog**ged** drop**ped**
4	When the base form of a two-syllable verb ends in a **c**onsonant + **v**owel + **c**onsonant (CVC) and the last syllable is stressed, **double the final consonant and add -ed**.	re·**fer** re·**gret**	referred regretted
5	For all other regular verbs, **add -ed**.	open destroy	opened destroyed

10 | Spelling Simple Past Regular Verbs Write the simple past form of each verb. `2.2 A`

Rule 1	Rule 2	Rule 3	Rule 4	Rule 5
agree _____*agreed*_____	carry _____	drip _____	admit _____	avoid _____
continue _____	copy _____	grin _____	commit _____	cook _____
damage _____	reply _____	hug _____	control _____	end _____
describe _____	try _____	rub _____	prefer _____	order _____

Think about It Add the simple past form of these verbs to the chart above.

dry	empty	enjoy	happen	increase	occur	permit	start	stop	wrap

11 | Using Irregular Verbs Write the simple past form of each verb. (For a list of irregular verbs, see the Resources, page R-3.) `2.2 B`

1. begin ____*began*____
2. buy _____
3. come _____
4. cut _____
5. eat _____
6. fall _____

7. fly _____
8. get _____
9. give _____
10. go _____
11. have _____
12. know _____

13. leave _____
14. run _____
15. see _____
16. sleep _____
17. win _____
18. write _____

Write about It Use ten of the verbs in Activity 11 to write sentences about your childhood. (Look back at Chart 2.1B for help with time expressions.)

I began school at the age of 5.

12 | Using Regular and Irregular Past Forms Complete this story with the simple past form of the verbs in parentheses. `2.2 A–B`

○ ○ ○

Sailing Around the World

Zac Sunderland _____*learned*_____
(1. learn)
to sail a boat at the age of 4! Thirteen

years later, Zac _____
(2. become)
one of the youngest people to

sail around the world by himself.

Zac _____ by the
(3. grow up)
water in California. As a child, he

_____ many hours sailing, surfing, and rock climbing.
(4. spend)
His father, Laurence, _____ a love of exploration to
(5. pass on)
his son. Laurence _____ Zac and his seven brothers
(6. take)
and sisters around Mexico, Australia, and New Zealand by sailboat.

After that, Zac _____ hard to buy his own sailboat and
(7. work)
_____ planning his trip around the world. At the age
(8. begin)
of 16, Zac _____ on his journey. The trip was hard, and
(9. leave)
Zac _____ through a lot of bad weather. He sometimes
(10. sail)
_____ lonely, but he _____ his journey in 13
(11. feel)   (12. finish)
months and two days.

STUDY STRATEGY

When you are learning irregular verbs, group them into categories that make sense to you. For example:

Verbs with different spelling but the same vowel sound

make   **made**
send   **sent**

Verbs with different spelling and different vowel sounds

feel   **felt**
say   **said**

Verbs that have the same spelling and pronunciation

cut   **cut**
put   **put**

Talk about It Close your book. Write three things you learned about Zac Sunderland. Then compare ideas with your classmates.

Think about It What time expressions did the writer use in the story above? Circle them. What other time expressions can you use in the sentences?

In sentence 2, you can use "At the age of 17" instead of "Thirteen years later."

13 | Error Correction   Correct any errors in these sentences. (Some sentences may not have any errors.)

1. For several years, she worked during the day and attend college at night.
2. I sat and think for a long time. Then I remembered the answer.
3. He try hard to finish college.
4. I told my parents and they agree with me.
5. At that time, not many people like her paintings. Later they admire her pictures a lot.
6. My uncle teached me everything about his work.
7. I meet him last year when I start my first class.
8. As a child, I usually finish all my homework and do well in school.

2.3   Simple Past Negative Statements and Questions

A

NEGATIVE STATEMENTS

		did + not	base form
1	I You He She It We You They	**did not** **didn't**	**go.**

We use the **helping verb** *did* + **not** + the **base form of a main verb** for simple past negative statements, as in **1**. In conversation, we usually use the contraction *didn't*.

B

YES/NO QUESTIONS

	did	subject	base form
2	**Did**	I you he she it we you they	**go?**

SHORT ANSWERS

			did (+ not)
3	Yes,	you I he she it	**did.**
	No,	you we they	**didn't.**

We use *did* and the **base form of a main verb** to form simple past *yes/no* questions, as in **2**.

We use *did* to give a short answer to a *yes/no* question, as in **3**. In negative short answers, we often use contractions.

C

WH- QUESTIONS

	wh- word	did	subject	base form
4	What		I	**do?**
5	Where		you	**live?**
6	When	**did**	he	**leave?**
7	Why		she	**quit?**
8	Who		it	**hurt?**
9	How long		they	**stay?**

For *wh-* questions, we use a **wh- word** + *did* and the **base form of a main verb**, as in **4 – 9**.

WH- QUESTIONS ABOUT THE SUBJECT

	subject	past verb form
10	What	**happened?**
11	Who	**called?**

When the *wh-* word is the subject, we use a **wh- word** + the **past form of a main verb**, as in **10 – 11**. We don't use *did*.

D

CORRECT THE COMMON ERRORS (See page R-14.)

12 ✗ They don't go shopping last weekend.

13 ✗ I no hear the news last night.

14 ✗ Who go with you?

15 ✗ When you get there?

14 | Using Positive and Negative Statements Complete these conversations with the positive or negative simple past form of the verb in parentheses. Then practice with a partner. `2.3 A`

1. A: What's the matter? You look upset.

   B: It's Amanda. She passed me on the street, but she _____didn't_____
   even ____say____ hello. (say)

   A: Maybe she _____ you. (see)

2. A: Are you OK?

   B: I'm just a little worried. I left a message for David, but he
   _____ me back. (call)

   A: Maybe he just _____ too busy. (get)

3. A: Why are you angry with Anna?

   B: Because she took my car, but she _____ first. (ask)

   A: Maybe she asked, but you _____ her. (hear)

4. A: Why are you firing Toshi?

   B: Because he _____ a lot of mistakes last week. (make)

   A: Maybe he _____ the task. (understand)

   B: That's possible, but he _____ to me with any questions either. (come)

5. A: Don't you think it's strange?

   B: What?

   A: John and Emma came all the way down here, and they _____ to visit us. (stop)

   B: Maybe they _____ time. (have)

6. A: Why is the front door unlocked?

   B: Maybe you _____ to lock it this morning. (forget)

   A: But I'm sure I did.

FYI

We sometimes use the word *even* to show that something is surprising.

He saw me, but he didn't **even** say hello.

She can't **even** remember my name.

15 | Asking *Yes/No* Questions about the Past Complete these conversations with the words in parentheses. Then practice with a partner. `2.3 B`

1. A: _____Did anyone call_____? (anyone/call)

   B: Yes, your wife called about an hour ago.

2. A: These cookies are delicious. _____ them? (you/make)

   B: No, I bought them.

3. A: _____ this photo? (your friend/take)

   B: Uh-huh. Do you like it?

   A: Yes. It's really nice.

4. A: _____ a good trip? (you/have)

   B: Yeah. We really enjoyed Sydney.

   A: _____ anywhere else in Australia? (you/go)

   B: Yes, we spent a week in Perth.

5. A: _____ the homework for today? (everyone/do)

   B: What homework?

6. A: _____ you about my award? (I/tell)

   B: Yes, three times.

7. A: _____ that? (you/see)

   B: See what?

   A: That car. It just went through a red light.

   B: _____ the license plate number? (you/get)

   A: No, it's too dark.

8. A: _____ my email? (you/get)

   B: What email? _____ me something? (you/send)

   A: Yeah, I sent an email this morning. It was important.

   B: Well, I didn't get it.

9. A: The food tasted good, but the waiter was kind of rude.

   B: Yeah. _____ him a tip? (you/leave)

   A: Yes, but not a very big one.

10. A: _____ anything to eat? (you/bring)

    B: No, I forgot.

Think about It Write each past verb in Activity 15 under the correct group in the chart below.

Regular simple past verbs	Irregular simple past verbs
called	*bought*

16 | Asking *Wh-* Questions about the Past Complete these questions with *you* and the simple past form of the verb in parentheses. `2.3 C`

ASKING QUESTIONS ABOUT A TRIP

1. Where _____*did you go*_____? (go)

2. When _____ this trip? (take)

3. How _____ there? (get)

4. Who _____ with? (travel)

5. What _____ there? (do)

6. What _____ best about the trip? (like)

7. What problems _____ on the trip? (have)

Write about It Choose a trip you took in the past. Write your own answers to the questions in Activity 16. Then ask and answer them with a partner.

A: *Where did you go?*
B: *I went to Thailand.*

17 | Asking *Yes/No* and *Wh-* Questions about the Past Read one person's personal timeline and complete the questions. Then match the questions with the answers below. **2.3 B–C**

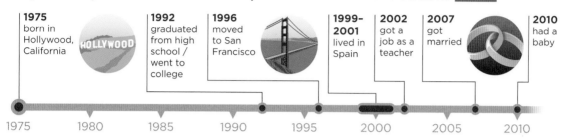

| **1975** born in Hollywood, California | **1992** graduated from high school / went to college | **1996** moved to San Francisco | **1999–2001** lived in Spain | **2002** got a job as a teacher | **2007** got married | **2010** had a baby |

1975   1980   1985   1990   1995   2000   2005   2010

QUESTIONS   **ANSWERS**

1. _____Did_____ you _____get_____ good grades in high school? (get)   _g_

2. _____ _____ you _____ to college? (where/go)   ____

3. _____ _____ you _____ in college? (what/study)   ____

4. _____ _____ you _____ to San Francisco? (why/move)   ____

5. _____ you _____ your time in San Francisco? (enjoy)   ____

6. _____ _____ you _____ best about Spain? (what/like)   ____

7. _____ _____ you _____ in 2002? (what/teach)   ____

8. _____ you _____ at a high school or college? (work)   ____

9. _____ you _____ a big wedding? (have)   ____

10. _____ you _____ a girl or a boy? (have)   ____

11. _____ _____ in 2008? (what/happen)   ____

ANSWERS

a. I taught Spanish.
b. Yes, I did, but it's an expensive city.
c. No, we had a very small wedding.
d. The people and the food.
e. I studied history and languages.
f. To look for a job.

g. Yes, I did. I was a pretty good student.
h. Nothing special.
i. In New York.
j. A girl.
k. At a high school.

Talk about It Add dates and ten facts about your life to the timeline below. Exchange timelines with a partner and ask your partner questions to get more information. Tell your classmates what you learned about your partner.

TIMELINE

18 | Error Correction Correct any errors in these sentences. (Some sentences may not have any errors.)

1. On that day, we didn't had anything to eat.
2. What kind of car do you buy?
3. Who did came?
4. They not do anything about the problem last week.
5. What go wrong yesterday?
6. Did he had much fun on the trip?
7. What happen to you yesterday?
8. Who took my books?

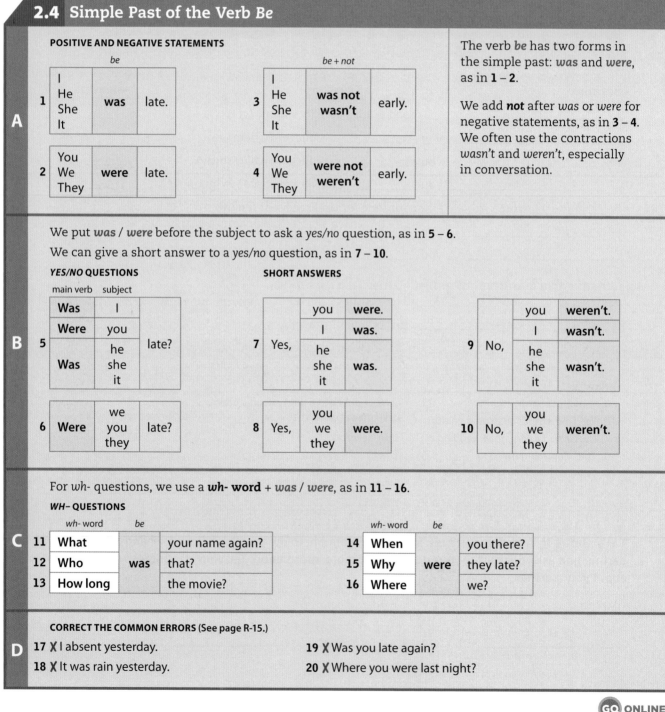

2.4 Simple Past of the Verb *Be*

A

POSITIVE AND NEGATIVE STATEMENTS

be

| 1 | I He She It | **was** | late. |

| 2 | You We They | **were** | late. |

be + not

| 3 | I He She It | **was not** **wasn't** | early. |

| 4 | You We They | **were not** **weren't** | early. |

The verb *be* has two forms in the simple past: *was* and *were*, as in **1 – 2**.

We add **not** after *was* or *were* for negative statements, as in **3 – 4**. We often use the contractions *wasn't* and *weren't*, especially in conversation.

B

We put *was / were* before the subject to ask a yes/no question, as in **5 – 6**.

We can give a short answer to a yes/no question, as in **7 – 10**.

YES/NO QUESTIONS

main verb   subject

5	**Was**	I	late?
	Were	you	
	Was	he she it	

| 6 | **Were** | we you they | late? |

SHORT ANSWERS

7	Yes,	you	were.
		I	was.
		he she it	was.

| 8 | Yes, | you we they | were. |

9	No,	you	weren't.
		I	wasn't.
		he she it	wasn't.

| 10 | No, | you we they | weren't. |

C

For *wh-* questions, we use a **wh- word** + *was / were*, as in **11 – 16**.

WH– QUESTIONS

wh- word   be

11	What		your name again?
12	Who	was	that?
13	How long		the movie?

wh- word   be

14	When		you there?
15	Why	were	they late?
16	Where		we?

D

CORRECT THE COMMON ERRORS (See page R-15.)

17 ✗ I absent yesterday.
18 ✗ It was rain yesterday.
19 ✗ Was you late again?
20 ✗ Where you were last night?

19 | *Was or Were?* Circle *was* or *were* in the first part of each sentence. Then match the beginnings of the sentences with the endings. (More than one answer may be possible, but only one is correct.) **2.4 A**

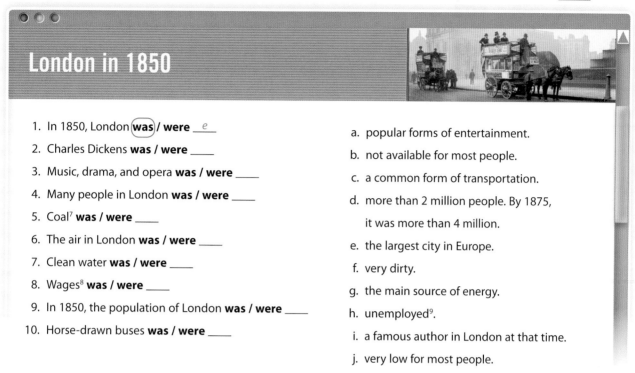

London in 1850

1. In 1850, London **was** / were __e__
2. Charles Dickens **was / were** ____
3. Music, drama, and opera **was / were** ____
4. Many people in London **was / were** ____
5. Coal⁷ **was / were** ____
6. The air in London **was / were** ____
7. Clean water **was / were** ____
8. Wages⁸ **was / were** ____
9. In 1850, the population of London **was / were** ____
10. Horse-drawn buses **was / were** ____

a. popular forms of entertainment.
b. not available for most people.
c. a common form of transportation.
d. more than 2 million people. By 1875, it was more than 4 million.
e. the largest city in Europe.
f. very dirty.
g. the main source of energy.
h. unemployed⁹.
i. a famous author in London at that time.
j. very low for most people.

20 | **Positive or Negative?** Complete these sentences with *was, wasn't, were,* or *weren't.* **2.4 A**

WHAT WAS YOUR FIRST SCHOOL LIKE?

1. My first school _____ very big.
2. The school building _____ very new.
3. The desks _____ very comfortable.
4. The teachers _____ very strict.
5. Sports _____ very important at my school.
6. Music _____ important at my school.
7. My first teacher _____ a man.
8. Girls and boys _____ in separate classes.
9. We _____ in school all day.
10. Summer vacation _____ very long.
11. My favorite school subject back then _____ math.
12. My grades in school _____ very good.

Talk about It Compare your sentences above with a partner. How were your schools similar?

"Our schools were very big."
"The desks at our schools weren't very comfortable."

---

⁷**coal:** a black mineral used as fuel
⁸**wages:** payment for work; salary

⁹**unemployed:** without a job

21 | Asking *Yes/No* Questions with *Was* and *Were* For each statement, think of a follow-up *yes/no* question with *was* or *were*. Use a word from the list on the right. (Many different questions may be possible.) `2.4 B`

1. Kate didn't go to work yesterday. _Was she sick?_____
2. I lost Matt's phone. _____
3. Mary spoke in front of 200 people last night. _____
4. We missed the bus this morning. _____
5. My brother didn't get on the football team. _____
6. My boss yelled at me. _____
7. I slept all day yesterday. _____
8. We went on a school picnic last week. _____
9. We watched a movie last night. _____
10. It was very hot during the last Olympic Games. _____
11. Nobody called or texted Rob yesterday. _____
12. Mr. Lee didn't come to class last week. _____

angry
disappointed
early
excited
fun
good
late
nervous
sick
there
tired
upset

Talk about It Work with a partner. Use the statements and questions above to make your own conversations. Add answers to the questions you wrote.

A: *Kate didn't go to work yesterday.*
B: *Really? Was she sick?*
A: *No, one of her kids was sick.*

22 | Asking *Wh-* Questions with *Was* and *Were* Complete these questions with a *wh-* word (*what, where, who,* or *how often*) and *was* or *were*. `2.4 C`

QUESTIONS ABOUT YOUR CHILDHOOD

1. _____What was_____ your favorite sport as a child?
2. _____ your favorite TV programs?
3. _____ your best childhood friend?
4. _____ you on your first birthday?
5. _____ your favorite toy as a child?
6. _____ you in trouble?
7. _____ your favorite food?
8. _____ your childhood heroes?
9. _____ your oldest relative?
10. _____ one of your childhood accomplishments?
11. _____ your first school?
12. _____ your parents angry at you?

Talk about It Ask a partner the questions above. Then tell your classmates something interesting you learned about your partner.

A: *What was your favorite sport as a child?*
B: *I didn't really play sports, but I watched a lot of basketball.*

2.5 Using *And / But / So* with the Simple Past

A

1 I called and made an appointment.

2 She read books and watched movies about mountain climbing.

3 The car skidded, hit a wall, and turned over.

We use **and** to connect two verb phrases, as in **1 – 2**. We use the same form for both verbs—in this case, the **simple past**.

When we connect three or more verb phrases, we use **commas (,)** + **and**, as in **3**.

B

4 | subject | verb | | subject | verb |

| We | **drove** | and | John | **walked**. |

| main clause | | | main clause | |

5 | The computer **was** old | but | it **worked**. |

6 | No one **came** | so | we **canceled** the meeting. |

7 Life **wasn't** easy in 1900, **and** the average person **didn't live** very long.

8 A few people **had** cars, **but** most people **traveled** by electric streetcar.

We use **and**, **but**, or **so** to connect two main clauses, as in **4 – 6**. Each main clause has a subject and a verb. We use

- **and** to connect two similar and equally important ideas, as in **4**
- **but** to connect two contrasting ideas, as in **5**
- **so** to say the result of something, as in **6**

We put a **comma (,)** before *and*, *but*, or *so* when it connects two longer clauses, as in **7 – 8**.

GRAMMAR TERM: A **main clause** is a group of words with a subject and a verb. A sentence with two main clauses connected by *and*, *but*, or *so* is called a **compound sentence**.

 GO ONLINE

23 | Using More Than One Verb Complete each sentence with a verb phrase from the box. Remember to use the simple past form of the verb. **2.5 A**

1. He went home and _____ *took a nap* _____.

2. He opened the refrigerator and _____.

3. They sat down at the table and _____.

4. She opened the car door and _____.

5. I turned around and _____.

6. He put on his coat and _____.

7. I pulled up a chair and _____.

8. He picked up a rock and _____.

9. He put his clothes in the washing machine and _____.

10. She turned on her computer and _____.

11. We opened our books and _____.

12. I went outside without a coat and _____.

13. The ball went through the window, hit the mirror, and _____.

14. The thief grabbed the money, put it in his pocket, and _____.

begin studying	see him behind me
break it	sit down
catch a cold	start eating
get in	take a nap
leave immediately	take out some food
read her emails	throw it
run out of the store	turn it on

Talk about It Think of a different way to complete each sentence above.

"He went home and went to bed."
"He went home and watched a movie."
"He went home and had something to eat."

24 | Combining Sentences In each pair of sentences, the subject is the same. Use *and* to combine the information in each pair of sentences. Make one sentence with one subject and two verbs. `2.5 A`

LIFE EVENTS

1. I grew up in Thailand. I moved to China in 2007 after college.

   I grew up in Thailand and moved to China in 2007 after college.

2. My grandfather left his parents in Poland. He started a new family here.
3. As children, we played together. We had a lot of fun.
4. He met many people on his trip. He made friends everywhere.
5. He graduated from college. He went to work for CARE International.
6. My brother studied engineering at school. He had many different jobs there.
7. I graduated from high school in 2010. I started college the next year.
8. At my first job, I checked business contracts. I also studied business disputes[10].
9. Two months later, I left Iran. I went to Turkey.
10. My father worked for a shipping company. He traveled a lot.

Think about It When you combine the sentences above, why can you leave out the second subject?

25 | Distinguishing *And*, *But*, and *So* Complete these sentences with the simple past. Then explain why the speaker used *and, but,* or *so*. Choose a reason from the box below. `2.5 B`

BEST EXCUSES FOR NOT DOING YOUR HOMEWORK   REASON

1. I _____opened_____ the car window, and my essay _____fell out_____.   _a_
   (open)   (fall out)
2. I _____ to finish my homework, but I _____ asleep.   ____
   (try)   (fall)
3. My mother _____ it was trash, so she _____ it out.   ____
   (think)   (throw)
4. My computer _____, and I _____ all my work.   ____
   (crash)   (lose)
5. I _____ to do my homework, but I _____ my book.   ____
   (want)   (forget)
6. I _____ my essay, but my printer _____ ink.   ____
   (write)   (run out of)
7. My friend _____ my glasses, so I _____ the homework assignment.   ____
   (break)   (not see)
8. I _____ my head and _____ my memory, so I _____ to do it.   ____
   (hit)   (lose)   (forget)
9. I _____ it in my shirt pocket, and then my mother _____ my shirt.   ____
   (put)   (wash)
10. My brother _____ it into a paper airplane, and it _____ on the roof. ____
    (make)   (land)
11. My friend _____ to do it for me, but she _____ busy.   ____
    (promise)   (get)
12. I _____ to do it but I _____ too tired.   ____
    (want)   (be)

REASON

The second part of the sentence is:
 a. a similar and equally important idea
 b. a contrasting idea
 c. a result of something

FYI

We sometimes use *and* + *then* to show that one action comes after another action.

I did all my homework, **and then** my brother spilled a glass of water on it.

[10]**disputes:** disagreements; debates

Write about It Write three other excuses like the ones in Activity 25. Try to use *and, but,* or *so.*

26 | Connecting Ideas with *And, But,* or *So* Which clause best completes each sentence? Match each main clause on the left with a main clause on the right. `2.5 B`

1. I had a headache, but ___c___
2. I had a headache, so ____
3. I had a headache, and ____

a. I didn't go to the meeting.
b. my back hurt.
c. I went to the meeting anyway.

4. We found a wallet on the street, but ____
5. We found a wallet on the street, so ____
6. We found a wallet on the street, and ____

a. it didn't have anyone's name inside.
b. we called the police.
c. it had a lot of money inside.

7. I called my mother, but ____
8. I called my mother, so ____
9. I called my mother, and ____

a. now she's happy.
b. she answered right away.
c. she didn't answer.

10. The kids were naughty, but ____
11. The kids were naughty, so ____
12. The kids were naughty, and ____

a. their mother sent them to bed early.
b. their parents didn't do anything.
c. they thought it was funny.

13. My brother didn't like school, but ____
14. My brother didn't like school, so ____
15. My brother didn't like school, and ____

a. he was a good student.
b. his teachers knew it.
c. he didn't go to college.

Write about It Choose one group of sentences above. Think of a different way to complete each sentence in the group.

I had a headache, but it wasn't very bad.
I had a headache, so I took some aspirin.
I had a headache, and my sister had a stomachache.

27 | Choosing *And, But,* or *So* Complete these sentences with *and, but,* or *so.* `2.5 B`

FOOD IN HISTORY

1. Plates weren't available for most people in fourteenth-century England, _____so_____ they ate their food on thick slices of bread instead.

2. In the 1800s in the U.S., many people bought tomato sauce, _____ they didn't put it on their food. They thought tomato sauce was a medicine, _____ they drank it when they were sick.

a fourteenth-century baker

3. Today, potatoes are popular in many parts of the world, _____ in the 1500s, they weren't. People thought potatoes were poisonous[11], _____ they refused to eat them.

4. When the first Europeans saw an avocado, they thought it was a pear, _____ they ate it for dessert. They told everyone that the avocado was delicious, _____ for a long time, people in Europe didn't want to eat this fruit.

SPORTS IN HISTORY

5. A football (soccer ball) in the 1870s was very heavy, _____ it was impossible to kick it very far, _____ hitting the ball with your head was very dangerous.

6. Golf was an Olympic sport in 1900 and 1904, _____ in 1908, the organizers of the Olympics decided to remove this sport from the Games.

7. The first modern Olympic Games took place in 1896. There were 311 male athletes, _____ there weren't any female competitors.

a football game in nineteenth-century England

2.6 Time Clauses with the Simple Past

A

	subject	verb
1	He was upset	when she **left**.
	main clause	time clause

2	I remember	when I **came** here in 2009.
	main clause	time clause

3	When I **was** ten,	we moved to Australia.
	time clause	main clause

We often use the simple past in a **time clause**, as in **1 – 3**. The time clause tells when something happened.

Notice that a time clause:

- has a subject and a verb
- needs a **main clause** to be a complete sentence
- can go before or after the main clause

We use a comma (,) at the end of a time clause when it comes before a main clause, as in **3**.

B

4	I had a headache	**when** I got up.
5	He made a lot of friends	**while** he was in Laos.
6	I changed my clothes	**before** I went to work.
7	**After** she moved away,	I never saw her again.

Time clauses often begin with the words *when*, *while*, *before*, or *after*, as in **4 – 7**.

> **when** = at that time
> **while** = during that time

We often use the simple past form of a verb in both a main clause and a time clause.

For more information on time clauses, see Unit 12, page 372.

C

CORRECT THE COMMON ERRORS (See page R-15.)

8 ✗ After left the class, something happened.

9 ✗ I meet her last week when I start the class.

10 ✗ I left, before she got there.

11 ✗ He gave me advice when I need it.

---

[11] **poisonous:** harmful; dangerous to eat or drink

28 | Noticing Time Clauses Underline the time clauses in these sentences. Then answer the questions below. 2.6 A

Great Achievements

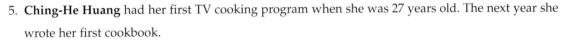

1. **Tamae Watanabe** was 63 years old <u>when she climbed Mount Everest for the first time</u>. Then, when she was 73 years old, she climbed Mount Everest again.

2. When **Zac Sunderland** was just 16 years old, he sailed alone around the world.

3. **Isaac Asimov** wrote more than 400 books during his life, but he started late. He was 30 years old when he wrote his first one.

4. **Wilma Rudolph** was sick most of the time when she was a child. As an adult, however, she won three gold medals at the Olympics.

5. **Ching-He Huang** had her first TV cooking program when she was 27 years old. The next year she wrote her first cookbook.

6. **Dikembe Mutombo** came to the U.S. to study, and then he became a professional basketball player. When he had enough money, he built a hospital in his native country.

7. **Bill Gates** was just 19 years old when he co-founded Microsoft.

8. **Farrah Gray** started his first business when he was 6 years old. What was his business? He painted rocks by hand and sold them. He later started his own radio program and wrote several books. Today Gray is a wealthy man.

QUESTIONS

1. What are the subject and verb in each time clause?
2. What are the subject and verb in each main clause?
3. In some of the sentences, the writer put the time clause before the main clause. Can you think of any reasons for doing this?
4. Which person is the most interesting to you? Why?

29 | Adding Time Clauses Complete each time clause with information about your childhood. (Many different answers are possible.) Then compare with a partner. 2.6 A

WHEN I WAS A CHILD . . .

1. I started school when _____.
2. I had a lot of friends when _____.
3. I had fun when _____.
4. I began studying English when _____.
5. I sometimes got angry when _____.
6. I was ten years old when _____.
7. I hated it when _____.
8. As a child, I was always happy when _____.

30 | Using the Simple Past in Time Clauses Read this text. Complete the story with the simple past. Then complete the sentences below with *when, while, before,* or *after.* 2.6 B

THE BURNING AIRPLANE

During World War II, Nicholas Alkemade was in the

British Royal Air Force. On March 25, 1944, he was on

a mission[12] when his airplane _____*caught*_____ fire.
(1. catch)

When the fire _____ to spread, the pilot
(2. start)

and the other crew members quickly _____
(3. put on)

their parachutes and _____ out of the
(4. jump)

burning plane. Nicholas turned to get his parachute and _____ that it was on fire. He
(5. see)

had to make a quick decision—burn in the airplane or jump without a parachute?

Nicholas _____ to jump. When he jumped, his plane _____ 6,000 meters
(6. decide)   (7. be)

above the ground. He _____ quickly, moving at about 185 kilometers per hour, but he
(8. fall)

didn't die. Nicholas was very lucky. The thick branches of some trees _____ his fall
(9. slow)

before he _____ on the deep snow below. Amazingly, Nicholas was not seriously injured.
(10. land)

He _____ burns on his legs, hands, and feet from the fire. He _____ his back
(11. have)   (12. hurt)

and knee when he landed, but he didn't break any bones. Nicholas Alkemade survived the war and

_____ to be an old man.
(13. live)

SENTENCES

1. _____ he was in the Air Force, Nicholas flew on many missions.

2. The pilot jumped from the airplane _____ Nicholas turned to get his parachute.

3. His parachute caught on fire _____ he could put it on.

4. _____ Nicholas jumped from the airplane, the fire burned his legs.

5. Nicholas was not seriously injured _____ he landed on the ground.

6. He lived for many years _____ the war ended.

Think about It What other time expressions did the writer use in the story above? Circle them.

31 | Error Correction Correct any errors in these sentences. (Some sentences may not have any errors.)

1. I met her last month when I start this class.

2. When I came here, I study very hard.

3. When I got here, my friends always help me.

4. When I saw the picture.

5. After I get to know him, we became very good friends.

6. I didn't speak any English before I came here.

7. When I was 15, my father take a job far away from my home.

8. When I was in a bad mood, my friends always make me laugh.

[12]**mission:** a trip to do a special job

2.7 Using the Past Progressive

1 I **was** still **doing** my homework at ten last night.

10 O'CLOCK

NOW

I WAS DOING MY HOMEWORK.

2 We **were** just **talking** about you.

3 The trains **weren't running** all day yesterday.

We use the **past progressive** to describe something in progress at a particular time in the past, as in **1 – 3**.

A

POSITIVE AND NEGATIVE STATEMENTS

	be (+ not)	*verb + -ing*	
4 I He She It	**was** **was not** **wasn't**	**working**	yesterday.

5 We You They	**were** **were not** **weren't**	**working**	yesterday.

We form the past progressive with *was / were* + (**not**) + the **-ing form of a main verb**, as in **4 – 5**.

With the past progressive, *was / were* (the past of *be*) are helping verbs.

For a list of spelling rules for the *-ing* form of verbs, see the Resources, page R-4.

B

PAST PROGRESSIVE IN TIME CLAUSES

6 I **was thinking** about her **while** she **was driving** across the country. (= I was thinking about her during the time she was driving.)

7 She **called while** I **was thinking** about her.
(= She called during the time I was thinking about her.)

8 I **was thinking** about her **when** she **called**.
(= I was thinking about her and then she called.)

We often use the **past progressive** in a sentence with a time clause. We sometimes use:

- **while** to connect two activities in progress at the same time, as in **6**
- **while** + the past progressive to show that an activity was in progress when another action (usually in the **simple past**) took place, as in **7**
- **when** + the simple past to show that an action interrupted an activity in progress, as in **8**

C

YES/NO QUESTIONS

	be	subject	*verb + -ing*
9	**Was**	I / he / she / it	**sleeping?**
10	**Were**	you / we / they	**sleeping?**

To form yes/no questions, we put *was / were* before the subject and use the **-ing form of a main verb**, as in **9 – 10**.

D

To form *wh-* questions, we use a **wh- word** + *was / were* and the **-ing form of a main verb**, as in **11 – 14**. In **15 – 16**, the *wh-* word is the subject.

WH- QUESTIONS

	wh- word	*be*	subject	*verb + -ing*
11	How	**was**	she	**doing?**
12	Why		he	**laughing?**

13	Where	**were**	you	**going?**
14	Why		they	**laughing?**

WH- QUESTIONS ABOUT THE SUBJECT

	subject	*be*	*verb + -ing*
15	What	**was**	**happening?**
16	Who		**laughing?**

32 | Using the Past Progressive in Statements Complete the sentences below with the past progressive form of the verb in parentheses. Then read Sam's schedule and check (✓) *True* or *False*. [2.7 A]

Wi-Fi 📶		7:30 AM		65% 🔋
YESTERDAY	8 a.m.	take children to school	2 p.m.	interview new staff member
	10 a.m.	doctor's appointment	4 p.m.	project meeting
	12 p.m.	lunch with client	6 p.m.	football game at high school

WHAT WAS SAM DOING AT THESE TIMES YESTERDAY?   TRUE   FALSE

1. At 8 in the morning, Sam _____*was taking*_____ his children to school. (take)   ☐   ☐

2. At 10:30, he _____ in the doctor's office. (sit)   ☐   ☐

3. At 12:30 yesterday, he _____ lunch at his desk. (have)   ☐   ☐

4. At 2:15 in the afternoon, he _____ a new staff member. (interview)   ☐   ☐

5. At 4:30 in the afternoon, he _____ his son's football game. (watch)   ☐   ☐

6. At 6:30 in the evening, he _____ a project meeting. (attend)   ☐   ☐

Talk about It Work with a partner. Talk about what you were doing at the same times yesterday.

"At 8 in the morning, I was riding the train to school."

---

33 | Noticing Past Progressive Verbs Read this text. Underline the past progressive verbs. [2.7 A–B]

Lightning Strikes Twice!

Does lightning ever hit the same thing twice? Absolutely. Just ask Roy Sullivan. In fact, lightning struck him four times! When lightning hit Sullivan the first time, he was climbing down from a lookout tower in a U.S. national park. Then, 27 years later, lightning hit Sullivan again. This time Sullivan was driving a truck. The next time lightning struck Sullivan, he was standing in his yard. Several years later, Sullivan was working at a campsite when lightning hit him again. Amazingly, lightning never seriously injured Roy Sullivan.

Think about It What are the four actions in progress in the story above? List them in the chart below. Then identify the specific action that interrupts each one.

Action in progress	Specific event that interrupts the action in progress
1.	
2.	
3.	
4.	

34 | Simple Past or Past Progressive? Complete these sentences with the verbs in parentheses. Use the simple past or the past progressive. `2.7 A-B`

ACCIDENTS

1. One time I _____*cut*_____ my finger while I _____*was making*_____ a sandwich.
   (cut)   (make)

2. My father once _____ his back when he _____ off the roof of our house.
   (hurt)   (fall)

3. I _____ to my car when I _____ on the ice and _____ down.
   (walk)   (slip)   (fall)

4. Back in 2009, a horse _____ on my foot and _____ my toe.
   (step)   (break)

5. My best friend _____ something at the stove when her shirt _____ on fire.
   (cook)   (catch)

6. One time I _____ my bike when a dog _____ into the street and _____
   (ride)   (run)   (bite)
   my leg.

7. I _____ the stove and _____ my arm while I _____ dinner.
   (touch)   (burn)   (make)

8. My brother _____ his arm when a boy _____ into him while they
   (break)   (run)
   _____ baseball.
   (play)

9. My best friend _____ his ankle while he _____ in his sleep.
   (twist)   (walk)

10. One time at the gym, I _____ on a treadmill when I _____ my footing and
    (run)   (lose)
    _____ down.
    (fall)

Talk about It Work with a partner. Take turns telling about an accident you had in the past. Ask questions to get more information.

A: One time I cut my leg while I was swimming.
B: Where were you swimming?
A: In a pool.
B: How did you cut your leg?

35 | Using Time Clauses Use each group of words to write a sentence. More than one sentence may be possible. `2.7 B`

1. I/hear a loud noise outside/talk on the phone/when

   I was talking on the phone when I heard a loud noise outside.

2. My friends/drive home from school/see something terrible/while

3. My friend/hurt his leg/walk to school/while

4. I/a customer/start yelling/work at the restaurant one night/while

5. I/the lights go out/work on my laptop/when

6. My brother/jump into the swimming pool/wear his new suit/when

7. I/stand on a street corner/hear someone call my name/when

8. I/listen to the radio/drive my car/while

Write about It Choose one or more of the sentences above. What do you think happened? Write your ideas.

I was talking on the phone when I heard a loud noise outside. I looked outside and saw two
men next to a car. The car had a big dent in it, and the men were yelling at each other.

36 | Simple Past or Past Progressive? Complete these conversations with the simple past or the past progressive. (More than one answer may be possible.) Then practice with a partner. `2.7 C-D`

1. A: _____Did_____ you _____talk_____ to James yesterday? (talk)

   B: Yeah, we had lunch together.

2. A: _____ you _____ to someone when I called you yesterday? (talk)

   B: Yeah. Isabel was here, and we were planning our vacation.

3. A: _____ your brother _____ TV when you got home last night? (watch)

   B: No, he was already in bed.

4. A: _____ you _____ the football game last night? (watch)

   B: Yeah, it was a great game.

5. A: What _____ you _____ when you fell down? (do)

   B: I was running down the stairs to answer the door.

6. A: What _____ you _____ when you cut your hand? (do)

   B: I put pressure on the cut.

7. A: Why _____ you and Mika _____ while I was giving my speech? (sleep)

   B: Sorry about that. We were up all night last night studying.

8. A: _____ you _____ OK last night? (sleep)

   B: Yes. I didn't wake up once.

9. A: _____ you _____ to Jen's house yesterday? (go)

   B: Yes, but I didn't stay very long.

10. A: Did I see your car downtown yesterday?

    B: Maybe. I was there in the afternoon.

    A: Where _____ you _____? (go)

    B: To the movies.

> **RESEARCH SAYS...**
>
> Sometimes it is possible to use either the simple past or the past progressive. The past progressive gives more emphasis to the ongoing nature of the activity.
>
> I **worked** all day yesterday.
> I **was working** all day yesterday.

37 | Error Correction Correct any errors in these sentences. (Some sentences may not have any errors.)

1. While I going to that school, I also had a job.
2. When I was deciding to leave, I made $10 an hour.
3. One week later, I was getting a new job.
4. She tried to wake me while I slept.
5. I felt sick when I got up this morning.
6. I was plan to go there, but then my mother called and asked me to help her.
7. Why you were laughing when I came in?
8. He looked at me while I fell down, but he didn't help me up.
9. She turned around while I was looking at her.
10. Where you going when I saw you yesterday?

2.8 Using Past Forms in Speaking

A

ASKING FOR REPETITION

1 A: Her number is 666-4549.
B: **Did** you **say** 4549?

2 A: I put your keys on the table.
B: Sorry. What **was** that?

3 A: Your dinner's on the stove.
B: Sorry. What **did** you **say**?

We often use the **simple past** when we ask for repetition, as in **1 – 3**.

B

USING *DID* IN POSITIVE STATEMENTS

4 A: I thought you had a key to the office.
B: I **did have** one, but I lost it.

5 A: Why didn't you buy coffee at the store?
B: I **did buy** coffee.

In a positive statement, we sometimes add the helping verb *did* before the main verb to give extra emphasis or show a contrast, as in **4 – 5**.

Remember: We use the base form of the main verb after *did*.

USING *DID NOT* AND *WAS NOT*

6 A: You ate all the ice cream.
B: I **did not**.

7 A: You were late.
B: I **was not**.

In conversation, we often use the contractions *didn't* and *wasn't*. However, we sometimes use *did not* and *was not* for extra emphasis, as in **6 – 7**.

C

CONNECTING SEVERAL CLAUSES

8 Sorry I'm late, **but** I had a bunch of stuff to deal with at home, **and** the traffic was bumper to bumper, **and** it was a real nightmare.

When people talk about past experiences in everyday conversation, they connect several clauses using *and*, *but*, or *so*, as in **8**. We don't do this in writing.

38 | Asking for Repetition Listen and write the missing question in each conversation. Then practice with a partner. **2.8 A**

1. A: Tom just called.
   B: _What was that?_
   A: Tom just called. He needs Sue's phone number.
   B: Oh, OK.

2. A: Hurry up. The train leaves at ten.
   B: _____
   A: Yes, ten.

3. A: Where's Sun-Hee?
   B: She's at the library.
   A: _____
   B: That's right.

4. A: Did you talk to Hassan this morning?
   B: _____
   A: Did you talk to Hassan?
   B: Yep.

5. A: John wants you to call him at 555-1212.
   B: _____
   A: No, I said 555-1212.

6. A: Could you get some milk at the store?
   B: _____
   A: Milk. Could you pick up some milk?
   B: Sure. No problem.

7. A: Did you go anywhere fun on vacation?
   B: Yeah. We went to China.
   A: _____
   B: Yeah. We spent three weeks there.

8. A: Please turn down the TV.
   B: _____
   A: I said, turn the TV down.
   B: Oh, OK.

39 | Adding Emphasis Listen and write the missing words. Then practice with a partner. `2.8 B`

1. A: Why didn't you call last night?

   B: _I did call_____, but you didn't answer.

2. A: I thought you had a headache.

   B: _____, but now I feel better.

3. A: I heard you didn't go to school today.

   B: But _____.

4. A: Matt said you fell asleep in class again.

   B: Yeah, _____ for a few minutes, but that's all.

5. A: Why were you downtown this morning?

   B: I wasn't downtown.

   A: Yes, you were.

   B: _____

6. A: I can't believe it. You ate my sandwich.

   B: No, I didn't.

   A: But you did.

   B: _____

7. A: Where's the remote?

   B: I put it on the table.

   A: Well, it's not there now.

   B: But _____.

8. A: That's my pen. You took it.

   B: I _____. This is my pen. Yours is on the floor over there.

40 | Noticing Long Sentences Listen and write the missing words: *and*, *but*, or *so*. `2.8 C`

SPOKEN DESCRIPTIONS

1. I left on time, ___*but*___ the traffic was terrible, _____ then I was late to that meeting, _____ it was important, _____ my boss was so angry.

2. Kate and I got together last night, _____ we were trying to do the homework, _____ it was really hard, _____ the instructions weren't clear, _____ we finally gave up.

3. This weather is weird, like it's hot out, _____ then the wind blows _____ it's cold, _____ I don't even know what to wear.

4. I was watching this movie, _____ then I had to go somewhere or something, _____ it was just when you called.

5. I didn't see Khalid today, _____ he called, _____ we decided to meet tomorrow, _____ I didn't go anywhere all day.

6. I saw Tom downtown, _____ I waved to him, _____ he didn't wave back, _____ maybe he didn't even see me. I don't know.

2.9 Using Past Forms in Writing

COMPARE

A	**1a** When J. Paul Getty died in 1976, he was one of the richest people in the world. He was also one of the stingiest. For example, Getty refused to turn on the heat in his home when he had visitors. He also installed a pay phone at home for his guests. **1b** J. Paul Getty died in 1976. He was one of the richest people in the world. He was also one of the stingiest. He refused to turn on the heat in his home. He also installed a pay phone at home for his guests.	Good writers combine information in different ways and use different sentence lengths to make their writing more interesting. This is true for stories and historical accounts about the past, as in **1a**. Using a lot of short sentences can be repetitive and boring, as in **1b**.
B	**2** Vanessa-Mae had her first piano lesson **when she was only three years old. Two years later**, she started playing the violin. **Then, at the age of eight**, she had to choose between the piano and the violin.	We often use **time expressions** and **time clauses** when we write about a sequence of events, as in **2**. They help us connect ideas from one sentence to the next. This helps the reader follow our ideas.
C	**3** One evening my brothers and I **were sitting** around the dinner table. Suddenly we **heard** a loud noise outside, and smoke **began** to fill the house. . . .	We sometimes use the **past progressive** to set the scene for a story, as in **3**. We then use the **simple past** to describe the events in the story.

41 | Noticing Sentence Variety Read two versions of the same story. Answer these questions. `2.9 A`

1. Which version of the story has fewer sentences? Why?
2. How many time clauses do you see in each version? Underline them.
3. Which version do you prefer? Why?
4. Choose one of the paragraphs in Version 1. Rewrite it in a different way.

Version 1

My father took a new job in Saudi Arabia. I was eight years old. I didn't want to leave my school to go there. I didn't want to leave my friends.

We arrived in Saudi Arabia. I was very nervous. I didn't know anybody there. The food tasted very different. I didn't speak the language. Then I started school. I quickly made a lot of new friends. It was fun to visit my classmates' homes. I discovered that the food was really delicious! I also began to study Arabic. I learned the language quickly.

This experience gave me the opportunity to meet new people. I also got to do new things. As a result, I now love to travel. I am also more adventurous. I meet new people, but I don't feel so shy. Sometimes I don't want to do something. Then I think about my time in Saudi Arabia. I remember that it is important to try new things.

Version 2

When I was eight years old, my father took a new job in Saudi Arabia. I didn't want to leave my school and my friends to go there.

When we first arrived in Saudi Arabia, I was very nervous. I didn't know anybody there. The food tasted very different, and I didn't speak the language. However, when I started school, I quickly made a lot of new friends. It was fun to visit my classmates' homes, and I discovered that the food was really delicious! I also began to study Arabic, and I learned the language quickly.

This experience gave me the opportunity to meet new people and do new things. As a result, I now love to travel, and I am more adventurous. I am also not so shy when I meet new people. Now, when I don't want to do something, I think about my time in Saudi Arabia, and I remember that it is important to try new things.

42 | Adding Sentence Variety Rewrite these paragraphs. Add more variety and use different sentence lengths. You can leave out words or add new words. (Many different answers are possible.) `2.9 A`

A TRIP TO COSTA RICA

In 2010, I spent six months in Costa Rica. I was 26 years old. I wanted to learn Spanish. I also wanted to make friends with people from a different culture.

I didn't know anyone at first. I was very lonely. None of the other students at my school spoke my language (German). I didn't have anyone to talk to. Many of the students were native speakers of English. They spent a lot of time together after class. Unfortunately, my English isn't very good. I didn't want to hang out with them.

After a few weeks, I made friends with a Costa Rican family. I went to their house every weekend for dinner. They taught me how to make some Costa Rican dishes. They helped me speak Spanish. They took me to a beautiful beach. They introduced me to some Costa Rican students. Before long I was speaking Spanish pretty well.

43 | Connecting Ideas in a Piece of Writing Read this story. Circle the time expressions. Underline the time clauses. `2.9 B`

From Bookworm to World Adventurer

When Lei Wang was young, no one thought she would become a world adventurer. She was a "bookworm[13]," her mother said. Wang did well in school, and after she earned an undergraduate degree at Tsinghua University in Beijing, she moved to the U.S. to study computer science at the University of North Carolina.

After Wang got her master's degree in computer science, she took a job in New York. Then, in 2001, she decided to go back to school to get a graduate degree. While she was in school, she went on a mountain-climbing trip in Ecuador. That trip excited her about mountain climbing. Soon after the trip, Wang began working out at the gym to build her strength. She also read books and watched movies about mountaineering. She was determined to excel[14] at her new sport.

Of course, most serious mountain climbers want to climb Mount Everest, and Wang was no exception. To prepare for Everest, she climbed the highest mountain on the six other continents. Then, in May of 2010, Wang climbed to the top of the highest mountain in the world.

Write about It Rewrite the story about Lei Wang above. For example, you might want to combine the information in different ways and use different time expressions and time clauses.

No one thought Lei Wang would become a world adventurer when she was a child. . . .

---

[13] **bookworm:** a person who loves to read books
[14] **excel:** to succeed; to do very well

44 | Setting the Scene Number the sentences in this story in order from 1 (first) to 7 (last). 2.9 C

THE LITTLE MICE

_____ The cat heard the barking of a dog and ran away.

_____ The mother mouse turned to her children and said, "You see, it's very important to know a second language."

_____ Then she yelled, "Woof, woof, woof[15]!"

_____ They were looking for something to eat when they heard a loud noise. "Meow[16]! Hiss! Meow!" It was a cat!

_____ The cat ran toward the mother mouse, but she didn't move.

_1_ One day a mother mouse and her young children were walking in the garden.

_____ Instead, she looked him in the eye and raised her paw.

Think about It Which words helped you to know the order of the sentences in the story above?

WRAP-UP Demonstrate Your Knowledge

A | INTERVIEW Think of ten things you did yesterday. List them below. Use the simple past form of the verb.

Things I Did Yesterday
1.
2.
3.
4.
5.
6.
7.
8.
9.
10.

Exchange your list above with a partner. Ask your partner questions to get more details about each activity.

A: _I walked for an hour yesterday._
B: _Where did you walk?_

---

[15] **woof:** the sound a dog makes
[16] **meow:** the sound a cat makes

B | SURVEY Ask a partner about the times in the chart below and complete it with the information. (You can also ask follow-up questions.)

				Yesterday				
	8 a.m.	10 a.m.	Noon	2 p.m.	4 p.m.	6 p.m.	8 p.m.	10 p.m.
Where?								
What?								
How?								

A: **Where** were you at 8 a.m. yesterday?
B: At home.
A: **What** were you doing?
B: I was reading.
A: What were you reading?
B: A magazine.
A: **How** were you feeling at the time?
B: Very good.

A: **Where** were you at _____ yesterday?
B: _____
A: **What** were you doing?
B: _____
A: **How** were you feeling at the time?
B: _____

How good was your partner's day yesterday? Use your partner's answers to make a line graph. Then show the graph to the class. For example:

	8 a.m.	10 a.m.	Noon	2 p.m.	4 p.m.	6 p.m.	8 p.m.	10 p.m.
HOW?	Very good	Good	Good	Very good	Very good	Terrible	Very good	Good
Very good								
Good								
OK								
So-so								
Terrible								

C | WEB SEARCH Choose one of the people mentioned in this unit. Think of three more things you want to know about this person. Write questions. Then look for the information online and write the answers.

PERSON:

Questions	Answers

EXAMPLE: Ingmar Bergman

What movies did he direct?   What was his most famous movie?   Where was he from?

D | WRITING Choose a topic from the box or think of your own. Write four to five sentences on your topic. Then read a classmate's writing. Think of three more things you would like to know about your classmate's story. Write your ideas as questions and give them to your classmate.

a childhood memory

a favorite game

a favorite teacher

a gift you received

2.10 Summary of the Simple Past and Past Progressive

SIMPLE PAST

STATEMENTS	I You He She It We They	worked. did not work. didn't work.

USES

We use the **simple past** for something that:
- began and ended at a specific time in the past
- took place over a period of time in the past
- took place regularly in the past

YES / NO QUESTIONS	Did	I / you / he / she / it / we / they	work?

WH- QUESTIONS	Where	did	I / you / he / she / it / we / they	work?

	Who	worked	here?

SIMPLE PAST OF THE VERB *BE*

STATEMENTS	I He She It	was was not wasn't	there.
	You We They	were were not weren't	

USES

The simple past uses of the verb **be** are similar to the simple past uses of other verbs—see above.

YES / NO QUESTIONS	Was	I / he / she / it	there?
	Were	you / we / they	

WH- QUESTIONS	Where	was	I / he / she / it?
		were	you / we / they?
	Who	was	that?

PAST PROGRESSIVE

STATEMENTS	I He She It	was was not wasn't	working.
	You We They	were were not weren't	

USES

We use the **past progressive** to show that something was in progress:
- at a particular time in the past
- when another event (usually in the simple past) took place

YES / NO QUESTIONS	Was	I / he / she / it	working?
	Were	you / we / they	

WH- QUESTIONS	Where	was	I / he / she / it	working?
		were	you / we / they	

	Who	was working?

3 Nouns and Articles

I find television very educational. The minute somebody turns it on, I go to the library and read a good book.

—GROUCHO MARX,
COMEDIAN
(1890–1977)

Talk about It What does the quotation above mean? Do you think television is educational? Why or why not?

WARM-UP

A | Circle one answer for each question. Then compare answers with your classmates. Which answer to each question was the most popular?

Personal Preferences

1. What do you usually eat for **breakfast**?
   a. **some cereal**
   b. **an egg** and **some toast**
   c. **nothing**
   d. other: _____

2. What is your favorite **school subject**?
   a. **math**
   b. **history**
   c. **English**
   d. other: _____

3. What do you like to do in your free time?
   a. watch **television**
   b. read **a book**
   c. get together with **friends**
   d. other: _____

4. Which **place** would you most like to visit?
   a. **the moon**
   b. **Antarctica**
   c. **Paris**
   d. **Australia**

5. What is most important to you?
   a. **money**
   b. **love**
   c. **friendship**
   d. other: _____

6. What do you worry about most?
   a. **the economy**
   b. **the environment**
   c. **crime**
   d. other: _____

B | Answer these questions about the words in the survey above.
1. The words in blue are nouns. Are any nouns capitalized? Which ones?
2. The words in green are articles. What are the words?
3. Do we always use an article before a noun?

C | Look back at the quotation on page 76. Identify any nouns or articles.

3.1 Overview of Nouns

Nouns are labels or names for people, places, things, and ideas.

A

PEOPLE		PLACES		THINGS		IDEAS	
child	friend	city	Japan	book	money	advice	power
Dr. Sanchez	Mary	country	library	computer	movie	fun	problem
father	sister	hospital	Sydney	game	television	peace	work

B

We use nouns in different places in a sentence, as in **1 – 4**.

1 [subject] **Friendship** | is | important.

3 I | went out | with | [object of preposition] **friends**.

2 I | have | [object of verb] **friends** | here.

4 We | are | [complement] **friends**.

C

NOUN PHRASE			
articles	adjectives	nouns	prepositional phrase
5		information	
6 a		computer	
7 some		money	
8 an	excellent	dinner	
9 the		members	**of a** team
10	serious	problems	

Sometimes we use nouns alone, as in **5**. We can also use nouns together with other "describing" words. For example:

- We can use nouns with *a/an*, *the*, and *some*, as in **6 – 9**. (These words are called articles.)
- We can use nouns with adjectives, as in **8** and **10**. Adjectives explain "what kind of" noun.
- We can add a prepositional phrase after a noun, as in **9**.

 GO ONLINE

1 | Grouping Nouns Read this information about symbols. Write each **bold** noun under the correct group in the chart on page 79. (Some nouns may fit into more than one group.) **3.1 A**

1. **People** wear green **ribbons** to show their **concern** for the **environment**.

3. The two olive **branches** on the United Nations flag represent **peace**.

5. A wedding ring is a **symbol** of **love** and **commitment**[3].

2. The **rings** on the Olympic **flag** represent the five main **regions**[1] of the **world**.

4. The **eagle**, a kind of **bird**, represents **courage**[2], **power**, and **strength**.

6. The **Taj Mahal** in **India** is the **tomb**[4] of the wife of **Emperor Shah Jahan**. The **building** is a symbol of the emperor's love.

---

[1] **regions:** areas
[2] **courage:** the ability to do something difficult or dangerous

[3] **commitment:** a promise to do something
[4] **tomb:** burial place

People	Places	Things you can see, hear, or touch	Ideas
people			

Write about It Add five more nouns to each group in the chart above. Then share ideas with your classmates.

2 | Using Nouns in Sentences Choose nouns from the box to complete each fact. `3.1 B`

ball	event	sport	television	women
countries	players	teams	Uruguay	the United States

TEN FACTS ABOUT FOOTBALL

Noun as subject

1. Only 8 _____*countries*_____ have won the World Cup.

2. _____ run for 3.5 or 4.5 kilometers during a game.

3. Today, more than 20 million _____ play football.

Noun as complement

4. Football is the most popular team _____ in the world.

5. Football became an Olympic _____ in 1908.

Noun as object of preposition

6. In _____, football is called soccer.

7. The World Cup was not on _____ until 1954.

8. The first World Cup took place in 1930 in _____.

9. Football players cannot run with the _____ in their hands.

Noun as object of verb

10. Only 13 countries sent _____ to the first World Cup.

Think about It We use a **complement** (not an object) after a linking verb to rename or describe the subject of the sentence. What are the linking verbs in sentences 4 and 5 above?

Write about It Work with a partner. Choose a different sport and write two facts like the ones above. Read your facts to your classmates. Ask them to identify the nouns in each one.

Ice hockey is the most popular sport in Canada.

3 | Usage Note: Prepositional Phrases Read the note. Then do Activities 4–5.

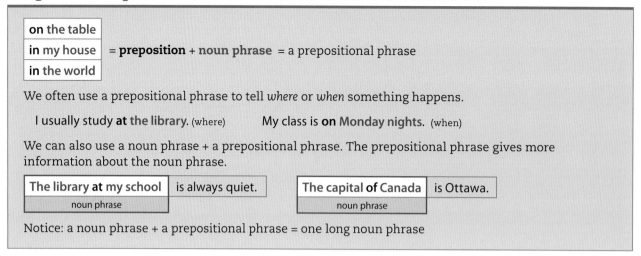

on the table
in my house   = **preposition** + **noun phrase** = a prepositional phrase
in the world

We often use a prepositional phrase to tell *where* or *when* something happens.

I usually study **at the library.** (where)   My class is **on Monday nights.** (when)

We can also use a noun phrase + a prepositional phrase. The prepositional phrase gives more information about the noun phrase.

The library **at my school** is always quiet.   The capital **of Canada** is Ottawa.
noun phrase   noun phrase

Notice: a noun phrase + a prepositional phrase = one long noun phrase

4 | Using Nouns with Describing Words Listen and write the missing word(s) in each question. `3.1 C`

	Article	Adjective	Noun	Prepositional phrase
1. Do you have	*a*		car?	
2. How expensive is	a		computer?	
3. How much is	a		cell phone?	
4. What is	the	largest	city	?
5. Do you like		scary	?	
6. What's the name of	an		movie?	
7. Do you like to wear		expensive	?	
8. Are you		hard	worker?	
9. Do you know			people	?
10. Do you want to be			engineer?	
11. What is	the			of a famous university?
12. What is	the	best	restaurant	?
13. Did you eat			breakfast?	
14. Would you like	some		?	

Talk about It Ask a partner the questions above.

A: *Do you have a car?*
B: *No, I don't. I don't like to drive.*

Think about It Look at the questions above. When do English speakers use *an* instead of *a*?

5 | Prepositions + Nouns Circle the nouns in each **bold** noun phrase. Then listen and add the missing prepositions. `3.1 C`

RESEARCH SAYS...

The most common prepositions are *of*, *in*, and *to*.

CORPUS

TORONTO, CANADA

1. Toronto is **the largest (city)** *in* **(Canada)**.

2. **The population ___ Toronto** is 2.48 million people.

3. Toronto is **one of the most multicultural cities ___ the world**.

4. **Twenty percent ___ all immigrants ___ Canada** live in Toronto.

5. There are **more than 1,400 parks ___ Toronto**.

6. Yonge Street in Toronto is **the longest street ___ the world**.

7. **More than 30 percent of the people ___ Toronto** speak a foreign language at home.

8. According to *Fortune Magazine*, Toronto was **the safest city ___ North America** in 1996.

9. **Over half ___ the workforce** has a university degree or college diploma.

10. The Toronto International Film Festival takes place **every year ___ September**.

Write about It Choose a city and write two sentences about it. Try to use a prepositional phrase in each sentence.

Beibei is a small city in China.

3.2 Proper Nouns and Common Nouns

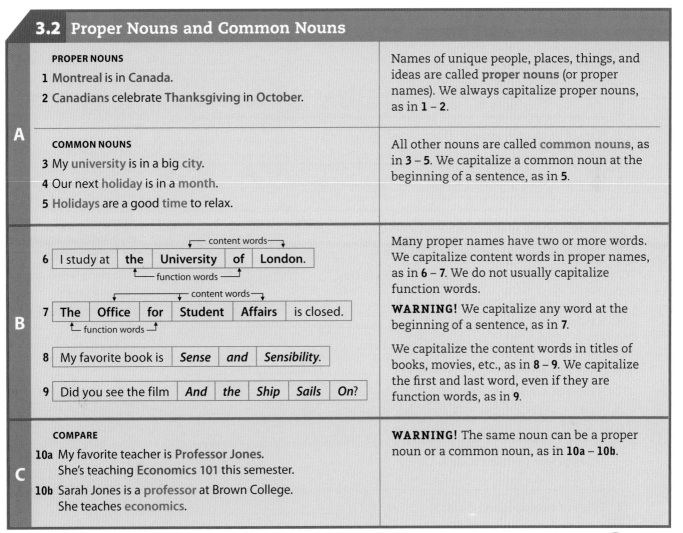

A

PROPER NOUNS

1 Montreal is in Canada.

2 Canadians celebrate Thanksgiving in October.

Names of unique people, places, things, and ideas are called **proper nouns** (or proper names). We always capitalize proper nouns, as in **1 – 2**.

COMMON NOUNS

3 My university is in a big city.

4 Our next holiday is in a month.

5 Holidays are a good time to relax.

All other nouns are called **common nouns**, as in **3 – 5**. We capitalize a common noun at the beginning of a sentence, as in **5**.

B

```
            ┌─── content words ───┐
6 │ I study at │ the │ University │ of │ London. │
                └─── function words ───┘
```

```
        ┌─── content words ───┐
7 │ The │ Office │ for │ Student │ Affairs │ is closed. │
      └─ function words ─┘
```

8 │ My favorite book is │ *Sense* │ *and* │ *Sensibility.* │

9 │ Did you see the film │ *And* │ *the* │ *Ship* │ *Sails* │ *On?* │

Many proper names have two or more words. We capitalize content words in proper names, as in **6 – 7**. We do not usually capitalize function words.

WARNING! We capitalize any word at the beginning of a sentence, as in **7**.

We capitalize the content words in titles of books, movies, etc., as in **8 – 9**. We capitalize the first and last word, even if they are function words, as in **9**.

C

COMPARE

10a My favorite teacher is **Professor Jones**. She's teaching **Economics 101** this semester.

10b Sarah Jones is a **professor** at Brown College. She teaches **economics**.

WARNING! The same noun can be a proper noun or a common noun, as in **10a – 10b**.

6 | Noticing Proper and Common Nouns Underline the nouns in these sentences. Then write each noun under the correct group in the chart below. 3.2 A

BIOGRAPHICAL INFORMATION

1. My first <u>name</u> is Linda.
2. I was born in Mexico in the month of August.
3. I have one brother. His name is Manuel.
4. I speak two languages: Spanish and English.
5. My first teacher was Mrs. Vargas.
6. I have classes on Wednesdays and Fridays.
7. I'd like to travel to Hawaii with a good friend.
8. I'm interested in science and art.

Proper nouns	Common nouns
	name

Write about It Change any of the nouns in the sentences above to make the sentences true for you.

My first name is _____ .

7 | Exploring Categories of Proper Nouns Add one more proper noun to each category. Then share ideas with your classmates. 3.2 A–B

1. **Names of countries:** Turkey, Brazil, _____
2. **Names of towns and cities:** Tokyo, San Salvador, _____
   _____
3. **Names of specific streets:** Abbey Road, Yonge Street, _____
   _____
4. **Names of rivers, lakes, etc.:** the Nile, the Indian Ocean, _____
   _____
5. **Months of the year:** February, October, _____
6. **Days of the week:** Wednesday, Saturday, _____
7. **Names of holidays:** Ramadan, New Year's Day, _____
   _____
8. **Nationalities:** Italian, Costa Rican, _____
9. **Names of languages:** Russian, Arabic, Farsi, _____
10. **Names of schools:** Oxford University, _____
11. **Names of school courses:** Intro to Astronomy, _____
    _____
12. **People's names:** Albert Einstein, _____
13. **Titles before people's names:** Dr. Smith, Mr. Jones, _____
    _____
14. **Titles of books, movies, etc.:** *Never Let Me Go,* _____
    _____

> **F Y I**
>
> We use *the* before some proper nouns. These include:
>
> - rivers, lakes, etc.
>   the Amazon
>   the Pacific Ocean
>
> - plural geographical names
>   the United Arab Emirates
>   the Solomon Islands
>
> - most newspapers and some magazines
>   *The Manchester Guardian*
>   *The New Republic*

15. **Names of organizations:** the United Nations (UN), _____

_____

16. **Abbreviations of academic degrees:** MA (master of arts), _____

_____

17. **Brand names:** Apple, Coke, _____

8 | Identifying Proper Nouns Underline the proper nouns in each paragraph. Then match each proper noun with a category from Activity 7. Write the number of the category above the proper noun. `3.2 A–B`

Excerpts from a University Catalog

                    10
<u>The School of Liberal Arts and Sciences</u> offers courses in biology, chemistry, English,

history, mathematics, music, psychology, and Spanish. This school is near Central Lake—

only two hours away from the city of Portland. The university bus system provides[5] free

transportation between the downtown area and the campus. Buses run from Thursday to

Sunday (Friday to Sunday in July and August) except during holidays.

Professor Nancy Lim is the director of the English Language Institute. Professor Lim is

from Korea. After receiving her MA and PhD in the United States, she taught English in

Costa Rica. In addition to her responsibilities as the director of the program, Professor

Lim teaches English Composition. She is the author of *Developing Your Writing Skills.*

Think about It In the information above, the following nouns are NOT capitalized: *history, city, university, downtown,* and *director.* Why is that?

9 | Capitalizing Words Rewrite these sentences and capitalize the correct words. `3.2 B`

1. my friend likes the magazine *reader's digest.*

    My friend likes the magazine <u>Reader's Digest</u>.

2. one of my favorite books is *the sea* by john banville.
3. my sister and I just watched the movie *beauty and the beast.*
4. my brother is a student at the university of california.
5. the london school of economics is a famous school.
6. aravind adiga wrote *the white tiger.*
7. we saw a great exhibit at the museum of modern art.
8. the president of brazil lives in the palace of the dawn.

> **F Y I**
>
> When we write on a computer, we usually *italicize* the titles of books, magazines, newspapers, films, etc. When we write by hand, we usually <u>underline</u> a title.

---

[5] **provide:** to offer; to give

10 | Capitalizing Words Read these paragraphs. Capitalize the correct words. `3.2 A–B`

AUSTRALIA

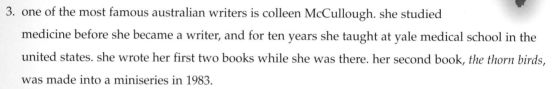

1. *A*
   australia is the sixth largest country in the world. in fact, it's 50 percent larger than europe. australia also has more beaches than any other country in the world. bondi beach, one of the most famous beaches in the world, is on the east coast of australia.

2. australia is a multicultural country. the most common languages after english are mandarin, italian, arabic, and cantonese.

3. one of the most famous australian writers is colleen McCullough. she studied medicine before she became a writer, and for ten years she taught at yale medical school in the united states. she wrote her first two books while she was there. her second book, *the thorn birds*, was made into a miniseries in 1983.

4. one of the most famous buildings in the world is the sydney opera house. this beautiful building was designed by a danish architect, jorn utzon. queen elizabeth II came to australia in 1973 to open the building. the first performance at the opera house was *war and peace* by sergei prokofiev.

Write about It Choose a country and write several sentences about it. Share your writing with your classmates and ask if you capitalized all the necessary words.

Hungary is a small country in Europe. The capital of Hungary is Budapest.

11 | Writing Common and Proper Nouns Ask a classmate these questions and write your classmate's answers. Be sure to capitalize the correct words. `3.2 A–B`

1. Where were you born?
2. What's your favorite kind of car?
3. What's the name of a good movie?
4. What's your favorite school subject?
5. Where did you live last year?
6. What is your favorite month of the year?
7. What languages did you study in school?
8. What city do you want to visit someday?
9. What is the name of a website you often visit?
10. What is your favorite holiday?

Write about It Write three sentences with information about a classmate. Collect the papers and mix them up. Then take turns reading the sentences aloud. The rest of the class can guess the person.

This person's favorite school subject is math. Last year, this person lived in Canada. This person often uses Facebook.

12 | Proper Noun or Common Noun? Rewrite these sentences and correct any errors in capitalization. (Some sentences may not have any errors.) `3.2 C`

1. a. One of my Professors always looks at my papers and gives me advice.
   b. I have a meeting with professor Henley on Friday.
2. a. What do you know about president Dilma Rousseff of brazil?
   b. Dilma Rousseff was the first female president of brazil.

Dilma Rousseff

3. a. My house is the first house on Castro street, next to the library.

   b. We live on a beautiful street with lots of trees.

4. a. I want to study Business in college.

   b. Between my final math 101 and spanish 201 exams, I drove home.

5. a. When the problems began in my country, I was still a student. I wanted to leave the University, but my parents told me to stay there.

   b. My parents visited North Carolina last year because my brother is studying engineering at Duke university.

6. a. My favorite movies are *the King's speech* and *Raiders Of The Lost Ark*.

   b. I always take my rings off when I go swimming.

3.3 Singular Nouns and Plural Nouns

A

singular	plural
one computer	two computers
one place	two places
one class	two classes

1

To form most **plural** nouns, add *-s* or *-es* to the **singular** form, as in **1**.

singular	plural
one life	two lives
one family	two families
one city	two cities

2

In some nouns, a letter changes when we add *-s* or *-es*, as in **2**.

For a complete list of spelling rules for plural nouns, see Activity 16, page 87.

B

singular	irregular plural
one child	two children
one foot	two feet
one man	two men
one person	two people
one tooth	two teeth
one woman	two women

3

A few nouns have irregular plural forms, as in **3**.

one fish	two fish
one species	two species

4

Some nouns have the same form for the singular and plural, as in **4**. These are often words for animals.

C

COMPARE NOUNS AND VERBS

5a Do you want a **copy** of this? (singular noun)

5b Please don't **copy** my paper. (verb)

5c Why do people **copy** me? (verb)

6a How many **watches** do you own? (plural noun)

6b My sister **watches** a lot of TV. (verb)

WARNING! Nouns and verbs can look the same.

- A singular noun can look like a verb, as in **5a** – **5c**.
- A plural noun can look like a verb, as in **6a** – **6b**.

D

7 The **French** are proud of their history.

(the French = all French people)

8 Are **the rich** different from you and me?

(the rich = all rich people)

We can use *the* + an adjective to describe a group of people that share one quality, as in **7** – **8**. *The* + adjective functions as a plural noun.

 ONLINE

13 | Singular or Plural Noun? It is sometimes difficult to hear the *-s* or *-es* ending on plural nouns. Listen and circle the letter of the sentence that you hear. `3.3 A`

1. a. Please write the **name** on the envelope.
   b. Please write the **names** on the envelope.
2. a. Don't forget to put your **paper** on my desk.
   b. Don't forget to put your **papers** on my desk.
3. a. Bring your **friend** to the meeting tonight.
   b. Bring your **friends** to the meeting tonight.
4. a. Please call the **number** below.
   b. Please call the **numbers** below.
5. a. Forward the **email** to my new address.
   b. Forward the **emails** to my new address.
6. a. Please pick up the **package** on my desk.
   b. Please pick up the **packages** on my desk.

7. a. Please finish the **report** by next week.
   b. Please finish the **reports** by next week.
8. a. Don't forget to leave the **box** on the table.
   b. Don't forget to leave the **boxes** on the table.
9. a. Please close the **window** when you leave.
   b. Please close the **windows** when you leave.
10. a. Make a copy of the **document** you found.
    b. Make a copy of the **documents** you found.
11. a. Leave the completed **form** on my desk.
    b. Leave the completed **forms** on my desk.
12. a. Did you find the **message** I left on your desk?
    b. Did you find the **messages** I left on your desk?

14 | Pronunciation Note: *-s* and *-es* Endings Listen to the note. Then do Activity 15.

Usually the plural ending *-s* or *-es* is just a consonant sound: /s/ or /z/.	When a singular noun ends in a hissing or buzzing sound, the plural *-s* or *-es* ending adds another syllable: / əz /. (These words are often spelled with a final *-s*, *-x*, *-z*, *-ce*, *-ge*, *-se*, *-ze*, *-sh*, and *-ss*.)

	SINGULAR	PLURAL	
1	one night	two nights	/ s /
2	one note·book	two note·books	
3	one her·o	two her·oes	/ z /
4	one cit·y	two cit·ies	

	SINGULAR	PLURAL	
5	one wish	two wish·es	
6	one size	two siz·es	+ 1 syllable / əz /
7	one page	two pag·es	
8	one sen·tence	two sen·ten·ces	

15 | Pronouncing Plural Nouns Listen to each pair of words. Check (✓) the ending you hear. `3.3 A`

			/ s / OR / z /	/ əz /
1.	sport	sports	☐	☐
2.	college	colleges	☐	☐
3.	symbol	symbols	☐	☐
4.	discovery	discoveries	☐	☐
5.	campus	campuses	☐	☐
6.	movie	movies	☐	☐
7.	course	courses	☐	☐
8.	place	places	☐	☐

			/ s / OR / z /	/ əz /
9.	language	languages	☐	☐
10.	similarity	similarities	☐	☐
11.	glass	glasses	☐	☐
12.	beach	beaches	☐	☐
13.	game	games	☐	☐
14.	name	names	☐	☐
15.	business	businesses	☐	☐
16.	suitcase	suitcases	☐	☐

Talk about It Work with a partner. One person reads aloud the singular nouns above. The other person listens and says the plural form. Then change roles.

Write about It Write three questions using plural nouns from the list above. Then ask your partner the questions.

How many movies did you watch last week?   *What are the similarities between Mexico and Spain?*

16│Spelling Note: -s and -es Endings Read the note. Then do Activities 17–19.

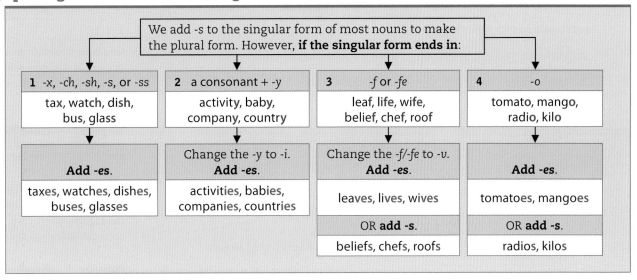

17│Spelling Plural Nouns Write the plural form of each noun. **3.3 A**

SINGULAR	PLURAL		SINGULAR	PLURAL
1. family	_____		10. lady	_____
2. dress	_____		11. match	_____
3. video	_____		12. hero	_____
4. story	_____		13. bush	_____
5. essay	_____		14. copy	_____
6. potato	_____		15. party	_____
7. box	_____		16. knife	_____
8. city	_____		17. chief	_____
9. day	_____		18. photo	_____

Think about It Work in a group of three. Each person checks the plural spelling of six words above.

18│Exploring Plural Nouns Write two more plural nouns for each category. **3.3 A**

1. Three things that people read: _magazines_ _____

2. Three things that people watch: _videos_ _____

3. Three things that people wear in cold weather: _coats_ _____

4. Three things that grow outdoors: _flowers_ _____

5. Three types of electronic devices: _cell phones_ _____

6. Three things you might see in a school: _students_ _____

7. Three kinds of fruit: _bananas_ _____

8. Three things you can use for cutting: _scissors_ _____

Write about It Compare your lists above with a partner and add any additional words.

Think about It Which of the words in your lists above changed spelling when you added -s or -es?

19│Using Plural Nouns Complete each question with the plural form of the noun in parentheses. Then choose an answer from the box below. `3.3 A–B`

QUESTIONS ABOUT NUMBERS

a. How many _____*sides*_____ does a square have? (side) *4*

b. How many _____ are in the number 1 million? (zero)

c. How many _____ are in one U.S. dollar? (penny)

d. How many _____ are there on a piano? (key)

e. How many _____ are there in a circle? (degree)

f. On average, how many years do _____ live? (elephant)

g. How many _____ are in a yard[6]? (foot)

h. How many _____ does a normal adult have? (tooth)

i. How many _____ does it take to make a whole? (half)

j. How many _____ do most humans have? (vertebra[7])

k. Approximately how many _____ are in 100 pounds? (kilo)

l. Approximately how many _____ are born in the world every second? (baby)

m. Approximately how many _____ in the world have more than 1 million people? (city)

> **F Y I**
> Words borrowed from other languages sometimes have an **irregular plural form**. For example:
>
> | Singular | Plural |
> |----------|--------|
> | crisis | crises |
> | hypothesis | hypotheses |
>
> In some cases, both the irregular plural form and the regular -s form are acceptable. For example:
>
> | Singular | Plural |
> |----------|--------|
> | appendix | appendixes |
> | | appendices |
> | vertebra | vertebrae |
> | | vertebras |

ANSWERS TO QUESTIONS ABOUT NUMBERS

2	3	4	4.5	6	32	33	45	60	88	100	360	480

Talk about It Work in a group of four. Ask and answer the questions above.

Write about It In your group, write three more questions with numbers for answers. Then ask another group the questions.

How many days are there in the longest month?

20│Distinguishing Nouns and Verbs Decide if the **bold** word is a noun or a verb. Write *N* (noun) or *V* (verb) above each word. `3.3 C`

1. Do you have a middle **name**? *(N)*

2. How did your parents choose your **name**?

3. Can you **name** the continents?

4. Do you have a **watch**?

5. Do you **watch** a lot of TV?

6. Who **watches** the most TV in your family?

7. Why are fewer people wearing **watches** these days?

8. Does your teacher **grade** all of your homework?

9. Are **grades** important to you?

---

[6] **yard:** a measure of length
[7] **vertebra:** a small bone in your back

10. Do you have a **plan** for your future?

11. What do you **plan** to do tomorrow?

12. Do you like to make **plans**?

13. Who **plans** the meals in your family?

14. What do family members sometimes **fight** about?

15. What is a good way to end a **fight**?

16. What are the basic **needs** of a baby?

17. How much water do you **need** to drink every day?

18. Do you ever feel the **need** to sleep during the day?

19. How many hours do you **need** to sleep at night?

Talk about It Ask a partner the questions in Activity 20.

A: Do you have a middle name?
B: No, I don't. But I have two last names.

21 | Using Adjectives as Nouns Use *the* + an adjective from the box to complete each question below. (You will use some adjectives more than once. Many different questions are possible.) `3.3 D`

educated	elderly[8]	poor	rich	uneducated	unemployed	young

QUESTIONS ABOUT GROUPS OF PEOPLE

1. Are _____ happier than other people?

2. Should _____ be allowed to make their own decisions?

3. Are _____ getting poorer?

4. Do _____ have more health problems than other people?

5. Are _____ likely to earn high salaries[9]?

6. Are _____ lazy?

7. Should _____ pay more taxes than other people?

8. Should young people take care of _____?

9. Is it difficult for _____ to find work these days?

Talk about It Choose one of your questions above and interview six classmates. Then report their answers to the class.

"I asked six classmates, 'Do the poor have more health problems than other people?'
Five people answered 'Yes' and one person answered 'No.'"

---

[8] **elderly:** old
[9] **salaries:** money that people receive for their work

3.4 Count Nouns and Noncount Nouns

When you use a noun, ask yourself, "Can I count this?" The things you can count are called **count nouns**. The things you can't count are called **noncount nouns**.

A

COUNT NOUNS

2 glasses

4 men

4 trees

NONCOUNT NOUNS

water

PEACE

flour

For a list of common noncount nouns, see the Resources, page R-10.

B

COUNT NOUNS

1 I have one **class** on Monday and two **classes** on Tuesday.

2 We spent a **day** in Boston and three **days** in New York.

NONCOUNT NOUNS

3 The **information** was correct. (NOT: ~~informations~~)

4 Your **advice** was very helpful. (NOT: ~~advices~~)

5 Did you buy some **furniture**? (NOT: ~~furnitures~~)

A count noun has a singular form and a plural form, as in **1 – 2**.

A noncount noun does not have a plural form because we think of it as a whole thing, as in **3 – 5**.

Sometimes "a whole thing" can have many parts, as in **5**. When we use a noncount noun, we are talking about all of the parts together.

C

COMPARE

6a Can I have three **coffees**, please? (coffees = cups of coffee)

6b Do you drink **coffee**? (coffee = the liquid drink)

7a I had a bad **experience** yesterday.
(experience = one separate event)

7b How much **experience** do you have with computers?
(experience = the skill or knowledge you learn)

Many nouns have a count meaning and a noncount meaning.

• Nouns have a count meaning when they are single, separate things, as in **6a** and **7a**.

• A noun has a noncount meaning when it is a thing or idea in general, as in **6b** and **7b**.

GO ONLINE

22 | Can You Count It? Think about each noun in this list. Is it something you can count? Check (✓) *Count* or *Noncount*. 3.4 A–B

	COUNT	NONCOUNT		COUNT	NONCOUNT
1. tomato	✓	☐	10. information	☐	☐
2. chemistry	☐	☐	11. knowledge	☐	☐
3. child	☐	☐	12. region	☐	☐
4. problem	☐	☐	13. university	☐	☐
5. advice	☐	☐	14. jewelry	☐	☐
6. excitement	☐	☐	15. library	☐	☐
7. job	☐	☐	16. furniture	☐	☐
8. fun	☐	☐	17. money	☐	☐
9. computer	☐	☐	18. holiday	☐	☐

Think about It Write the plural form of each count noun above.

tomatoes

23 | Distinguishing Count and Noncount Nouns Is the **bold** word in each question a singular count noun, a plural count noun, or a noncount noun? Check (✓) your answers. `3.4 A–B`

COMMON QUESTIONS FOR TEACHERS	SINGULAR COUNT	PLURAL COUNT	NONCOUNT
1. Did we have any **homework** for today?	☐	☐	✓
2. Do I need to bring my book to **school** every day?	☐	☐	☐
3. What **advice** do you have for someone studying English?	☐	☐	☐
4. Do I need a learner's **dictionary**?	☐	☐	☐
5. What is your **opinion** of electronic dictionaries?	☐	☐	☐
6. How often do you give **tests**?	☐	☐	☐
7. When is the next **holiday**?	☐	☐	☐
8. Why do we need to study **grammar**?	☐	☐	☐
9. How many **books** do we need for this class?	☐	☐	☐
10. Can we drink **coffee** in class?	☐	☐	☐
11. Does reading **literature** help you learn a new language?	☐	☐	☐
12. Can we work in **groups** today?	☐	☐	☐
13. Can we listen to some **music** today?	☐	☐	☐
14. Do we need to take **notes** in class?	☐	☐	☐

Talk about It Ask your teacher the questions above.

Student: Did we have any homework for today?
Teacher: No, but we're having a quiz!

24 | Identifying Count Nouns There is one count noun in each group of **bold** nouns. Circle the count noun. `3.4 A–B`

1. Do you like to talk about (**grammar** / the **weather** / **shopping** / (**books**)?
2. Do you like (**fruit** / **meat** / **sugar** / **beans**)?
3. Do you need special (**tools** / **equipment** / **clothing** / **knowledge**) to fix a car?
4. Do you hope to have (**money** / a good **job** / good **health** / **happiness**) in the future?
5. Do you like to watch (**baseball** / **movies** / **football** / **tennis**)?
6. Do you eat a lot of (**carrots** / **cheese** / **meat** / **bread**)?
7. Is it important to have (**courage** / good **health** / **friends** / **confidence**)?
8. Do you spend a lot of money on (**entertainment** / **books** / **clothing** / **food**)?
9. Did you buy any (**furniture** / **equipment** / **gasoline** / **shoes**) yesterday?
10. Where can you get (good **information** / good **advice** / a good **meal** / good **coffee**)?

Think about It What helped you to identify the count nouns above?

Talk about It Ask a partner the questions above. Use any of the **bold** nouns.

A: Do you like to talk about movies?
B: Sure. Do you like to talk about the weather?
A: Not really.

25 | Listening for Count and Noncount Nouns Listen and write the missing words. Then decide where each conversation takes place. Write your ideas in the boxes. (More than one answer is possible.)

`3.4 A–B`

1. Employee: Next, please.

   Customer: _____Tickets_____ for one adult and two _____, please.

   Employee: There you go. That will be seventeen _____.

1. Where?

2. Employee: Do you need some _____?

   Customer: Yes, do you sell _____?

   Employee: Yes, we do. Luggage is on the third _____.

2. Where?

3. Customer: Excuse me.

   Employee: Yes?

   Customer: I'm looking for some _____ about popular music in the 1960s.

   Employee: Did you look it up on the _____?

   Customer: Yes, I did, but I didn't have any _____.

3. Where?

4. Customer: Excuse me. How much are these _____?

   Employee: Let me look on the box. Um, it says five hundred dollars.

   Customer: Five hundred dollars! That's a lot of _____.

4. Where?

5. Employee: Are you ready to order?

   Customer: Yes, I'd like the broiled _____, please.

   Employee: Do you want that with _____ or _____?

5. Where?

6. Employee: Can I help you?

   Customer: I need to withdraw some _____, but I don't have my ATM card.

   Employee: Can I see some identification, please?

   Customer: Sure. Here's my _____.

6. Where?

7. Customer: Excuse me, where's the _____?

   Employee: It's in that aisle, next to the _____.

   Customer: Thanks.

7. Where?

8. Employee: How many _____ are you checking?

   Customer: Just one.

   Employee: Is that your _____? Do you want to check it, too?

   Customer: No, my _____ is in it.

8. Where?

Think about It Circle all of the nouns in the conversations in Activity 25. Then write each noun under the correct group in the chart below.

Count nouns	Noncount nouns
tickets	

Write about It Work with a partner. Write another conversation for one of the places in Activity 25.

---

26 | Using Noncount Nouns Use the nouns in the box to complete the quotations below. (More than one noun may be possible, but only one is correct.) `3.4 A–B`

advice	education	information	music	money
	education	information	music	money
	education	information	music	money

FAMOUS QUOTATIONS

1. All _____*music*_____ is beautiful. (*Billy Strayhorn, composer*)

2. _____ is only a tool. (*Ayn Rand, writer*)

3. _____ is not knowledge. (*Albert Einstein, physicist*)

4. _____ is a fantastic[10] peacekeeper of the world. (*Xun Zi, philosopher*)

5. _____ is the most powerful weapon which you can use to change the world.

    (*Nelson Mandela, president of South Africa*)

6. _____ is the universal language of mankind. (*Henry Wadsworth Longfellow, writer*)

7. _____ is only useful when you get rid of[11] it. (*Evelyn Waugh, writer*)

8. _____ is seldom[12] welcome, and those who need it the most, like it the least.

    (*Lord Chesterfield, statesman*)

9. _____ is the oxygen of the modern age. (*Ronald Reagan, U.S. president*)

10. _____ is the root of[13] all evil. (*Louisa May Alcott, writer*)

11. _____ is a source of[14] learning. (*William Pollard, physicist*)

12. _____ is not preparation for life; _____ is life itself. (*John Dewey, philosopher*)

Talk about It Take turns reading the quotations above aloud with a partner. What does each quotation mean? Do you agree or disagree?

Think about It Do an online search for other quotations about money, music, information, education, or advice and share them with your classmates.

---

[10] **fantastic:** excellent; very good
[11] **get rid of:** to throw away or use up
[12] **seldom:** not often

[13] **the root of:** the cause of
[14] **a source of:** a person or thing that something comes from

27 | Choosing the Correct Meaning Match the **bold** words with the dictionary definitions. Write the number of the definition. `3.4 C`

> **or·gan·i·za·tion** 🔑 /ˌɔrɡənəˈzeɪʃn/ *noun*
> **1** [*count*] a group of people who work together for a special purpose: *He works for an organization that helps old people.*
> **2** [*noncount*] the activity of planning or arranging something; the way that something is planned or arranged: *She's busy with the organization of her daughter's wedding.*

> **room** 🔑 /rum/ *noun*
> **1** [*count*] one of the spaces in a building that has walls around it: *How many rooms do you have in your house?* • *a classroom*
> **2** [*noncount*] space; enough space: *There's no room for you in the car.*

1. The United Nations is an international **organization**. __1__
2. I belong to a student **organization** at my school. ____
3. Your desk needs a bit of **organization**. ____
4. She volunteers at an **organization** for the homeless. ____
5. Success in school depends on good **organization**. ____
6. We aren't all good at **organization**. ____
7. My apartment only has two **rooms**. ____
8. Is there **room** for 50 chairs in your classroom? ____
9. A hotel **room** in New York can be expensive. ____
10. My car only has **room** for four people. ____
11. There isn't **room** on my shelf for another book. ____
12. I'm renting a **room** in a private house. ____

Dictionary entries are from the *Oxford Basic American Dictionary for learners of English* © Oxford University Press 2011.

28 | Count or Noncount Meaning? Decide if the **bold** word in each sentence has a count meaning or a noncount meaning. Check (✓) your answers. `3.4 C`

		COUNT	NONCOUNT
1.	a. Do you like **football**?	☐	✓
	b. Do you own a **football**?	☐	☐
2.	a. Are you interested in studying **law**?	☐	☐
	b. Is there a **law** against talking on your cell phone while driving?	☐	☐
3.	a. We had many **adventures** on our trip to the Arctic.	☐	☐
	b. She had lots of excitement and **adventure** in her life.	☐	☐
4.	a. Please don't make so much **noise**!	☐	☐
	b. I heard a loud **noise**.	☐	☐
5.	a. She felt a sharp **pain** in her stomach.	☐	☐
	b. We could see the **pain** in her eyes.	☐	☐
6.	a. We took a tour bus to see the **sights** of Paris.	☐	☐
	b. Don't let the children get out of **sight**.	☐	☐
7.	a. I hope you have **success** in your new job.	☐	☐
	b. The dinner was a great **success**.	☐	☐

Think about It What helped you identify the count nouns above?

Write about It Look up one of the words below in a learner's dictionary. Write sentences using the count and noncount meanings. Read your sentences to your classmates and ask them to identify the count and noncount meanings.

> action   alarm   authority   chocolate   danger   production

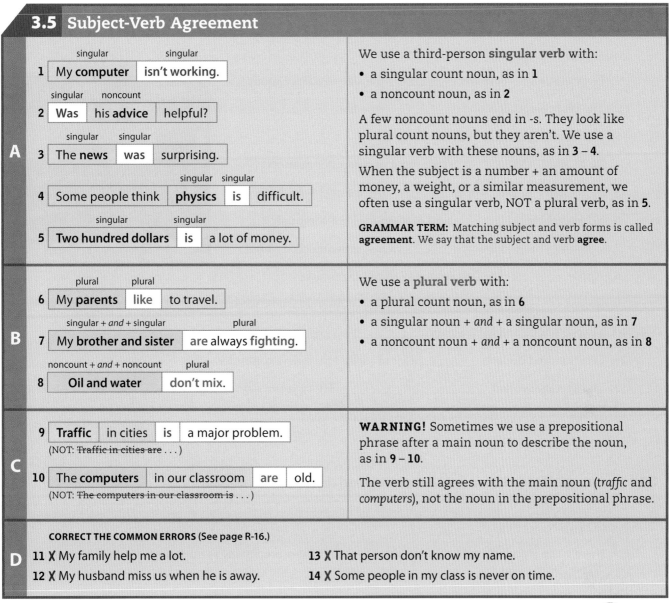

3.5 Subject-Verb Agreement

A

	singular	singular
1	My **computer**	isn't working.

	singular	noncount	
2	Was	his **advice**	helpful?

	singular	singular	
3	The **news**	was	surprising.

		singular	singular	
4	Some people think	**physics**	is	difficult.

	singular	singular	
5	**Two hundred dollars**	is	a lot of money.

We use a third-person **singular verb** with:

• a singular count noun, as in **1**

• a noncount noun, as in **2**

A few noncount nouns end in -s. They look like plural count nouns, but they aren't. We use a singular verb with these nouns, as in **3 – 4**.

When the subject is a number + an amount of money, a weight, or a similar measurement, we often use a singular verb, NOT a plural verb, as in **5**.

GRAMMAR TERM: Matching subject and verb forms is called **agreement**. We say that the subject and verb **agree**.

B

	plural	plural	
6	My **parents**	like	to travel.

	singular + *and* + singular	plural	
7	My **brother and sister**	are always **fighting**.

	noncount + *and* + noncount	plural
8	**Oil and water**	don't mix.

We use a **plural verb** with:

• a plural count noun, as in **6**

• a singular noun + *and* + a singular noun, as in **7**

• a noncount noun + *and* + a noncount noun, as in **8**

C

9	**Traffic**	in cities	is	a major problem.

(NOT: ~~Traffic in cities are . . .~~)

10	The **computers**	in our classroom	are	old.

(NOT: ~~The computers in our classroom is . . .~~)

WARNING! Sometimes we use a prepositional phrase after a main noun to describe the noun, as in **9 – 10**.

The verb still agrees with the main noun (*traffic* and *computers*), not the noun in the prepositional phrase.

D

CORRECT THE COMMON ERRORS (See page R-16.)

11 ✗ My family help me a lot.

12 ✗ My husband miss us when he is away.

13 ✗ That person don't know my name.

14 ✗ Some people in my class is never on time.

 ONLINE

29 | Noticing Singular Subjects and Verbs Circle the subject and underline the verb(s) in these questions. **3.5 A**

1. <u>Is</u> (fruit) good for you?
2. What is a popular sport in your country?
3. How important is money to you?
4. When is the news on TV?
5. Is physics an interesting subject?

6. Is anger ever useful?
7. What is your favorite movie?
8. Does your mother speak English?
9. What makes a good home?
10. Is exercise an important part of your life?

Talk about It Ask a partner the questions above. Then ask each question again with a different subject.

A: Is fruit good for you?
B: Yes, it is.

A: Is ice cream good for you?
B: No, it isn't, but it's delicious.

Think about It Look back at the subjects you circled in the questions above. Write *SC* over the singular count nouns. Write *NC* over the noncount nouns.

30 | Distinguishing Singular and Plural Subjects Complete these sentences with the correct form of the verb. `3.5 A–B`

COMPUTERS

1. Early electronic computers ___were___ the size of a large room.
   (was / were)
2. The first computer mouse _____ wooden.
   (was / were)
3. A laptop _____ a portable computer.
   (is / are)
4. ROM and RAM _____ two types of computer memory.
   (is / are)
5. More than 2 billion people _____ the Internet worldwide.
   (uses / use)
6. 512 megabytes _____ a lot of memory for a computer.
   (isn't / aren't)
7. Computer programming _____ a fast-growing occupation.
   (is / are)
8. Apple _____ the first company to sell the mouse.
   (wasn't / weren't)
9. Iceland _____ the highest percentage of Internet users: 95 percent.
   (has / have)
10. My cell phone and MP3 player _____ small computers inside.
    (has / have)
11. One hundred dollars _____ a lot of money for a new computer.
    (isn't / aren't)
12. The average worker _____ or _____ 110 emails a day.
    (sends / send)   (receives / receive)
13. 123456 _____ the most common email password.
    (is / are)

31 | Language Note: *There is/There are* Read the note. Then do Activity 32.

We sometimes use *there* + *be* at the beginning of a sentence. In these sentences, *there* has little meaning. We call it "empty *there*."

| There's | no place like home. |

| There are | many opportunities for work here. |

Notice that the verb *be* agrees with the main noun after it.

| There is | too much **information** on the Internet. |

| There are | over 20 billion **Web pages** on the Internet. |

There + *be* signals that new information is coming next. It often introduces a new topic.

There are many ways to greet people. For example, you can . . .

32 | Using *There + Be* Write *There is* or *There are* to complete these sentences. Is each sentence true or false? Check (✓) your answer and then compare with a partner. `3.5 A–B`

TOPIC SENTENCES		TRUE	FALSE
1. *There is* a possibility of rain tomorrow.		☐	☐
2. _____ 30 days in February.		☐	☐
3. _____ many different ways to lose weight.		☐	☐
4. _____ very little sugar in candy.		☐	☐
5. _____ many interesting things to do in a big city.		☐	☐
6. _____ beautiful places in every country.		☐	☐
7. _____ always a danger of war.		☐	☐

8. I think _____ a connection between cell phones and cancer.   ☐   ☐

9. I think _____ a lot of ads on TV.   ☐   ☐

10. _____ few living things in the oceans.   ☐   ☐

11. _____ life on Mars.   ☐   ☐

12. _____ a difference between happiness and joy.   ☐   ☐

Think about It Which of the sentences in Activity 32 could you use as a topic sentence for a paragraph or longer pieces of writing? Why?

33 | Using Prepositional Phrases Complete each sentence with a phrase from the box. **3.5 C**

in Africa	in South America	in your body	of India	of the earth
in North America	in 2 billion	of art	of Mount Everest	of the horse

1. The ancestors[15] _____ *of the horse* _____ were only a foot tall.

2. The longest river _____ is the Amazon.

3. The longest rivers _____ are the Nile and the Congo.

4. The diameter _____ is 12,756 kilometers (7,926 miles).

5. The height _____ is 8,848 meters (29,029 feet).

6. The earliest works _____ are animal paintings in a cave in France.

7. The capital _____ is New Delhi.

8. One person _____ will live to be 116 or older.

9. The highest mountain _____ is in Alaska.

10. The longest bone _____ is in the leg.

34 | Singular or Plural Verb? Choose verbs from the boxes to complete the article. **3.5 A–C**

Common Surnames[16] in the United States

There _____ now six million different surnames in the U.S. The most common surname _____ Smith. More than two million people _____ that name. Johnson, Williams, Brown, Jones, Miller, and Davis _____ the next most common surnames. More than a million people _____ each of those names. Garcia and Rodriguez, two Hispanic surnames, _____ now on the list of the top 10 surnames in the U.S. The surname Lee _____ on the list of the top 25 most common names. Many people with the surname Lee _____ of Asian descent.

1. is/are

2. is/are

3. has/have

4. is/are

5. has/have

6. is/are

7. is/are

8. is/are

[15] **ancestors:** the animals in the past that developed into modern animals   [16] **surnames:** family names

Talk about It Activity 34 lists some common surnames in the U.S. What are some common surnames in other countries? Share ideas with your classmates.

"The most common surnames in Argentina are Fernandez, Rodriguez, and Gonzalez."

35 | Error Correction Correct any errors in these sentences. (Some sentences may not have any errors.)

1. My friends likes me a lot, but they are also a little jealous of me.

   My friends like me a lot, but they are also a little jealous of me.

2. The blue stripes on the Nicaraguan flag represents the Pacific Ocean and Caribbean Sea.
3. Many people wants a good job, but they don't have the necessary skills.
4. The news are always very bad.
5. The programs on television isn't very good.
6. Fresh food keep you healthy.
7. Computers make it easier to learn about other countries without traveling.
8. A college education provide you with the tools to get a good job.
9. My brother have a serious problem.
10. When children is young, they don't understand money.
11. Four dollars is a lot of money for a cup of coffee.
12. Food and water is all we need.
13. The food in most restaurants here is expensive.
14. There are some moneys for you on the table.

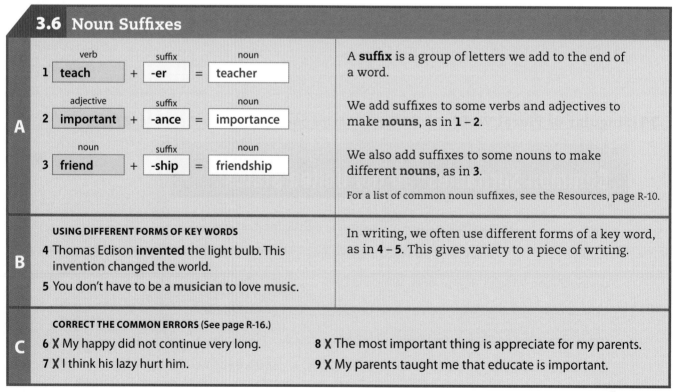

3.6 Noun Suffixes

A

verb		suffix		noun
1 **teach**	+	**-er**	=	teacher

adjective		suffix		noun
2 **important**	+	**-ance**	=	importance

noun		suffix		noun
3 **friend**	+	**-ship**	=	friendship

A **suffix** is a group of letters we add to the end of a word.

We add suffixes to some verbs and adjectives to make **nouns**, as in **1 – 2**.

We also add suffixes to some nouns to make different **nouns**, as in **3**.

For a list of common noun suffixes, see the Resources, page R-10.

B

USING DIFFERENT FORMS OF KEY WORDS

4 Thomas Edison **invented** the light bulb. This **invention** changed the world.

5 You don't have to be a **musician** to love **music**.

In writing, we often use different forms of a key word, as in **4 – 5**. This gives variety to a piece of writing.

C

CORRECT THE COMMON ERRORS (See page R-16.)

6 ✗ My happy did not continue very long.

7 ✗ I think his lazy hurt him.

8 ✗ The most important thing is appreciate for my parents.

9 ✗ My parents taught me that educate is important.

36 | Identifying Suffixes Complete this chart. Write the missing noun or suffix. 3.6 A

Verb + suffix	= Noun
1. achieve + -ment	= *achievement*
2. act + ___ion___	= action
3. appear + _____	= appearance
4. arrange + -ment	=
5. connect + _____	= connection
6. contain + -er	=
7. develop + _____	= development
8. differ + -ence	=
9. direct + -ion	=
10. disagree + _____	= disagreement
11. discuss + _____	= discussion
12. employ + _____	= employer
13. excite + _____	= excitement
14. fail + _____	= failure
15. lead + _____	= leader
16. press + -ure	=

Adjective + suffix	= Noun
17. difficult + -y	=
18. free + -dom	=
19. kind + _____	= kindness
20. real + -ity	=
21. sad + -ness	=
22. similar + _____	= similarity
23. weak + _____	= weakness

Noun + suffix	= New noun
24. art + -ist	=
25. child + _____	= childhood
26. music + -ian	=
27. office + _____	= officer
28. poet + _____	= poetry
29. prison + -er	=
30. relation + -ship	=

Think about It Use a dictionary to check the meaning of any words above that you don't know.

37 | Spelling Note: Noun Suffixes Read the note. Then do Activities 38–39.

Some words need a spelling change when we add a suffix. For example:

VERB		NOUN	VERB		NOUN
decide	(-de + -sion)	= decision	describe	(-be + -ption)	= description
combine	(-e + -ation)	= combination	argue	(-e + -ment)	= argument
compare	(-e + -ison)	= comparison	behave	(-e + -ior)	= behavior

There is no easy way to know which suffix to add to a word. You learn suffixes by seeing the words (by reading a lot) and practicing them. You can also look in a dictionary. Notice that the noun is often listed separately from the verb.

> **re·duce** 🔑 /rɪˈdus/ *verb* (re·duc·es, re·duc·ing, re·duced)
> to make something smaller or less: *This shirt was reduced from $50 to $30.* ◆ *Reduce speed now* (= words on a road sign). ⊃ **ANTONYM increase**

> **re·duc·tion**
> /rɪˈdʌkʃn/ *noun* [count]
> making something smaller or less: *price reductions* ◆ *a reduction in the number of students*

Dictionary entries are from the *Oxford Basic American Dictionary for learners of English* © Oxford University Press 2011.

38 | Using Noun Suffixes Complete these test prompts with the noun form of the words in parentheses. Use a dictionary if necessary. [3.6 A]

COMMON TEST PROMPTS

1. What are some qualities of a good _____supervisor_____? (supervise)
2. If you were an employer, for what reasons would you fire an _____? (employ)
3. _____ is the most important factor in the _____ of a country. Do you agree? (educate/develop)
4. Do the benefits of study abroad justify the _____? (difficult)
5. Money can't buy _____. Do you agree? (happy)
6. Should the _____ spend money on space _____? (govern/explore)
7. How do movies and television influence people's _____? (behave)
8. There will always be _____ in the world. Agree or disagree? (violent)
9. Should foreign language _____ begin in kindergarten? Why or why not? (instruct)
10. Parents should make important _____ for their older (15- to 18-year-old) children. Agree or disagree? (decide)

Talk about It Talk about one of the questions above with a partner.

A: What are some qualities of a good supervisor?
B: Well, I think a supervisor should be patient. . . .

39 | Using Different Forms of a Word Complete these sentences with the noun form of the **bold** word. (You can use a dictionary if necessary.) [3.6 B]

ESSAY BEGINNINGS

1. The Internet has changed the way people **interact**. For example, today there is less need for face-to-face _____interaction_____.
2. My friends are **similar** in a number of ways. Perhaps the most important _____ is their love of sports.
3. It's not easy to **decide** what to do with your life, but it's a _____ we all have to make.
4. If you want your children to **behave** well, you should pay attention to your own _____.
5. Football and soccer **differ** in several ways. One important _____ is how the players use the ball.
6. My parents **collect** old jazz records. Their _____ fills an entire room.
7. Awards and prizes **motivate** people to work hard. Simple praise can also be a good _____.
8. It may take years to **recover** from a brain injury, but a complete _____ is possible.
9. For homework, we had to **describe** a beautiful place. I decided to write a _____ of my hometown.
10. We all **fail** sometimes. We just can't allow _____ to discourage us.

Write about It Choose one of the essay beginnings above. What do you think the writer says next? Write your idea in a sentence. (You don't need to use the bold word in your sentence.)

The Internet has changed the way people interact. For example, today there is less need for face-to-face interaction. People don't need to meet in person to make friends.

40 | Error Correction Correct any errors in these sentences. (Some sentences may not have any errors.)

1. The organize of my paragraph wasn't very good.

   The organization of my paragraph wasn't very good.

2. Last year I took a course in art appreciate.

3. There are many different between my language and English.

4. When I was young, my brother always tried to protect me from dangerous.

5. I think confident makes us perform better.

6. It is not easy to accept the true sometimes.

7. The behave of many people on airplanes is very surprising.

8. When does adult begin? Is it when a person can drive a car?

9. The organization and develop of my essay need improvement.

10. I failed the exam because of its difficultness.

11. Teachers and their teenaged students discuss lots of different things in class. That's why teenagers and their teachers have a special relation.

12. Everyone fails sometimes. When you know the cause of your fail, you can change your actions.

3.7 Using *A/An* and *Some*

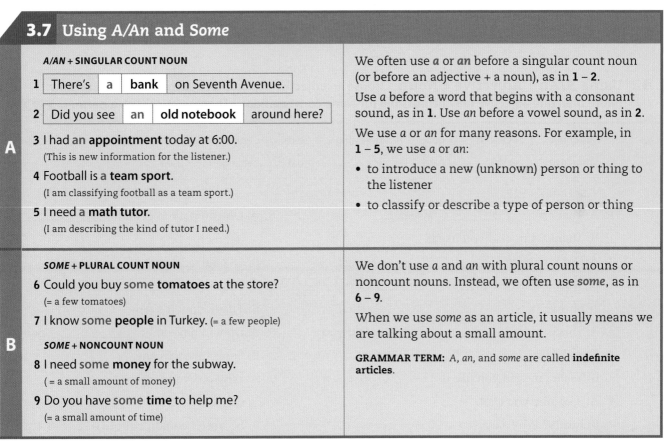

A/AN + SINGULAR COUNT NOUN

A

1 | There's | a | bank | on Seventh Avenue.

2 | Did you see | an | old notebook | around here?

3 I had **an appointment** today at 6:00.
(This is new information for the listener.)

4 Football is **a team sport**.
(I am classifying football as a team sport.)

5 I need **a math tutor**.
(I am describing the kind of tutor I need.)

We often use *a* or *an* before a singular count noun (or before an adjective + a noun), as in **1 – 2**.

Use *a* before a word that begins with a consonant sound, as in **1**. Use *an* before a vowel sound, as in **2**.

We use *a* or *an* for many reasons. For example, in **1 – 5**, we use *a* or *an*:

• to introduce a new (unknown) person or thing to the listener

• to classify or describe a type of person or thing

B

SOME + PLURAL COUNT NOUN

6 Could you buy some **tomatoes** at the store?
(= a few tomatoes)

7 I know some **people** in Turkey. (= a few people)

SOME + NONCOUNT NOUN

8 I need some **money** for the subway.
(= a small amount of money)

9 Do you have some **time** to help me?
(= a small amount of time)

We don't use *a* and *an* with plural count nouns or noncount nouns. Instead, we often use *some*, as in **6 – 9**.

When we use *some* as an article, it usually means we are talking about a small amount.

GRAMMAR TERM: *A, an,* and *some* are called **indefinite articles**.

ONLINE

NOUNS AND ARTICLES 101

41 | Using _A_ and _An_ Complete these sentences with _a_ or _an_. `3.7 A`

SPORTS

1. Gymnastics is _an_ ancient[17] sport.

2. Football is ____ team sport.

3. Golf is ____ individual sport, not a team sport.

4. Car racing is ____ dangerous sport.

5. Volleyball is ____ awesome[18] sport.

6. Kite flying is ____ professional sport in Thailand.

7. Golf was ____ Olympic sport in 1900 and 1904.

8. You can't play polo without ____ horse.

9. A football game lasts for about ____ hour and a half.

10. The World Cup takes place in ____ different country every four years.

11. There are six players on ____ ice hockey team.

PRONUNCIATION

For words that begin with the letter _u_:

- use _an_ when the _u_ has a vowel sound:
  an unusual sport, **an u**mbrella

- use _a_ when the _u_ has a consonant sound:
  a unique sport, **a u**niversity

For words that begin with the letter _h_:

- use _an_ when the _h_ is silent:
  an hour, **an h**onest man

- use _a_ when the _h_ is pronounced:
  a hospital, **a h**ard test

Write about It Write your own sentences about six different sports. Then share ideas with your classmates.

_____ is (a/an) _____ sport.
(name of sport)   _(adjective)_

---

42 | Using _A/An_ + Adjective + Noun Choose an adjective to complete each conversation below. (More than one adjective may be possible for some conversations.) Then practice with a partner. `3.7 A`

academic	delicious	good	interesting	nice	only	unusual
attractive	extra	hard	new	old	strange	used

1. A: That's a _____ _nice_ _____ sweater.
   B: Thanks. I'm glad you like it.

2. A: Did you have a _____ evening?
   B: Yeah, I watched an _____ movie on TV.

3. A: This is a _____ sandwich. Did you make it?
   B: Yeah. I'm glad you like it.

4. A: I admire you a lot.
   B: Really? Why's that?
   A: Because you're a _____ worker.

5. A: Is there anything good on TV tonight?
   B: Yeah, there's an _____ program about Antarctica at 8:00.

6. A: Do you plan to get an _____ degree?
   B: Of course. I want to be an engineer.

7. A: That's an _____ suit.
   B: Thank you. It's new.

8. A: Do you have an _____ pen?
   B: Sure. Take this one.

9. A: Why did you buy a _____ car?
   B: Because I couldn't afford a _____ car.

10. A: Are you an _____ child?
    B: No, I have two brothers.

---

[17]**ancient:** very old

[18]**awesome:** very good

43 | Choosing *A* or *An* Read this text and complete it with *a* or *an*. `3.7 A`

Who's Who at __a__ University
₁

Most college professors have ____ doctoral degree[19]. However, sometimes
₂

____ university will hire ____ person without one. The university calls this
₃   ₄

person ____ instructor. The instructor works to finish his or her PhD and
₅

can become ____ assistant professor after that. Assistant professors don't
₆

usually have ____ permanent job or tenure[20]. If they don't receive tenure
₇

after 5 to 7 years, they usually have ____ year to find another job.
₈

If ____ assistant professor gets tenure, he or she becomes ____ associate
₉   ₁₀

professor. Later, the associate professor can get ____ position as ____ full
₁₁   ₁₂

professor.

____ adjunct professor doesn't have ____ permanent position and
₁₃   ₁₄

teaches ____ small number of classes. ____ visiting professor is from one
₁₅   ₁₆

university, but teaches at another school for ____ year or two.
₁₇

---

44 | Using *A*, *An*, and *Some* Complete these questions with *a*, *an*, or *some*. `3.7 A–B`

1. Do you have ___*some*___ money with you today?

2. Can you drive _____ car?

3. Can you give me _____ information about your country?

4. Is there _____ bank around here?

5. Do you have _____ favorite restaurant?

6. Do you know _____ good place for breakfast?

7. Do you live in _____ apartment?

8. Can you give me _____ help with my homework?

9. Where's a good place to buy _____ clothes?

10. Would you like _____ coffee right now?

11. Can you name _____ funny movies?

Talk about It Ask a partner the questions above.

A: Do you have some money with you today?
B: Yes, I do. What about you?
A: I do too.

---

[19] **doctoral degree:** the most advanced academic degree; also called a doctorate or PhD

[20] **tenure:** the right to keep a job as long as you want it

Think about It Write each noun phrase in Activity 44 under the correct group in this chart.

A/An + singular count noun	Some + plural noun	Some + noncount noun
		some money

---

45 | Using *A*, *An*, and *Some* What would you take on each trip below? Choose two trips and list six things for each trip. Then tell your classmates about the things on your list. `3.7 A–B`

"For trip number 1, I would take some sunscreen, a hat, . . . "

Trip #1: Spend a hot summer day on a sailboat with three friends. Lunch is NOT included.	**Trip #3:** Spend three days in a cabin on a lake. Enjoy the warm weather in a place without electricity.
Trip #2: Take a working vacation. Work on a farm in France for five days. Take care of the farm animals and work in the field. Learn to make cheese. Room and food are included.	**Trip #4:** Spend two nights in one of New York City's best hotels. Free tickets to a Broadway play and the Museum of Modern Art are included.

3.8 Using *The*

A	**1** Who is **the new teacher**? **2** Who are **the best students in class**? **3** **The light** in my eyes was too bright.	We can use ***the*** before: • singular or plural count nouns, as in **1 – 2** • noncount nouns, as in **3** **GRAMMAR TERM:** *The* is called the **definite article**.
B	**4** I met **the new teacher** yesterday. (I think the listener knows which specific teacher.) **5** **The earth** is in danger of overpopulation. (There is only one earth.) **6** I need to be at **the airport** by 10:00. (A city usually has only one airport.) **7** **The computer** in our classroom is old. ("In our classroom" identifies which computer is old.) **8** When's **the last bus**? (There is only one last bus.) **9** Who is **the youngest person** here? (There is only one youngest person.)	We can use ***the*** when: • we are talking about specific people or things • and we think our listener knows which one(s) we are talking about, as in **4** Our listener knows which one we are talking about when: • there is only one in the world and everyone knows about it, as in **5** • there is only one in a particular place (such as in a classroom or a city), as in **6 – 7** • we use the noun with an adjective that describes only one thing, such as *first, last, next, best,* or *oldest,* as in **8 – 9**
C	**COMPARE *THE* AND *A/AN*** **10a** Can you answer **the phone**, please? (= a specific phone) **10b** Do you hear **a phone** ringing? (= one of many possible phones)	We use ***the*** when we think the listener can identify the person or thing, as in **10a**. We use ***a*** or ***an*** when we don't think the listener can identify the person or thing, as in **10b**.

46 | Using *The* with Count Nouns and Noncount Nouns Read this recipe. Write each **bold** noun phrase under the correct group in the chart below. `3.8 A`

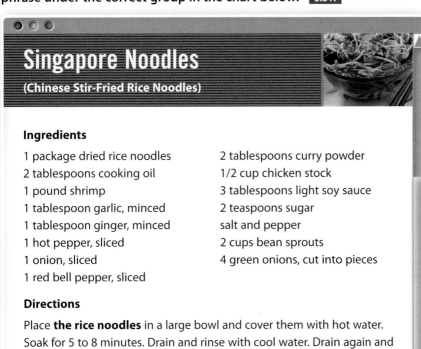

Singapore Noodles
(Chinese Stir-Fried Rice Noodles)

Ingredients

1 package dried rice noodles	2 tablespoons curry powder
2 tablespoons cooking oil	1/2 cup chicken stock
1 pound shrimp	3 tablespoons light soy sauce
1 tablespoon garlic, minced	2 teaspoons sugar
1 tablespoon ginger, minced	salt and pepper
1 hot pepper, sliced	2 cups bean sprouts
1 onion, sliced	4 green onions, cut into pieces
1 red bell pepper, sliced	

Directions

Place **the rice noodles** in a large bowl and cover them with hot water. Soak for 5 to 8 minutes. Drain and rinse with cool water. Drain again and set aside.

Heat **the oil** in a wok over a high flame. Add **the shrimp** and stir-fry for 1 to 2 minutes. Remove the shrimp and set aside.

Add more oil to **the wok** if necessary. Add **the garlic**, **ginger**, and **hot pepper**. Stir-fry for about 30 seconds. Next, add **the onion** and **red pepper** and stir-fry for another 2 to 3 minutes or until **the vegetables** are cooked but still crisp.

Stir in **the curry powder** and stir-fry for about 30 seconds. Then reduce **the heat** to medium and stir in **the chicken stock**, **soy sauce**, **sugar**, **salt**, and **pepper**. Simmer for about a minute.

Stir in **the drained noodles**, **sprouts**, and **green onions**. Toss to coat **the noodles** with **the sauce** and heat them through. Adjust seasoning to taste and serve hot.

> **FYI**
>
> In recipes and instructions, writers sometimes drop *the* before nouns in a series.
>
> Add **the** garlic, ginger, and pepper. =
>
> Add **the** garlic, **the** ginger, and **the** pepper.

The + singular count noun	*The* + plural count noun	*The* + noncount noun
	the rice noodles	

Think about It Was it difficult to group any of the nouns in the recipe above? Why?

47 | Talking about Specific Things Match the sentence beginnings with the sentence endings. `3.8 B`

FACT BOOK

1. **The** first plane flight ___*i*___
2. **The** earth's atmosphere ____
3. **The** first ocean liners ____
4. **The** first trains ____
5. In 2011, **the** tallest building in **the** world ____
6. **The** fastest way to travel ____
7. **The** ground floor of a building ____
8. By **the** 1930s, ocean liners ____
9. **The** capital of Australia ____
10. **The** flag of Singapore ____
11. Countries near **the** equator ____

a. is Canberra.
b. is by plane.
c. crossed **the** Atlantic Ocean in **the** 1840s.
d. is red and white.
e. could cross **the** Atlantic Ocean in about four days.
f. traveled at less than 16 kph (10 mph).
g. are very hot.
h. contains various gases.
i. was in 1903.
j. was in Dubai.
k. is usually **the** first floor.

Think about It Why did the writer use *the* in each sentence above? Choose from these reasons.

a. There is only one in the world and everyone knows about it.
b. The noun is used with an adjective that describes only one thing.

48 | Using *A/An* or *The* Read each conversation and add *a/an* or *the*. Then practice with a partner. `3.8 C`

AT SCHOOL

1. A: Do you know ___*the*___ new science teacher?
   B: Yes, her name is Ms. Hernandez.
2. A: Did you write down ____ homework assignment?
   B: Yes, do you need it?
3. A: Did Mr. Thompson give us ____ assignment for today?
   B: I hope not.
4. A: Can I borrow ____ dictionary?
   B: Sorry. This is ____ only dictionary in the room.
5. A: When is ____ first day of classes?
   B: ____ sixth of September, I think.
6. A: Did you find ____ phone in here?
   B: Does it have ____ red case?
   A: Yes, that's it.
7. A: Why are you late?
   B: There was ____ accident on the highway.
8. A: When's ____ meeting tomorrow?
   B: I think it's at 7.

AT HOME

9. A: Where's ____ car?
   B: I put it in ____ garage.
10. A: Could you get me ____ tomato from ____ fridge?
    B: Just one?
    A: Yep[21], just one.
11. A: Did you eat ____ last piece of cake?
    B: Sorry. Were you saving it?
12. A: Do we have ____ first aid kit?
    B: Yes, it's in ____ bathroom closet.
13. A: Do you have ____ remote?
    B: No, it's over there on ____ chair.
14. A: Please don't play football in ____ house.
    B: But it's raining outside.
15. A: Did you see ____ weather forecast for tomorrow?
    B: No, I missed it.
16. A: What's ____ box for?
    B: I'm sending some things to Ben.

[21] **yep:** yes (informal)

49 | Using *A/An* or *The* Write *a/an* or *the* to complete the sentences in each set. **3.8 C**

1. a. _____ last bus is at 10.

   b. I think there's _____ bus at 10 tomorrow.

   c. Are you going to take _____ 10 o'clock bus?

   d. Is there _____ bus to the zoo?

2. a. We just saw _____ great movie.

   b. I love _____ movie *The Last Emperor*.

   c. We watch _____ movie every weekend.

   d. Is there _____ movie on TV tonight?

3. a. Let's go home _____ different way.

   b. I think this is _____ only way to go.

   c. We went _____ wrong way.

   d. Is there _____ faster way to go?

> **FYI**
>
> When we use *there is* to introduce a new thing or idea, we use *a* or *an* with singular count nouns—NOT *the*.
>
> Hey, **there's a bug** in my soup.
> **There is a great show** on TV tonight.

3.9 Using No Article (Ø)

A

Ø + PLURAL COUNT NOUN

1 I like Ø **old movies.**
(I enjoy old movies in general.)

2 Are Ø **trains** safe?
(In general, are all trains safe?)

Ø + NONCOUNT NOUN

3 Ø **Life** in the 1800s was difficult.
(a general statement about life in the 1800s)

4 Ø **Education** should be free.
(In general, education should be free.)

Sometimes we don't use an article before a noun at all. We use **no article (Ø)** because we are talking about people or things in general, as in **1 – 4**.

We can use no article before:

- plural count nouns, as in **1 – 2**
- noncount nouns, as in **3 – 4**

GRAMMAR TERM: No article (Ø) is also called the **zero article**.

B

COMPARE Ø AND *SOME*

5a I need **some money** for the bus.

5b She always needs Ø **money.**

6a Can we have **some tomatoes** for lunch?

6b He made a pasta dish with Ø **fresh tomatoes.**

7 It's not hard to grow Ø **tomatoes.**
(NOT: ~~It's not hard to grow some tomatoes.~~)

We can use *some* or **no article (Ø)** before a plural count or noncount noun. We use *some* to talk about a small amount, as in **5a – 6a**. When we use no article, we are not giving any information about amount, as in **5b – 6b**.

WARNING! We don't use *some* when we are talking about something in general, as in **7**. Use no article instead.

C

CORRECT THE COMMON ERRORS (See page R-16.)

8 ✗ He gave me sandwich for breakfast.

9 ✗ Tokyo and Kyoto are some cities in Japan.

10 ✗ I learned that the friends are very important.

50 | Writing General Statements
Complete these proverbs with the words from the box. (More than one answer may be possible, but only one is correct.) Then say what each proverb means. **3.9 A**

PROVERBS

1. Life is _short_ .
2. Time is _____ .
3. Knowledge is _____ .
4. Charity[22] begins _____ .
5. Clothes make _____ .
6. Actions speak _____ .
7. Walls have _____ .
8. Money doesn't grow _____ .
9. Misery[23] loves _____ .
10. Laughter is _____ .
11. Bad news travels _____ .

at home
company[24]
ears
fast
louder than words
money
on trees
power
short
the best medicine
the man

F Y I
Proverbs are short, familiar statements. They often give advice or a general truth about life.

Think about It Circle all of the nouns and noun phrases in the proverbs above. Then write them under the correct group in the chart below.

Ø + plural count noun	Ø + noncount noun	*The* + singular count noun	*The* + noncount noun
	life		

Write about It Choose three sentence beginnings above. Think of different ways to complete them.

Money doesn't grow in my wallet.   *Money doesn't grow like weeds.*

51 | Making General Statements
Add the missing verb to each sentence. Then check (✓) *Agree* or *Disagree*. **3.9 A**

WHAT'S YOUR OPINION?   AGREE   DISAGREE

1. Life _____ more difficult now than a hundred years ago.   ☐   ☐
   (is / are)
2. Women _____ better parents than men.   ☐   ☐
   (is / are)
3. Medical care _____ to be free for everyone.   ☐   ☐
   (needs / need)
4. People _____ too much free time nowadays.   ☐   ☐
   (has / have)
5. Politicians _____ always dishonest.   ☐   ☐
   (is / are)
6. Parents _____ to spend time with their children.   ☐   ☐
   (needs / need)

[22] **charity:** kindness to others
[23] **misery:** great unhappiness
[24] **company:** other people

Talk about It Take turns reading the sentences in Activity 51 aloud with a partner. See if your partner agrees or disagrees and why.

A: Life is more difficult now than a hundred years ago.
B: I agree with that. OR *B: I'm not sure about that. I think...*

52 | Using *Some* and No Article Read the texts. Where possible, add *some* before the **bold** words. **3.9 B**

What Do You Like to Do in Your Free Time?

1. When I have **free time**, I like to sit down and read a good book. I like **novels** best—especially **stories** about
   some
   detectives or **crime**. I often bring **books** to the kitchen so I can read while I am eating. At **night**, I usually read until I fall asleep. Reading lets you enter a different world for a short time. You meet **new people** there and have **exciting adventures**. It is like a vacation from **real life**.

2. I enjoy cooking in my free time. I especially like to make **bread** and **fancy desserts**. Usually, **bread** takes a long time to prepare, so I can do other things at the same time. I often put on **good music** and make myself **tea** while I am working in the kitchen.

Write about It What do you like to do in your free time? Write two or three sentences. Then read them to a partner.

53 | Error Correction Correct any errors in these sentences. (Some sentences may not have any errors.)

1. I got my high school diploma in 2009, and after that, I went to the college.

   I got my high school diploma in 2009, and after that, I went to college.

2. We took a physical education every year in high school.
3. I hope that I always have a good health.
4. I prefer to travel with friend.
5. When my brother was baby, he was very sick.
6. I like to write an article for my blog.
7. Last night I went to concert of Arabic music.
8. Don't be afraid to ask for a help.
9. My grandmother always had a beautiful clothes.
10. I love this restaurant because it has a delicious food.
11. I want to get better job so that I can get a better health care.
12. I moved here from Colombia after I finished my senior year of the high school.
13. Some money can ruin a good friendship.
14. My goal was to go to the university in my country and get a degree in engineering.

3.10 Using Nouns and Articles in Speaking

A

1 I can't talk now. I'm **in a hurry.** (= "ina hurry")

2 I'll see you **in an hour.** (= "ina nour")

3 Let's sit **in the back.** (= "inthuh back")

4 **In the end**, we got home safely. (= "inthee end")

5 I need **some money.** (= "sm money")

Articles are often difficult to hear. This is because they are short, and we don't usually stress them in conversation. With unstressed articles, we often "reduce" the vowel, as in **1 – 5**.

We pronounce *the* in two ways:

B

We say "thuh" before **consonant sounds**, as in **6 – 9**.

6 | Can I take | the | car?

7 | Please pass me | the | bread.

8 | What's | the | problem?

WARNING! The letter *u* is a vowel, but sometimes it has a consonant sound, as in **9**.

9 | He's a student at | the | university.

We say "thee" before **vowel sounds**, as in **10 – 13**.

10 | I don't understand | the | answer.

11 | The | elevator | isn't working.

12 | Please pass me | the | olives.

WARNING! The letter *h* is a consonant, but sometimes it has a vowel sound, as in **13**.

13 | She belongs to | the | Honor Society.

C

SUGGESTING ANSWERS

14 Who wrote this? Peter?

15 What's for dessert? Ice cream?

16 Where are you going? To school?

We sometimes suggest an answer to our own question. This might be the **name of a person, place, or thing**, as in **14 – 16**.

We usually use rising intonation to suggest an answer.

GO ONLINE

54 | Pronouncing Articles Listen and complete these common expressions. Then practice saying them. Pay special attention to the pronunciation of the articles. **3.10 A**

1. Don't worry about ____*a*____ thing.

2. Let's try again _____ other time.

3. What's _____ problem?

4. Thank you for _____ lovely evening.

5. I have _____ idea.

6. I'll be with you in _____ minute.

7. Could I leave _____ message?

8. Have _____ good day.

9. Could I have _____ check, please?

10. Give me _____ call later.

11. That's out of _____ question[25].

12. Don't breathe _____ word[26] of this to anyone.

13. Let's call it _____ day[27].

14. I've been under _____ weather[28].

Talk about It Work with a partner. Choose one of the expressions above and use it to create a short conversation. Present your conversation to the class.

A: *I don't think I can finish all this work.*
B: *Don't worry about a thing. I can help you.*
A: *That would be great. . . .*

---

[25] **out of . . . question:** impossible
[26] **don't breathe . . . word:** don't say anything

[27] **call it . . . day:** to stop working for the day
[28] **under . . . weather:** sick

110

55 | Pronouncing *The* Listen to the questions. Do you hear "thee" or "thuh"? Check (✓) your answers.

3.10 B

	"Thee"	"Thuh"			"Thee"	"Thuh"
1.	✓	☐	7.		☐	☐
2.	☐	☐	8.		☐	☐
3.	☐	☐	9.		☐	☐
4.	☐	☐	10.		☐	☐
5.	☐	☐	11.		☐	☐
6.	☐	☐	12.		☐	☐

RESEARCH SAYS...

English speakers do not always pronounce *the* according to the rules in Chart 3.10. You may hear "thee" before consonant sounds and "thuh" before vowel sounds. This does not change the meaning of the nouns.

CORPUS

Talk about It Listen again and write the words you hear after *the*. Then practice saying the questions. Pay attention to the pronunciation of *the*.

DID YOU . . . ?

1. bring the _____umbrella_____
2. turn off the _____
3. watch the _____
4. go to the _____
5. read the _____
6. lock the _____
7. eat the _____
8. wash the _____
9. pay the _____
10. stop at the _____
11. go to the _____
12. drink all the _____

56 | Suggesting Answers Choose the correct word(s) from each box on the right to suggest an answer to each question. Then practice with a partner. Be sure to use rising intonation with your suggestion.   **3.10 C**

1. A: What do you want for lunch? ____A sandwich____?
   B: Sure. Sounds great.

2. A: Where are you going? To _____?
   B: No, I have to go to work.

3. A: When are you coming back? _____?
   B: Yes, probably.

4. A: What did you buy? _____?
   B: No, I didn't buy anything.

5. A: What are you watching? _____?
   B: No, it's a movie.

6. A: What are you wearing to the concert? _____?
   B: I'm not sure yet.

7. A: How are we going to get there? _____?
   B: No, that's too expensive.

8. A: What are you eating? _____?
   B: No, it's soup.

1. a restaurant/a sandwich/a glass

2. the gym/a cup of coffee/the teachers

3. the car/tonight/a store

4. the city/a sweater/a new teacher

5. the news/tomorrow/a dictionary

6. the truth/some food/a suit

7. on Monday/some cars/by taxi

8. a cold drink/a new shirt/cereal

Talk about It Ask a partner the questions above again. Use your own ideas to suggest answers.

A: *What do you want for lunch? Some soup?*
B: *Sure. Sounds great.*

3.11 Using Nouns and Articles in Writing

A	**USING NOUNS IN A LIST** **1** My classmates come from **Korea, Turkey, Brazil, and** Spain. **2** Television, newspapers, **and** magazines give too much attention to the lives of famous people.	When we use three or more **nouns in a list**, we separate them with commas, as in **1 – 2**. We use *and* before the last noun only. **WARNING!** Some style manuals leave out the comma after the next-to-last noun.
B	**FIRST MENTION–SECOND MENTION** **3** When I was eight years old, my parents gave me **a gold ring. The ring** wasn't valuable, but I didn't know that. . . . (The writer starts with *a gold ring* because she is talking about it for the first time. She then says *the ring* because the reader knows what she is talking about.)	We sometimes use *a* or *an* to introduce a noun (talk or write about it for the first time). When we mention the noun again, we use *the*, as in **3**. **GRAMMAR TERM:** When we introduce a noun with *a/an*, we call it **first mention**. When we later use *the*, we can call it **second mention**.
	4 The first televisions looked very different from our modern ones. **The screens** were very small, and **the pictures** were only in black and white. (the screens = the screens on the first televisions) (the pictures = the pictures on the first televisions)	In writing, we use *the* with nouns that we think the reader already knows. We can also use *the* when a new noun is related to a previous noun, as in **4**.
C	**IDENTIFYING NOUNS WITH PREPOSITIONAL PHRASES** **5** In Russia, I visited **the homes of some great artists.** ("Of some great artists" identifies which homes.) **6** He stayed there for **the rest of his life.** ("Of his life" identifies what "the rest" is.)	We often use prepositional phrases with *in, on, for, of,* etc., to add information after a noun. Then we can use *the* before the noun phrase because the noun is identifiable, as in **5 – 6**.

57 | Using Nouns in a List Add the missing commas to these sentences. **3.11 A**

1. Brazil, Colombia, and Peru are all countries in South America.
2. Hungarian Finnish and Chinese are difficult languages to learn.
3. In biology class, students learn about plants animals and even humans.
4. Playing a sport requires energy concentration and determination.
5. The most important qualities of a good boss are patience fairness and flexibility.
6. The Nigerian writer Chinua Achebe has written novels essays and poems.
7. In a large city, there are many opportunities for work education and entertainment.
8. You can't be a good parent without love caring and commitment.
9. People live longer today because of vaccinations new workplace safety rules and a decrease in smoking.
10. Hemingway Steinbeck and Morrison are well-known writers.

Write about It Rewrite two of the sentences above with your own ideas.

Japan, Korea, and Vietnam are all countries in Asia.
Learning a new language requires determination, intelligence, and time.

THE OWL AND THE RABBITS

_An_ owl saw two rabbits on the ground. ____ owl flew down
1   2
and grabbed one rabbit in each foot. ____ rabbits started
3
running, and they pulled ____ owl behind them. ____ owl's wife
4   5
yelled, "Let one of them go."

"But winter is coming and we'll be hungry," ____ owl replied.
6
"We'll need both of ____ rabbits."
7

The rabbits ran until they came to ____ big rock. One rabbit ran to ____ left of the rock. ____ other
8   9   10
rabbit ran to ____ right of ____ rock. ____ poor owl hit ____ rock, and ____ two rabbits ran away.
11   12   13   14   15

THE BOY WHO CRIED WOLF

____ young boy, alone all day, got bored taking care of his
1
sheep. For fun, ____ boy shouted, "Wolf! Wolf!"
2

People in town heard ____ boy and came running to help him.
3
But when they arrived, ____ boy just laughed at them. "I was
4
only kidding," ____ boy said to ____ townspeople. "I didn't really
5   6
see ____ wolf."
7

A few days later, ____ boy cried again, "Wolf! Wolf!" Again
8
____ people in town came running. And once more, ____ boy
9   10
laughed at them.

In time, ____ wolf really did come. ____ boy screamed, "Wolf!
11   12
Wolf!" But this time no one came.

Think about It Look at the answers for 7 and 11 in the second story above. Why did you choose the
article you did?

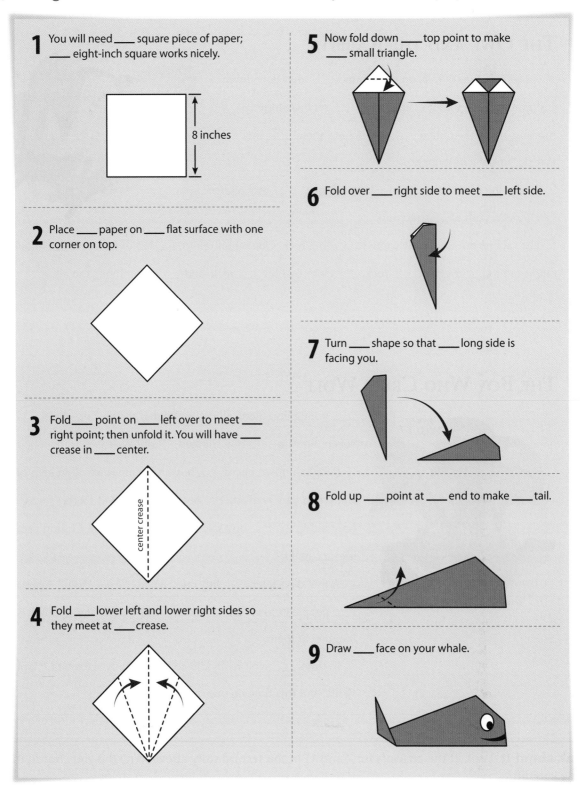

1 You will need ____ square piece of paper; ____ eight-inch square works nicely.

8 inches

2 Place ____ paper on ____ flat surface with one corner on top.

3 Fold ____ point on ____ left over to meet ____ right point; then unfold it. You will have ____ crease in ____ center.

center crease

4 Fold ____ lower left and lower right sides so they meet at ____ crease.

5 Now fold down ____ top point to make ____ small triangle.

6 Fold over ____ right side to meet ____ left side.

7 Turn ____ shape so that ____ long side is facing you.

8 Fold up ____ point at ____ end to make ____ tail.

9 Draw ____ face on your whale.

Write about It Think of something you can do or make. Write the instructions for your classmates to read.

60 | **Adding Information to a Noun** Look at the **bold** words in these questions. Think of two more prepositional phrases you could use instead. Rewrite the questions with your new ideas. **3.11 C**

1. What is the value **of recreation**?

   What is the value of music?
   _____

2. What are the important qualities **of a good parent**?

   _____
   _____

3. Should the government spend money **on space exploration**?

   _____
   _____

4. Is the traditional role **of fathers** changing?

   _____
   _____

5. What are the main reasons **for poverty**?

   _____
   _____

Write about It Choose two of the questions above. List two or more answers to each question.

What is the value of recreation?
1. Recreation is good for your health.
2. It helps you relax.

WRAP-UP Demonstrate Your Knowledge

A | DISCUSSION Think of at least six things you would find in each place in this chart. Work with a small group to list your ideas.

In an airplane	In a car	In a movie theater	In a kitchen
seats seat belts			

Work in your group and look at each list above. Decide which thing on each list is the least important. Why? Report your group's answers to the class.

LEAST IMPORTANT

_____ _____ _____ _____

B | GROUPING NOUNS Study this example. Then choose one of the quotations below and add the **bold** nouns to the correct groups.

Example

Quotation: **Experience** is the **name** everyone gives to their **mistakes**.—**Oscar Wilde**

Quotation: _____

_____

```
                    NOUNS
     experience, name, mistakes, Oscar Wilde
         │                      │
   COMMON NOUNS           PROPER NOUNS
experience, name, mistakes    Oscar Wilde
      │
  ┌───────┴────────┐
COUNT NOUNS    NONCOUNT NOUNS
name, mistakes    experience
  │
┌─────┴──────┐
SINGULAR NOUNS  PLURAL NOUNS
   name          mistakes
```

```
                    NOUNS

         │                      │
   COMMON NOUNS           PROPER NOUNS

      │
  ┌───────┴────────┐
COUNT NOUNS    NONCOUNT NOUNS

  │
┌─────┴──────┐
SINGULAR NOUNS  PLURAL NOUNS
```

- The **man** who has no **imagination** has no **wings**.—**Muhammad Ali**
- Your **children** need your **presence** more than your **presents**.—**Jesse Jackson**
- **Talent** wins **games**, but **teamwork** and **intelligence** win **championships**.—**Michael Jordan**

C | WRITING Use the pictures below and the words in the box to write a story. Think about how you use *a/an*, *the*, *Ø*, and *some* in your story.

| ambulance | ice pack | knock herself out | leak | paramedics | plumber | sink | stretcher |

3.12 Summary of Nouns and Articles

NOUNS

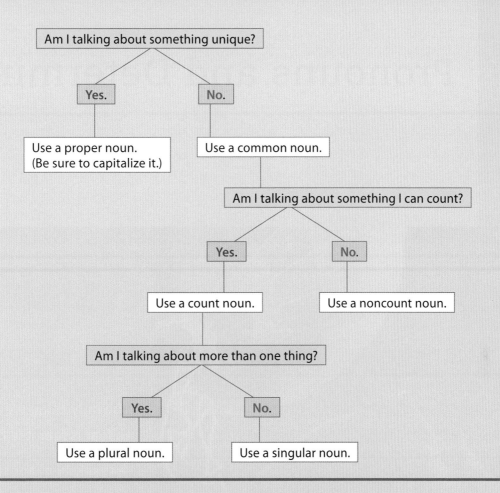

ARTICLES

	COUNT NOUNS		NONCOUNT NOUNS	USE
	SINGULAR	PLURAL		
a / an	**a** message (before a consonant sound) **an** answer (before a vowel sound)	–	–	A person or thing that: • the listener can't identify • you talk or write about for the first time
some	–	**some** people	**some** money	Unknown people or things: • a small amount
Ø	–	**Ø** people	**Ø** money	People or things in general
the	**the** message **the** answer	**the** people	**the** money	People or things that: • the listener can identify • were already introduced

4 Pronouns and Determiners

The only thing we have
to fear is fear itself.

—FRANKLIN D. ROOSEVELT,
UNITED STATES PRESIDENT
(1882–1945)

Talk about It What does the quotation above mean? Do you agree or disagree? Why?

WARM-UP

A | Match the beginnings of these proverbs with the endings. Then choose one and tell a partner what it means. Do you agree or disagree with it?

Proverbs from Around the World

1. When **the** apple is ripe[1], **it** __d__
2. If **you** want to lose a friend, ____
3. To be rich is not **everything**, but ____
4. What belongs to **everybody**, ____
5. **Many** hands ____
6. **You** can't have **your** cake and ____
7. If **you** want a thing done well, ____
8. Behind **every** great man, there ____

a. is a great woman.
b. do **it** **yourself**.
c. eat **it** too.
d. will fall.
e. **it** helps.
f. lend **him** money.
g. make light work.
h. belongs to **nobody**.

B | Answer these questions about the proverbs above.

1. The words in **blue** are **pronouns**. What are the words?
2. The words in **green** are **determiners**. What are the words?
3. Do we use a verb or a noun after a determiner?

C | Look back at the quotation on page 118. Identify any pronouns or determiners.

[1] **ripe:** ready to eat

4.1 Subject Pronouns

A

1 **My father** came here when **he** was young.
(he = my father)

2 Who are **the people over there**? Are **they** the new teachers? (they = the people over there)

3 **My brother and I** want to go, but **we** can't.
(we = my brother and I)

We often use a pronoun in place of a noun or noun phrase, as in **1 – 3**. This saves time when we speak or write.

GRAMMAR TERM: We say a pronoun "**refers to**" a noun phrase. For example, in **1**, he refers to *my father*.

B

4 A: Is **your brother** here?
B: No, **he's** at home.

5 **Ann** isn't coming to the meeting. **She's** busy.

6 A: Were **you and Tim** out last night?
B: No, **we** stayed at home.

7 A: Where's **the car**?
B: **It's** in the garage.

8 I love **music**. **It** relaxes me.

9 A: Do you know where **my keys** are?
B: **They're** on the table.

The **subject pronouns** are:

singular					plural		
I	you	he	she	it	we	you	they

We use the pronouns *I, you, he, she, we, you,* and *they* to refer to people, as in **4 – 6**.

When we refer to places, things, or ideas, we use:

- *it* in place of a singular count noun, as in **7**
- *it* in place of a noncount noun, as in **8**
- *they* in place of a plural count noun, as in **9**

C

SUBJECT-VERB AGREEMENT

10 I like ice cream, but **it isn't** good for me.

11 My brothers are smart, but **they don't study** very hard.

12 A: Do you know Sam?
B: Sure. **He and I are** good friends.

With subject pronouns, we use:

| a singular pronoun | + a singular verb, as in **10** |

| a plural pronoun | + a plural verb, as in **11** |

| a pronoun + *and* + a pronoun | + a plural verb, as in **12** |

1 | Understanding Subject Pronouns What do the **bold** pronouns refer to in these sentences? Write your answers in the boxes. `4.1 A`

EIGHT FACTS ABOUT NEW ZEALAND

1. The name *New Zealand* comes from the Dutch language. **It** probably means "new sea land."

2. New Zealand and Japan are about the same size, but in other ways, **they** are very different.

3. New Zealand has a population of only 4 million, so **it's** not a very crowded country.

4. People love to watch rugby in New Zealand, but **it** isn't the most popular sport to play. Golf is.

5. The singer Kiri Te Kanawa grew up in New Zealand. **She** has performed around the world and has made many recordings.

6. Sir Edmund Hillary was a famous mountain climber from New Zealand. **He** and Tenzing Norgay were the first people to climb to the top of Mount Everest.

7. Wellington has great weather 12 months a year. **It** is the capital of New Zealand.

8. Kiwi birds live on both the north and the south islands of New Zealand. **They** can't fly, but they can run very fast.

1. it = *New Zealand*

2. they =

3. it =

4. it =

5. she =

6. he =

7. it =

8. they =

Write about It In Activity 1, you read facts about New Zealand. Write three facts about another country. (Use pronouns.)

São Paulo is the largest city in Brazil, but it is not the capital. Brasilia is the capital.

2 | Using Subject Pronouns Replace each **bold** noun phrase with a subject pronoun. `4.1 B`

1. A: Did you like the movie?

   B: Yeah, ~~the movie~~ *it* was great.

2. A: How did your parents get here?

   B: **My parents** took the train.

3. A: Does Maria really like this show?

   B: Yeah, **this show** is her favorite.

4. A: Hi, Mr. Ellis. How are you and Mrs. Ellis?

   B: **Mrs. Ellis and I** are fine, thanks.

5. A: Do you have this shirt in blue?

   B: No, I'm sorry. **This shirt** only comes in red.

6. A: How's your back? Feeling any better?

   B: No, **my back** is worse. Much worse.

7. A: I think Jenna's good at tennis.

   B: Who?

   A: Jenna. **Jenna** plays well.

   B: Oh, I wouldn't know.

   A: Don't you like tennis?

   B: No, **tennis** is boring.

8. A: Look at the two people over there. I think **the two people over there** are teachers at our school.

   B: I think you're right.

9. A: Is your brother still looking for a job?

   B: No, **my brother** just found one.

10. A: Why do you want to study physics?

    B: Because **physics** is interesting.

The movie was great.

My back is worse.

Talk about It Practice the conversations above with a partner. Use contractions where possible.

Think about It Why do we use subject pronouns? What do they help us do?

> **F Y I**
>
> We often contract verbs with subject pronouns. For example:
>
> I am = I**'m**
> you are = you**'re**
> she is = she**'s**

3 | Using the Correct Verb Form Complete these sentences with a pronoun and the simple present form of the verb in parentheses. `4.1 B–C`

GOOD THINGS/BAD THINGS

1. Fried food tastes good, but _____*it isn't*_____ good for you. (not/be)

2. Coffee may protect you from some kinds of cancer, and _____ good, too. (taste)

3. Games and other kinds of puzzles are fun. _____ your brain active, too. (keep)

4. Exercise is good for you, but _____ kind of boring. (be)

5. Vegetables are good for you, and _____ a lot. (not/cost)

6. The sun feels good, but _____ your skin. (damage)

7. Laughter is good for your health, and _____ free. (be)

8. Cars are useful, but _____ the air. (pollute)

9. It's important to read the news, but sometimes _____ depressing[2]. (be)

10. You can get a lot of information on the Internet, but _____ always accurate. (not/be)

11. Money is useful, but _____ happiness. (not/buy)

12. Volleyball and basketball are good sports for children because _____ dangerous. (not/be)

Write about It Write four sentences about things that are good for you.

____ is good for you, but ____.
____ are good for you, but ____.
____ is good for you, and ____.
____ are good for you, and ____.

4 | Error Correction Correct any errors in these sentences. (Some sentences may not have any errors.)

1. I love my brother. He always make me laugh.

   I love my brother. He always makes me laugh.

2. I and my parents arrived at the same time.
3. When children are young, they a big responsibility.
4. Spanish and electric guitars they have metal strings.
5. I like to eat fresh food because they are good for your health.
6. I and my older sister stayed there for eight days.
7. My brother works hard because he have a big family.
8. Andy and I usually does something together on Saturday night.
9. My friends and I, we always get together on the weekend.
10. My brothers they argue a lot, but we are still good friends.
11. I love music. They really make me happy.
12. Did you hear the news? It's really surprising.
13. She miss her family very much.

> **WARNING!**
>
> We don't use a subject pronoun after a noun subject. We only write the subject one time.
>
> **My friend** lives there.
> (NOT: ~~My friend he lives there.~~)
>
> When we connect two (or more) nouns and pronouns with *and*, the subject pronoun *I* comes last.
>
> **My brother and I live** with my parents.
> (NOT: ~~I and my brother . . .~~)

[2] **depressing:** making someone feel very sad

4.2 Subject Pronouns vs. Object Pronouns; *One and Ones*

A

SUBJECT PRONOUNS

1 A: Did you call Ann?
B: Yes, but **she** didn't answer.

VERBS + OBJECT PRONOUNS

2 I had Tom's email address, but now I **can't find it.**

3 A: Do you know Tim and Ray?
B: Yes, but I **don't see them** often.

PREPOSITIONS + OBJECT PRONOUNS

4 I have a message **for you.**

5 Tom forgot to bring his cell phone **with him.**

6 A: I'm leaving now.
B: Wait! Don't leave **without** John and **me.**

Like a noun, a pronoun can be:
- a subject, as in **1**
- an object of a verb, as in **2 – 3**
- an object of a preposition, as in **4 – 6**

Notice that **subject pronouns** and **object pronouns** have different forms.

	singular					plural		
SUBJECT	I	you	he	she	it	we	you	they
OBJECT	me	you	him	her	it	us	you	them

B

7 A: May I have a banana, please?
B: I'll have **one**, too. (= I'll have a banana, too.)

8 I hate scary movies. Let's watch **a funny one.**
(= a funny movie)

9 A: Which shoes do you like?
B: I think I like **the red ones.** (= the red shoes)

We can also use **one** or **ones** as pronouns. We use *one* in place of a singular count noun. We use *ones* in place of a plural count noun.
- We can use *one* alone, as in **7**.
- We can use *one* or *ones* after a word like *a* or *the* + an adjective, as in **8 – 9**.

C

CORRECT THE COMMON ERRORS (See page R-17.)

10 ✗ Her father gave she a new computer.

11 ✗ Tom talked to Lisa and I.

12 ✗ He saved some of his money and spent some of them.

13 ✗ We bought a lot of gifts for our friends. I hope they like it.

5 | Using Object Pronouns Complete these conversations with object pronouns. Then practice with a partner. `4.2 A`

1. A: What's the problem?

   B: My computer froze and I can't restart ____*it*____.

2. A: Tomorrow is Steve's birthday.

   B: Do you want to make a birthday cake for _____?

   A: Sure. Why not?

3. A: Did you talk to Jen?

   B: Yeah. I told _____ that you were sick yesterday.

4. A: Did you get the tickets for the game?

   B: Yes, I bought _____ yesterday.

5. A: Where's your book?

   B: I left _____ at school.

6. A: Did you call Jill?

   B: No, I asked _____ to call me.

7. A: Goodbye, Joe. I'll call you later.

   B: OK. Talk to _____ then.

8. A: Did you talk to Bob last night?

   B: No. I called _____ but he didn't call _____ back.

9. A: Do you and Chris need some help tomorrow?

   B: No, thanks. Jim is going to help _____.

10. A: Did you get the information?

    B: Yes, I found _____ on the Internet.

11. A: Why are you staring at that man?

    B: I'm not staring at _____. I'm looking at the car behind _____.

12. A: Is Carol late again?

    B: Yes, and I'm getting tired of waiting for _____.

Talk about It Choose one of the conversations in Activity 5. Add three or four more lines. See how many pronouns you can use. Then present it to your classmates.

A: What's the problem?
B: My computer froze, and I can't restart it.
A: Why don't you call Chris? He knows a lot about computers. Maybe he can help.
B: No. I think I'll just unplug it.

6 | Choosing Pronouns Read these paragraphs and complete them with the correct pronouns. `4.2 A`

Favorite Teachers

My favorite teacher in school was my second-grade teacher, Ms. Ellis. ___She___ was
1

the perfect teacher for young children. Ms. Ellis was strict[3], but _____ also treated
2

_____ like equals. And when _____ did well, she rewarded[4] _____. Ms. Ellis
3 4 5

made it clear that we could talk to _____ about anything. I learned a lot from
6

_____, and I knew that she wanted _____ to be successful.
7 8

1. she/her
2. she/her
3. we/us
4. we/us
5. we/us
6. she/her
7. she/her
8. I/me

Mr. Ochs was my freshman math teacher. _____ loved math, and by the end of the
9

semester, all of his students loved it, too—and we loved _____. In class, _____
10 11

usually worked together in groups to solve math problems. For _____, this was
12

more fun than working alone. Mr. Ochs also encouraged _____ to solve problems in
13

different ways. He really wanted _____ to be creative thinkers.
14

9. he/him
10. he/him
11. we/us
12. I/me
13. we/us
14. we/us

Write about It Describe one of your favorite teachers. Write three or more sentences.

---

[3] **strict:** making people follow rules [4] **reward:** to give something for good work

124

7 | Using Subject and Object Pronouns Add the missing pronoun to each conversation. Then practice with a partner. `4.2 A`

STATING A FACT

1. A: When's your best friend's birthday?

   B: I think ^it^ is in March.

2. A: Do you have your book with you today?

   B: No, I left at home.

3. A: Was there a lot of traffic on your way here?

   B: No, was pretty quiet.

4. A: Does your best friend live here?

   B: No, lives in Greece with his family.

5. A: Do you buy your clothes on the Internet?

   B: No, I always buy at a store.

GIVING AN OPINION

6. A: What's your opinion of American food?

   B: I'm not crazy about.

7. A: What did you think of your first teacher?

   B: Was great.

8. A: Do you like classical music?

   B: Yes, I do. I like a lot.

9. A: Do you like French movies?

   B: Yes, I love.

10. A: Do you have a favorite actor?

    B: Well, I'm a great fan of Michael Sheen. I loved in the movie *The Queen*.

Talk about It Ask a partner the questions above. Give your own answers.

A: When's your best friend's birthday?
B: It's on September 22.

8 | Understanding *One* What does the word *one* refer to in each sentence? Write the word(s) in the boxes. `4.2 B`

1. I brought some sandwiches from home today. Do you want **one**?
2. There's an umbrella in the closet if you need **one**.
3. There were fifty questions on the test and I only got **one** wrong.
4. My sister doesn't have a college degree yet, but she plans to get **one**.
5. I have a tissue in my purse if you need **one**.
6. My parents sold their house downtown and bought a new **one** in the country.
7. I didn't like the first book very much, but I liked the second **one** a lot.
8. A new computer is expensive, so I'm waiting until I've saved some more money before I buy **one**.

| 1. one = *a sandwich* |
| 2. one = |
| 3. one = |
| 4. one = |
| 5. one = |
| 6. one = |
| 7. one = |
| 8. one = |

Think about It Read the sentences below. Compare them with sentences 1–3 above. When do we use *it* instead of *one*?

1. I brought a sandwich, but I'm not hungry. Do you want it?
2. If you want my umbrella, it's in the closet.
3. The last question on the test was very hard. I think I got it wrong.

9 | Using *One* or *Ones* Complete these conversations with an adjective from the box + *one* or *ones*. (Use each adjective once.) `4.2 B`

best	important	large	only	right
easy	Italian	new	real	small

1. A: Your car doesn't sound very good.

   B: Yeah, I think I need a _____*new one*_____.

2. A: Can you bring home a pizza tonight?

   B: A large one or a _____?

3. A: Which movie do you want to watch first?

   B: Let's put on the _____.

4. A: Oh boy, my suitcase is really heavy.

   B: Why don't you take two small suitcases

   instead of a _____?

5. A: Where do you buy cakes and cookies?

   B: I think Jimmy's Bakery makes the

   _____.

6. A: How many people came to the meeting?

   B: We were the _____ there.

7. A: These are the wrong papers.

   B: Well, where are the _____?

8. A: Did we get any emails?

   B: Yes, but not any _____.

9. A: That's a beautiful diamond!

   B: It's not a _____. It's plastic.

10. A: How was the quiz?

    B: I was worried about it, but it was an

    _____.

Think about It What does the word *one* or *ones* refer to in each conversation above?

Talk about It Work with a partner. Choose one of the adjectives above. Write a new conversation using the adjective + *one* or *ones*. Present your conversation to the class.

A: Your stereo speakers don't sound very good.
B: Yeah, I think I need some new ones.

10 | Error Analysis One sentence in each pair has an incorrect pronoun. Circle the letter of the incorrect sentence and the error.

FAMILY MEMBERS

1. a. My brothers, sisters, and I are very close.
   b. My brothers, sisters, and (me) are very close.
2. a. I talk to my youngest brother a lot. I tell him everything.
   b. I talk to my youngest brother a lot. I tell her everything.
3. a. My brother helped me a lot. I learned a lot from him.
   b. My brother helped me a lot. I learned a lot from he.
4. a. My parents let my sister and I make our own decisions.
   b My parents let my sister and me make our own decisions.

> **WARNING!**
>
> We can connect two (or more) nouns and pronouns with *and*. Be careful to use the correct pronoun form after *and*.
>
> **Joe and I** are going to the movies. (NOT: ~~Joe and me~~)
>
> Do you want to come with **Joe and me**? (NOT: ~~Joe and I~~)

5. a. One of my brothers wants to be an artist, but my parents don't want them to.

   b. One of my brothers wants to be an artist, but my parents don't want him to.

6. a. My oldest sister often helped take care of I because I was the youngest.

   b. My oldest sister often helped take of me because I was the youngest.

7. a. My brothers and sisters and I were good children. My parents hardly ever punished us.

   b. My brothers and sisters and I were good children. My parents hardly ever punished them.

8. a. My sisters and I shared a bedroom. I loved to be with them because we talked and laughed a lot.

   b. My sisters and I shared a bedroom. I loved to be with her because we talked and laughed a lot.

Write about It Write several sentences about your family members like the ones in Activity 10. Pay special attention to the way you use pronouns in your sentences.

I'm the oldest child in my family. I have two younger brothers. I don't see them very often.

4.3 Reflexive Pronouns

A

OBJECT PRONOUNS

1 Sam saw **me** downtown.

2 Jen drove **them** to school.

3 Ian and Linda cooked dinner for **us**.

REFLEXIVE PRONOUNS

4 **Sam** saw **himself** in the mirror. (himself = Sam)

5 **Jen** drove **herself** to school. (herself = Jen)

6 **Ian and Linda** cooked dinner for **themselves**.
(themselves = Ian and Linda)

7 **History** repeats **itself**.

8 **I** told **myself** to hurry.

9 **You** can help **yourselves** to some coffee.

We often use an **object pronoun** after a verb or a preposition, as in **1 – 3**.

However, when the object is the same person or thing as the subject, we use a **reflexive pronoun**, as in **4 – 9**.

	OBJECT PRONOUN	REFLEXIVE PRONOUN
singular	me	myself
	you	yourself
	him	himself
	her	herself
	it	itself
plural	us	ourselves
	you	yourselves
	them	themselves

B

SPECIAL USES OF REFLEXIVE PRONOUNS

10 You have to bag the groceries **yourself**.
(yourself = without help)

11 He wants to tell us **himself**.
(himself = not a different person)

12 I prefer to study **by myself**. (by myself = alone)

We sometimes use a reflexive pronoun to add emphasis, as in **10 – 11**.

We can also use *by* + a reflexive pronoun to mean "alone," as in **12**.

C

CORRECT THE COMMON ERRORS (See page R-17.)

13 ✗ This society must help it self.

14 ✗ We always make tortillas ourself.

15 ✗ I can make a better future for me here.

16 ✗ We made a plan for spending ourself money.

11 | Using Reflexive Pronouns Ask a partner these questions. Make notes of your partner's answers.

4.3 A

YOU AND YOUR HABITS

Verb + Reflexive Pronoun

1. Do you like to get up early, or do you have to make yourself get up?

    A: Do you like to get up early, or do you have to make yourself get up?
    B: I usually have to make myself get up.

2. Do you consider yourself to be a good student?
3. Do you ever have to remind yourself to eat?
4. Do you ask yourself questions while you are reading?
5. Did you ever teach yourself to do something?
6. How would you describe yourself in one word?

Preposition + Reflexive Pronoun

7. How often do you look at yourself in a mirror?
8. Do you ever talk to yourself?
9. Do you ever get angry with yourself?
10. Do you usually cook for yourself?
11. Do you ever laugh at yourself?
12. How can you take better care of yourself?

PRONUNCIATION
Be careful not to stress the first syllable in a reflexive pronoun.
NOT: ~~MY~~self

Talk about It Tell your classmates two things you learned about your partner.

"Lin taught herself to play tennis."

12 | Reflexive Pronouns after Verbs Complete these statements with reflexive pronouns. Then draw an arrow from the reflexive pronoun to the subject. 4.3 A

COMMON VERBS

1. If you are feeling anxious, you should remind _____*yourself*_____ to breathe.
2. Linda told _____ to get up early this morning, but she didn't.
3. You and Amy need to give _____ more time to relax.
4. I often find _____ thinking about work.
5. Sometimes we have to force _____ to smile.
6. If you worry too much, you will make _____ sick.
7. What do the Chinese people call _____?
8. In the morning, my sister and I found _____ alone in the house.
9. I don't know why my brother lied. He needs to ask _____ that question.
10. My parents were in the U.S. for five years, but they didn't consider _____ to be American.

Think about It What verbs do we often use with reflexive pronouns? Make a list of the verbs in the sentences above. Then write a new sentence using each verb with a reflexive pronoun.

told   I told myself to eat a good breakfast this morning.

13 | Reflexive Pronouns after Prepositions Complete these statements with reflexive pronouns. Then check (✓) *Agree* or *Disagree*. `4.3 A`

WHAT DO YOU THINK?   AGREE   DISAGREE

1. I **owe it to** _____*myself*_____ to eat well and exercise.   ☐   ☐

2. If you want to remember someone's name, **repeat it to** _____   ☐   ☐
   a few times.

3. When I tell my friends a secret, I want them to **keep it to** _____.   ☐   ☐

4. You should always **listen to** _____.   ☐   ☐

5. Most people like to **hear** good things **about** _____.   ☐   ☐

6. A newborn⁵ animal can't **take care of** _____.   ☐   ☐

7. Children need to learn to **think for** _____.   ☐   ☐

8. You shouldn't **talk about** _____ all the time. It's rude.   ☐   ☐

Write about It Write a new sentence for each verb + preposition + reflexive pronoun above.

I owe it to myself to do something fun every day.

14 | Pronunciation Note: Reflexive Pronouns Listen to the note. Then do Activity 15.

> When we use a **reflexive pronoun for emphasis**, we often stress the second syllable.
>
> **1** Children shouldn't cook by them**SELVES**.
> **2** It's important to try and do the work your**SELF**.
> **3** Did the boy pay for that him**SELF**?

15 | Giving Emphasis with Reflexive Pronouns Complete these conversations with reflexive pronouns. Then listen and practice with a partner. `4.3 B`

1. A: Hey, Bob asked me to invite you to his house
      for dinner.
   B: Why doesn't he just invite me
      _____?
   A: I don't know. I guess he's really busy.

2. A: Could you get the phone, Matt?
   B: I can't. You'll have to get it _____.

3. A: Who helped you paint the rooms?
   B: Nobody. We did it _____.

4. A: Sorry I didn't call. I couldn't remember your
      phone number.
   B: Don't worry about it. I can never remember it
      _____.

5. A: Why are you upset?
   B: Sarah thinks I lost her phone.
   A: Did you?
   B: No. She lost it _____.

6. A: That's a nice sweater.
   B: Thanks. It's from Anna. She made it
      _____!

7. A: That was nice of your parents to give you
      their computer.
   B: Yeah, they didn't need it _____.

8. A: I can't find my cell phone.
   B: It's on the desk. You left it there
      _____.

⁵**newborn:** just born

Write about It Work with a partner. Write conversations like the ones in Activity 15 for each of these expressions. Then share your ideas with your classmates.

get it yourself   *make it yourself*   *do it yourself*   *just be yourself*

16 | Using Reflexive Pronouns with *By* Write answers to these questions with information about yourself and your opinions. `4.3 B`

DOING THINGS ALONE

1. What are three things you like to do by yourself?
2. What are three things you *don't* like to do by yourself?
3. What are three things young children shouldn't do by themselves?

Talk about It Ask a partner the questions above. Then tell the class about your partner.

"Leila likes to read by herself, but she doesn't like to eat out by herself."

17 | Error Correction Correct any errors in these sentences. (Some sentences may not have any errors.)

1. They expressed themself very well.
2. I ate the whole thing by my self.
3. I finally took my first trip with myself.
4. You should see your person in this picture. You look great.
5. My sister made all of the plans for the trip himself.
6. I often talk or sing to me while I am driving.
7. We had to do everything ourself. No one could help us.
8. Sometimes you need to do things for your family or for your own.

4.4 *Each Other and One Another*

A

1 Does Bill know you? Do you know Bill? =
Do **you and Bill** know **each other**?

2 **The children** pushed **one another**.
(= Each child pushed the other children in the group.)

3 **Tom and Joe** are staring at **each other**.
(= Tom is staring at Joe, and Joe is staring at Tom.)

4 How often do **your friends** talk to **one another**?

We can use *each other* and *one another* to refer back to two or more people. They are an easy way to combine ideas, as in **1**.

We usually use *each other* and *one another* as:

• an object of a verb, as in **1 – 2**
• an object of a preposition, as in **3 – 4**

GRAMMAR TERM: *Each other* and *one another* are called **reciprocal pronouns**.

B

COMPARE RECIPROCAL AND REFLEXIVE PRONOUNS

		reciprocal pronoun
5a	Vera and Tim	were angry with	**each other.**

		reflexive pronoun
5b	Vera and Tim	were angry with	**themselves.**

Reciprocal pronouns and **reflexive pronouns** have different meanings.

• In **5a**, Vera was angry with Tim, and Tim was angry with Vera.
• In **5b**, Vera was angry with herself, and Tim was angry with himself.

C

CORRECT THE COMMON ERRORS (See page R-18.)

6 ✗ They had a problem each other.

7 ✗ They didn't like one anothers.

8 ✗ My parents have a great relationship. They truly love themselves.

GO ONLINE

18 | Exploring Uses of *Each Other* Read these sentences and check (✓) your opinions. `4.4 A`

HOW IMPORTANT ARE THESE THINGS TO A GOOD MARRIAGE?	VERY IMPORTANT	SOMEWHAT IMPORTANT	NOT AT ALL IMPORTANT
1. A husband and wife should give each other expensive gifts.	☐	☐	☐
2. They shouldn't keep secrets from each other.	☐	☐	☐
3. They should always tell each other the truth.	☐	☐	☐
4. They should talk to each other every day.	☐	☐	☐
5. They should listen to each other carefully.	☐	☐	☐
6. They should spend time away from each other.	☐	☐	☐
7. They should know each other well before they get married.	☐	☐	☐
8. They should agree with each other about everything.	☐	☐	☐
9. They should like (not just love) each other.	☐	☐	☐

Think about It What verbs and expressions above do we use with *each other*? Write each verb and expression under the correct group in the chart below.

Verb + *each other*	Expression with preposition + *each other*
give each other something	*keep (something) from each other*

Write about It What else is important to a good marriage? Write three more sentences and then share them with your classmates.

19 | Using *Each Other* and *One Another* Rewrite each sentence using *each other* or *one another*. `4.4 A`

RELATIONSHIPS

1. I enjoy spending time with my older sister, and she enjoys spending time with me.

    My older sister and I _enjoy spending time with each other_____.

2. My new teacher knows my parents and my parents know my new teacher.

    My new teacher and my parents _____.

3. I email my brothers every day and they email me every day.

    My brothers and I _____.

4. I couldn't look at Sam and Sam couldn't look at me.

    Sam and I _____.

5. Kate respects her boss and her boss respects her.

    Kate and her boss _____.

> **RESEARCH SAYS...**
>
> *Each other* is more common when we are talking about just two people.
>
> My parents love **each other**.
>
> *One another* sounds more formal.
>
> The Internet has changed the way people communicate with **one another**.

CORPUS

6. My brother isn't talking to his best friend, and his best friend isn't talking to him.

My brother and his best friend _____.

7. I always speak Spanish with my grandfather, and my grandfather always speaks Spanish with me.

_____

8. My father never argues with my mother, and my mother never argues with my father.

_____

20 | *Each Other* or *Themselves*? Complete these sentences with *each other* or *themselves*. Then check (✓) *Agree* or *Disagree*. 4.4 B

WHAT'S YOUR OPINION?   AGREE   DISAGREE

1. People who speak different languages can't understand _____*each other*_____.   ☐   ☐

2. Family members shouldn't argue with _____.   ☐   ☐

3. It's not unusual for lonely people to talk to _____.   ☐   ☐

4. Friends shouldn't lie to _____.   ☐   ☐

5. Classmates should give answers to _____ during tests.   ☐   ☐

6. Most people think they know _____.   ☐   ☐

7. It's easier for friends to communicate with _____ these days. ☐   ☐

8. It's good for two people to face _____ when they talk.   ☐   ☐

9. People need to learn to work with _____.   ☐   ☐

10. Children should learn to cook for _____.   ☐   ☐

Talk about It Take turns reading the sentences above aloud with a partner. See if your partner agrees or disagrees and why.

A: People who speak different languages can't understand each other.
B: I disagree. If you don't speak the same language, you can point or draw pictures.

21 | Error Correction Correct any errors in these sentences. (Some sentences may not have any errors.)

COMMUNICATING AND INTERACTING

1. We talk each other many times during the day.

2. My friends all help each another.

3. In some cultures, people don't look at themselves when they talk.

4. I love my friends. I have a lot of fun with one another.

5. We introduced ourselves to each other.

6. My grandmother and I don't talk on the phone to ourselves very often because she can't hear very well.

7. We use the Internet to communicate with one anothers.

8. My two sisters had a big argument and now they aren't talking to themselves.

4.5 Indefinite Pronouns

<table>
<tr><td>

A

1 **Somebody** left a book here.
(A person left a book here. I don't know who.)

2 Please don't touch **anything.**
(Don't touch any of the things here.)

3 He says that to **everyone.**
(He says that to all people.)

4 Luckily, **nobody** got lost.
(Not one person got lost.)

</td><td>

We use **indefinite pronouns** when we can't or don't need to name a specific person or thing, as in **1 – 4.**

INDEFINITE PRONOUNS			
somebody	anybody	nobody	everybody
someone	anyone	no one	everyone
something	anything	nothing	everything

</td></tr>
<tr><td>

SUBJECT-VERB AGREEMENT

5 Everything **is** ready. (NOT: ~~Everything are~~ . . .)

6 Somebody **has** my book. (NOT: ~~Somebody have~~ . . .)

</td><td>

WARNING! Indefinite pronouns are always singular. We use a singular verb with them, as in **5 – 6.**

</td></tr>
<tr><td>

B

NEGATIVE VERB + *ANYBODY, ANYONE, OR ANYTHING*

7 We **didn't see** anyone there.
(NOT: ~~We didn't see someone~~ . . .)

8 I **can't throw** anything away.

</td><td>

We don't usually use *somebody, someone,* or *something* after *not.* We use *anybody, anyone,* or *anything* instead, as in **7 – 8.**

</td></tr>
<tr><td>

***NOBODY, NO ONE,* AND *NOTHING* WITH A POSITIVE VERB**

9 Nobody **called.** (NOT: ~~Nobody didn't call.~~)

10 There's **nothing** to eat. (NOT: ~~There isn't nothing~~ . . .)

</td><td>

Nobody, no one, and *nothing* have a negative meaning. We don't use them with *not,* as in **9 – 10.**

</td></tr>
<tr><td colspan="2">

C

CORRECT THE COMMON ERRORS (See page R-18.)

11 ✗ I didn't see nothing.

12 ✗ I thought everythings were free in the U.S.

13 ✗ Everyone want to come.

14 ✗ I don't want to see somebody.

</td></tr>
</table>

 GO ONLINE

22 | Understanding Indefinite Pronouns Rewrite these sentences. Replace the **bold** words with *someone, something, everyone, everything, no one, nothing, anyone,* or *anything.* `4.5 A`

1. I thought I heard **a person** outside. I don't know who it was.

   I thought I heard someone outside. I don't know who it was.

2. I like **all of the people** in my class.
3. I moved **all of the things** in my room.
4. **Not one person** called me last night.
5. When there is **a thing** you want to learn, you can look on the Internet.
6. **Not one thing** in the closet belongs to me.
7. We need to find **one person** to help us.
8. **Any person** can learn this.
9. Do you know **all of the people** here?
10. We didn't see **any person** in the building.
11. Do you want **a thing** to drink?
12. Did you write down **all of the things**?

> **F Y I**
>
> We use:
>
> - *some-* for one person or thing
> - *every-* for all the people or things in a group
> - *any-* for people and things in general
> - *no-* to say no people or things

23 | Pronunciation Note: Indefinite Pronouns Listen to the note. Then do Activity 24.

> When an indefinite pronoun is **new or contrasting information**, we can stress the first syllable, as in Example 1. In Example 2, the speaker does not stress the indefinite pronoun. (We don't stress the second syllable in an indefinite pronoun.)
>
> **EXAMPLE 1**
> A: Do you know that man over there?
> B: No, I don't know **ANY**one here.
>
> **EXAMPLE 2**
> A: Why didn't you ask for help?
> B: There was no one there to ask.

24 | Pronouncing Indefinite Pronouns Listen to the song titles and write the missing pronouns. Listen again and repeat the song titles. `4.5 A`

SONG TITLES

1. "____Everybody____ Loves Saturday Night"
2. "_____'s Talking"
3. "Say _____"
4. "Money Changes _____"
5. "_____ to Love Me"
6. "_____ Hurts Like Love"
7. "I've Got Plenty of _____"
8. "_____ about You"

9. "_____ Loves _____ Sometime"
10. "I'll Never Need _____ Anymore"
11. "We Must Be Doing _____ Right"
12. "_____ Knows the Trouble I've Seen"
13. "He's Done More for Me Than _____"
14. "Doesn't _____ Want to Be Wanted?"
15. "_____'s Looking for the Same Thing"
16. "_____ Is Different Now"

Write about It Complete these song titles with your own ideas. Then share titles with your classmates.

"Everybody Loves ____"   *"Nobody Knows ____"*
"____ Changes Everything"   *"Somebody Is ____"*
"____ Anything"

25 | Indefinite Pronoun + Verb Complete these conversations with the correct form of the verb in parentheses. Then practice with a partner. `4.5 A`

1. A: Can I help?
   B: No need. Everything _____is_____ ready. (be)
2. A: Nothing ever _____ here. (happen)
   B: That's not true.
3. A: Where's Marta?
   B: Nobody _____. (know)
4. A: _____ everything OK here? (be)
   B: Yes, I think so.
5. A: _____ somebody _____ my computer? (have)
   B: Yes, I'm using it.
6. A: Nobody called me last night.
   B: That's because nobody _____ your new phone number. (have)

RESEARCH SAYS...

More Formal
someone
anyone
no one

Less Formal
somebody
anybody
nobody

7. A: _____ anybody here yet? (be)

   B: Yep⁶. Lisa and Irene are both here.

8. A: Can I start the meeting?

   B: Yes, everyone _____ here. (be)

9. A: _____ anyone _____ a question for Mr. Wong? (have)

   B: Yes, I do.

10. A: I forgot to put salt in the soup. I hope nobody _____. (notice)

    B: Don't worry about it.

Think about It Look at conversations 7–10 above. In each conversation, where do you think the people are? Who are the people? Is the situation more formal or less formal?

26 | Using the Correct Pronoun Choose the correct pronoun to complete these conversations. Then practice with a partner. `4.5 B`

1. A: How was your day?

   B: OK. I didn't do ___*anything*___ special.
      (anything / nothing)

2. A: Are you going to play basketball today?

   B: No, there's _____ to play with.
      (anyone / no one)

3. A: Why didn't Sheila come to the concert?

   B: She said she didn't want to see

   _____.
   (anybody / nobody)

4. A: I think there's _____ on the
      (anything / something)
   floor. Be careful!

   B: Don't worry. It's just water.

5. A: Are you going to bring Peter?

   B: No, he doesn't want to do

   _____ this afternoon.
   (anything / something)

6. A: Was there an accident last night?

   B: Well, I didn't see _____.
      (nothing / anything)

7. A: What was that noise?

   B: I don't know. I looked outside, but there's

   _____ there.
   (nothing / anything)

8. A: Why didn't you come to the meeting?

   B: _____ told me about it.
      (nobody / somebody)

9. A: _____ is wrong with this bill.
      (anything / something)

   B: What do you mean?

   A: The numbers don't add up.

10. A: How come everybody knows my plans?

    B: I don't know. I didn't tell _____.
       (anyone / no one)

27 | Usage Note: *Some-* vs. *Any-* Read the note. Then do Activity 28.

We often use **somebody**, **someone**, and **something** in questions when we expect a particular answer, as in Example 1. We use **anybody**, **anyone**, and **anything** when we don't expect a particular answer, as in Example 2.

EXAMPLE 1

What's that noise? Is **somebody** there?
(I hear a noise so I expect a "yes" answer.)

EXAMPLE 2

Hello! Is **anybody** home?
(Someone may or may not be home. I don't know. I have no expectation.)

⁶**yep:** yes (informal)

28 | Asking Questions with Indefinite Pronouns Listen to these conversations and add the missing indefinite pronouns. 4.5 A

1. A: Excuse me, waiter?

   B: Yes, can I get you _____?

   A: Could I have some water, please?

   B: Sure.

3. A: What happened?

   B: There was a bad accident.

   A: Has _____ called the police?

   B: I don't know.

2. A: Dinner's almost ready.

   B: Is there _____ I can do to help?

   A: No, I don't think so.

4. A: What's the matter? Did you lose

   _____?

   B: Yeah. I dropped a contact lens.

Think about It Explain each speaker's choice of indefinite pronoun in the conversations above.

29 | Error Correction Correct any errors in these sentences. (Some sentences may not have any errors.)

1. Where were everyone?
2. Everybody in my class have a car except me.
3. We didn't talk to someone while we were in the city.
4. My brother and I are very different. I don't like nothing that he likes.
5. There weren't anythings we could do to help.
6. Everythings went wrong.
7. Is there anything you need?
8. I invited some body to have dinner with us.
9. Can I get you anything?
10. I can't find no one to help me.
11. My brother brought everythings with him. I didn't need to get anything.
12. Everyone in my family have red hair.
13. When my sister got here, she wouldn't talk to no one.
14. When the accident happened, there was no bodies around.
15. I know everybody here and everyone know me.
16. I don't know something about this city.

> **WARNING!**
> In informal conversations you may hear some English speakers use a double negative.
>
> "He didn't say nothing."

4.6 Demonstratives

A

DEMONSTRATIVE PRONOUNS

1 | This | is | a great movie. | (this = this movie)

2 | These | are | my best photos. | (these = these photos)

3 | What | is | that | on the roof? | (that = that thing)

4 | Whose books | are | those? | (those = those books)

We use the *pronouns this / that / these / those* to point out something, as in **1 – 4**. Notice:

	DEMONSTRATIVES	
singular	this	that
plural	these	those

things that are close   things that are farther away

B

DEMONSTRATIVE DETERMINERS

5 | This | information | is very interesting.

6 | These | dishes | are beautiful.

7 | That | window | over there is dirty.

8 | Could you bring down | those | books?

We can also use *this / that / these / those* + a *noun*, as in **5 – 8**. Notice:

| this | that | + singular count noun or noncount noun

| these | those | + plural count noun

When we use these words before a noun, they are determiners. Determiners help us "determine" important information about a noun.

GO ONLINE

🔊 **30 | Distinguishing *This, That, These,* and *Those*** Sometimes it's difficult to hear the words *this, that, these,* and *those*. **Listen to these sentences and write the missing words.** `4.6 A–B`

		PRONOUN	DETERMINER
1.	_This cake_ _____ is delicious.	☐	☐
2.	_____ are mine.	☐	☐
3.	Why are _____ here?	☐	☐
4.	I can't answer _____.	☐	☐
5.	Did you see _____?	☐	☐
6.	Do you think _____ is too small?	☐	☐
7.	_____ are my friends.	☐	☐
8.	_____ works best.	☐	☐
9.	_____ isn't possible.	☐	☐
10.	Is _____ for sale?	☐	☐
11.	_____ were the good days.	☐	☐
12.	_____ was difficult.	☐	☐
13.	Is _____ your pen?	☐	☐
14.	I never saw _____.	☐	☐
15.	Do you want _____?	☐	☐

Think about It In each sentence above, is *this, that, these,* or *those* a pronoun or a determiner? Check (✓) your answers.

31 | Using Demonstrative Determiners Choose the correct word to complete these sentences. `4.6 B`

1. I like most movies, but _____*this*_____ movie is terrible.
   (this / these)
2. Do you see _____ students over there? They're teaching assistants.
   (that / those)
3. Do you really know all of _____ people?
   (this / these)
4. Did you hear _____ loud noise?
   (that / those)
5. Are you really going to buy all of _____ things?
   (this / these)
6. _____ information is incorrect.
   (this / these)
7. I have lived in _____ country all my life.
   (this / these)
8. I didn't see _____ holes in the floor.
   (that / those)
9. A very smart person gave me _____ advice. She said, "Listen to yourself."
   (this / these)
10. You are as smart as Tom and Ali. Don't compare yourself to _____ guys.
    (that / those)
11. You know _____ beautiful pictures on our classroom wall? Our teacher painted them.
    (that / those)
12. Turn right here. _____ way is shorter.
    (this / these)

Think about It In which sentences above could you use a different demonstrative?

For number 1, you could say, "I like most movies, but that movie is terrible."
For number 2, you can't use a different demonstrative.

32 | Choosing *This, That, These,* and *Those* Read each situation and answer the question.
Use *this, that, these,* or *those* + a noun in your answer. `4.6 A-B`

1. **Situation:** You are doing homework with a friend. You think the homework is very difficult.
   What do you say to your friend?

   "This homework is really hard."

2. **Situation:** You are wearing some new shoes, and they are hurting your feet. What do you say to yourself?
3. **Situation:** You come home and see some flowers on the table. You want to know where they came from.
   What question do you ask?
4. **Situation:** Your friend made a delicious meal for you. You want to compliment her. What do you say?
5. **Situation:** You are listening to a song, and you don't like it. What do you say?
6. **Situation:** You are at a restaurant. A group of people across the room are very loud.
   What do you say to yourself?
7. **Situation:** There is a man across the room. You think you and your friend have met him.
   What question do you ask your friend?

33 | Error Correction Correct any errors in these sentences. (Some sentences may not have any errors.)

1. I really like these idea.
2. My friend gave me those advices.
3. I don't know all of this things.
4. Here. I want you to have that.
5. Those moneys belong to you.
6. Please take this. I want you to have them.
7. I couldn't do these homeworks.
8. I found this information in a library book.

4.7 Showing Possession

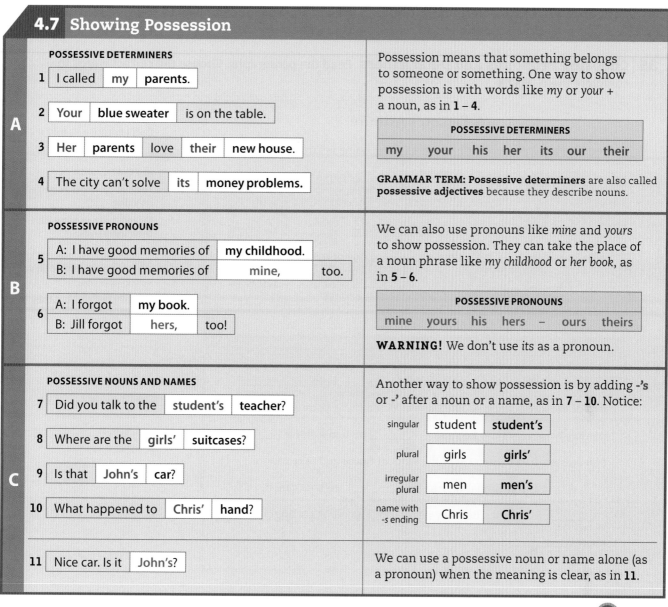

A

POSSESSIVE DETERMINERS

1 I called | my | parents.

2 Your | blue sweater | is on the table.

3 Her | parents | love | their | new house.

4 The city can't solve | its | money problems.

Possession means that something belongs to someone or something. One way to show possession is with words like *my* or *your* + a noun, as in **1 – 4**.

POSSESSIVE DETERMINERS						
my	your	his	her	its	our	their

GRAMMAR TERM: Possessive determiners are also called **possessive adjectives** because they describe nouns.

B

POSSESSIVE PRONOUNS

5 A: I have good memories of | my childhood.
B: I have good memories of | mine, | too.

6 A: I forgot | my book.
B: Jill forgot | hers, | too!

We can also use pronouns like *mine* and *yours* to show possession. They can take the place of a noun phrase like *my childhood* or *her book*, as in **5 – 6**.

POSSESSIVE PRONOUNS						
mine	yours	his	hers	–	ours	theirs

WARNING! We don't use *its* as a pronoun.

C

POSSESSIVE NOUNS AND NAMES

7 Did you talk to the | student's | teacher?

8 Where are the | girls' | suitcases?

9 Is that | John's | car?

10 What happened to | Chris' | hand?

Another way to show possession is by adding -'s or -' after a noun or a name, as in **7 – 10**. Notice:

singular	student	student's
plural	girls	girls'
irregular plural	men	men's
name with -s ending	Chris	Chris'

11 Nice car. Is it | John's?

We can use a possessive noun or name alone (as a pronoun) when the meaning is clear, as in **11**.

---

34 | Using Possessive Determiners Complete the proverbs with *my, your, his, her, its, our,* or *their*. `4.7 A`

PROVERBS

1. A chain is only as strong as ____*its*____ weakest link.

2. Fools[7] and _____ money are soon parted[8].

3. A leopard cannot change _____ spots.

4. A poor workman always blames _____ tools.

5. Cowards[9] may die many times before _____ death.

6. Sticks and stones may break _____ bones, but words will never hurt me.

7. Don't burn _____ bridges behind you.

8. Never judge a book by _____ cover[10].

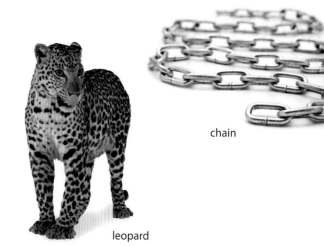

chain

leopard

[7]**fools:** foolish people
[8]**parted:** separated

[9]**cowards:** fearful people
[10]**cover:** the outside part of a book or magazine

Talk about It Choose one of the proverbs in Activity 34. What does it mean to you? Tell your classmates.

35 | Choosing Pronouns and Determiners   Read the paragraphs. Choose the correct words to complete them.   `4.7 A`

A Person I Admire

I admire my older brother a lot. _____*His*_____ name is Edgar, and
(1. he's / his)

_____ lives in Vancouver with _____ parents. Why do I
(2. he / his) (3. our / their)

admire _____ so much? Edgar is very good at working with
(4. his / him)

_____ hands. _____ can fix anything. _____ also very
(5. his / him) (6. he / his) (7. he's / his)

generous with _____ time. _____ one of his best qualities. If
(8. his / its) (9. its / it's)

you want _____ to fix something for _____, he'll stop what
(10. his / him) (11. you / your)

he's doing and fix _____ right away.
(12. it / them)

I have two older sisters, and I admire _____ both. _____
(13. their / them) (14. they're / their)

two of the most caring people I know. When I was young, _____
(15. our / us)

parents were very busy because _____ owned a store. _____
(16. their / they) (17. me / my)

older sisters had to do most of the work at home and take care of

_____. It was probably hard for _____ to take care of
(18. me / my) (19. their / them)

_____ little sister, but they never complained or got angry
(20. their / them)

about _____.
(21. it / its)

WARNING!

Don't confuse *its* and *it's* or *their* and *they're*.

***its* / *their* + noun**
The company lost 25 percent of **its value**.

My three sisters came with **their husbands**.

it* / *they* + *be
I like this restaurant but **it's** very expensive.

We have two cars but **they're** both old.

Write about It Write several sentences about someone you admire.

36 | Using Possessive Pronouns   Each of these **bold** sentences has a possessive phrase (such as *my new computer*). Change the phrase to a possessive pronoun. Then practice with a partner.   `4.7 B`

1. A: I love my new computer.
   mine
   B: **I like ~~my new computer~~, too.**

2. A: How old is your daughter?
   B: She's five. **Your daughter is seven, right?**
   A: No, she's six.

3. A: Our children love the new teacher.
   B: **Our children do, too.**

4. A: That isn't Tom and Jill's car.
   B: **How do you know it's not their car?**
   A: **Because their car is white.**

5. A: Is this Leila's phone?
   B: **No, her phone is upstairs.**
   A: Then whose is it?
   B: Let me see it. **Maybe it's my phone.**

6. A: Here are your keys. I found them in the car.

   B: **But those aren't my keys.**

   A: Then whose keys are they?

   B: I don't know. Pam was in the car today.
   Maybe they're her keys.

7. A: Can I use your computer?

   B: **What's the matter with your computer?**

   A: It's not working.

8. A: You and George both have nice singing voices!

   B: **I think George has a great voice, but my voice is terrible.**

   A: Not true. **Your voice is good, too.**

37 | Pronunciation Note: Possessive –'s Listen to the note. Then do Activity 38.

We pronounce the -'s endings on possessive nouns just like the -s endings on plural nouns.

Usually the -'s ending on a possessive noun is just a consonant sound: / s / or / z /.			When a singular noun ends in a hissing or buzzing sound, the possessive -'s adds another syllable: / əz /. (These words are often spelled with a final -s, -x, -z, -ce, -ge, -se, -ze, -sh, and -ss.)		
1	women	women**'s** clothing	/ z /	3	judge	the judge**'s** decision	/ əz / (+ 1 syllable)
2	president	the president**'s** family	/ s /	4	Liz	Liz**'s** house	

38 | Pronouncing Possessive Nouns Listen to each pair of words and check (✓) the ending you hear on the possessive noun. 4.7 C

		/ s / OR / z /	/ əz /
1. people	people**'s** problems	☐	☐
2. the horse	the horse**'s** tail	☐	☐
3. a father	a father**'s** role	☐	☐
4. my parents	my parents**'** friend	☐	☐
5. our children	our children**'s** future	☐	☐
6. someone else	someone else**'s** idea	☐	☐
7. the audience	the audience**'s** response	☐	☐
8. the college	the college**'s** president	☐	☐
9. an employee	an employee**'s** work	☐	☐
10. next month	next month**'s** bill	☐	☐
11. my boss	my boss**'** boss	☐	☐
12. the earth	the earth**'s** atmosphere	☐	☐
13. a good night	a good night**'s** sleep	☐	☐
14. our nation	our nation**'s** capital	☐	☐

F Y I

We can use a possessive determiner + a possessive noun or name.

my friend
my parents' friend

our future
our children's future

Write about It Choose five possessive phrases above and write sentences using them.

What's a father's role in a family?

39 | Possessive Names and Nouns Complete each question with the possessive form of the word in parentheses. Then match each question with an answer on the right. `4.7 C`

QUESTIONS ABOUT NAMES AND NOUNS

1. What was ___*Shakespeare's*___ first name? (Shakespeare)
2. What was the name of _____ first movie? (the Beatles)
3. What is the name of a popular _____ toy? (children)
4. What's a popular _____ name? (boy)
5. What is the name of the _____ largest library? (world)
6. What is a scientific name for the _____ moon? (Earth)

____	*A Hard Day's Night*
____	LEGOs
____	Library of Congress
____	Luna
____	Michael
____	William

7. What is a word for your _____ brother? (father)
8. What do we call our _____ father? (mother)
9. What is the word for an _____ nose? (elephant)
10. What do we call a _____ bed? (baby)
11. What is another word for a _____ bag? (woman)
12. What is one word for a _____ hat? (man)

____	crib
____	fedora
____	grandfather
____	purse
____	trunk
____	uncle

Talk about It Ask a partner the questions above.

40 | Using Possessive Forms Write ten questions using words from each column in the chart. Add -'s or -' after the **bold** noun. `4.7 C`

THE PEOPLE IN YOUR LIFE

What	is are	your best **friend** your **father** your **parents** your **classmates** our **teacher** the **school** your **brother** your **sister** most **children**	name(s)? phone number(s)? address(es)? favorite movie(s)? favorite food(s)? biggest concern(s)? favorite sport(s)?

Talk about It Ask a partner the questions you wrote above.

A: What is your best friend's favorite food?
B: He really likes Japanese food.

41 | Error Correction Correct any errors in these sentences. (Some sentences may not have any errors.)

1. Do you have mine paper?
2. That's my friend book. Do you want me to give it to her?
3. I want to have a job like my mother job. She is the manager of her parents' clothing store.
4. In my country capital, the street's are crowded, and it takes a long time to get anywhere.

5. My parents are very generous with my. They are helping me start a business.

6. My brother and I argue a lot. I don't always understand he's point of view, and he doesn't understand mine.

7. I live with my aunt. She's home is near the center of town.

8. I can't wear my brother's clothes because he is tall and I am short.

9. Most people know that smoking is not good for you health.

10. While I was there, my friends invited me to them home.

11. I'm lucky because I can watch my TV's roommate.

12. People should take care of theirs health. It's important.

4.8 Overview of Quantifiers

A

QUANTIFIER + SINGULAR NOUN

1 **Each person** is going to help.

2 I called **every student** in the class.

QUANTIFIER + PLURAL NOUN

3 **Many students** today need financial aid.

4 Wow, there are **a lot of people** here!

QUANTIFIER + NONCOUNT NOUN

5 I could use **a little help**.

6 I didn't bring **much money** with me.

We use a special group of determiners to describe *how much* or *how many*, as in **1 – 6**. We call these words **quantifiers**. Notice:

	singular count noun
each every either neither any +	car book boy

	plural count noun
a few some any many a lot of +	cars books boys

	noncount noun
a little some any much a lot of +	time food

ONLINE

42 | Noticing Quantifiers Read the text and circle the quantifiers + nouns. **4.8 A**

What Do You Do to Stay Healthy?

There are (many things) you can do to stay healthy. The right plan is different for every individual, but the most important things are eating right and exercising. I eat a lot of fruit and vegetables during the day, along with some bread and a little meat. I try not to eat many sweets even though I love them. When I can't resist, I try to eat just a few cookies or a little ice cream.

I also try to exercise to stay healthy. Many people go to a gym to exercise, but I prefer to exercise outdoors. Either way will make you feel better. I always feel good after exercising outdoors and have a lot of energy.

Think about It Write each quantifier + noun above under the correct group in the chart below.

Quantifier + singular count noun	Quantifier + plural count noun	Quantifier + noncount noun
	many things	

4.9 Quantifiers with Plural and Noncount Nouns

A

1 I need **some money.**
2 I need some new **clothes.**
3 He never has **any money.**
4 I don't have **any clothes** for the baby.

We use **some** and **any** with plural nouns and noncount nouns.

- We can use *some* in a positive statement to talk about a small number or amount, as in **1 – 2.**
- We can use *any* in a negative statement to mean "no," as in **3 – 4.**

B

5 We need **a lot of information.**
6 We didn't receive **many invitations.**
7 I have **a lot of money** with me.
8 I didn't bring **much money** with me.
(DON'T SAY: I brought much money with me.)

We use **many** or **a lot of** with plural nouns. We use **much** or **a lot of** with noncount nouns.

- We can use *a lot of* and *many* in both positive and negative statements, as in **5 – 7.**
- We usually use *much* in negative, NOT positive, statements, as in **8.**

C

A FEW / FEW + PLURAL NOUN
9 Luckily, **a few people** came. (= a small number)
10 Sadly, **very few people** came. (= almost no people)

A LITTLE / LITTLE + NONCOUNT NOUN
11 It's nice to have **a little free time.** (= a small amount)
12 Are you a busy person with **very little free time**?
(= almost no free time)

A few / few and *a little / little* look similar, but we use them differently. Notice the different meanings in **9 – 12.**

We often use *very* before *few* or *little*, as in **10** and **12.**

D

QUANTIFIERS AS PRONOUNS
13 A: Do you want **some soup?**
   B: Thanks, I'll have **a little.** (a little = a little soup)
   C: And I'll take **a lot.** (a lot = a lot of soup)
14 A: How many of **your friends** did you see today?
   B: **A few.** What about you?
   A: **None.** They were all working.

We can also use a **quantifier as a pronoun** in place of a noun or noun phrase, as in **13 – 14.**

WARNING! When we use *a lot* as a pronoun, we do not use *of*, as in **13.** We use *none* as a pronoun to mean "zero," as in **14.**

GO ONLINE

43 | *Some* and *Any* Complete the sentences with *some* or *any*. Then check (✓) *True* or *False*. 4.9 A

FACTS ABOUT YOU	TRUE	FALSE
1. I like to have ___*some*___ fun on the weekend.	☐	☐
2. I ate _____ cereal for breakfast this morning.	☐	☐
3. I didn't have _____ homework last night.	☐	☐
4. I have _____ money in my pocket.	☐	☐
5. I didn't see _____ good movies last year.	☐	☐
6. I have _____ friends in Canada.	☐	☐
7. I have _____ good reasons for studying English.	☐	☐
8. I usually ask _____ questions in class.	☐	☐
9. I never need _____ help with my homework.	☐	☐
10. I have _____ pictures of my family with me today.	☐	☐

	TRUE	FALSE
11. I have _____ concerns about the economy.	☐	☐
12. I don't have _____ trouble making big decisions.	☐	☐
13. I need _____ new clothes.	☐	☐
14. There isn't _____ furniture in my bedroom.	☐	☐

Write about It Rewrite the false statements in Activity 43 to make them true.

There is some furniture in my bedroom.

44 | *Much, Many, and A Lot of* Complete each sentence with your own ideas. 4.9 B

1. I don't have many _____ *friends* _____ here.
   _____ at home.
   _____ at school.
   _____ here.

2. I don't have much _____ at home.
   _____ for breakfast.
   _____ here.

3. There are a lot of _____ in a city.
   _____ on TV.
   _____ in the world.

4. There is a lot of _____ in a city.
   _____ on TV.
   _____ in the world.

5. There isn't much _____.
   _____
   _____

6. There are many _____.
   _____
   _____

> **RESEARCH SAYS...**
>
> In general, *a lot of* is less formal than *many* or *much*.
>
> CORPUS

Think about It Share the sentences you wrote above with a partner. How many quantifiers + nouns you can list in the chart below?

Many + plural count noun	*Much* + noncount noun	*A lot of* + plural count noun	*A lot of* + noncount noun
many friends	much time	a lot of people	a lot of violence

45 | A Few/Few and A Little/Little Complete each pair of sentences with the correct words. `4.9 C`

1. a. Everyone needs ___*a little*___ time to relax.

   b. Hurry up! We have _____ time.

2. a. My brothers live far away, so they are _____ help to my parents.

   b. Could you give me _____ help, please?

3. a. Can you wait ten more minutes? I still have _____ things to do.

   b. My boss is a great person. There are _____ things I dislike about her.

4. a. Let me read this letter while there is still _____ light.

   b. It's difficult to read when there is _____ light.

5. a. Tony Bennett is famous, but _____ people would recognize him.

   b. I thought the movie was funny, but only _____ people laughed.

6. a. My father takes care of himself. He doesn't smoke, and he eats

   _____ salt.

   b. This soup doesn't have much flavor. I think it needs _____ salt.

7. a. _____ people passed the test, but most didn't.

   b. We were lonely here at first because we knew _____ people.

1. a little/very little
2. a little/little
3. a few/few
4. a little/very little
5. a few/few
6. a little/very little
7. a few/very few

Write about It Look at the sentences above that use (*very*) *few* or (*very*) *little*. Rewrite them with *not . . . many/much*.

Hurry up! We don't have much time.

> **F Y I**
>
> In informal situations, we often use *not . . . many/much* instead of *few* and *little*.
>
> There are**n't many** people here.
> (= There are very few people here.)
>
> He does**n't** have **much** time.
> (= He has very little time.)

46 | Using Quantifiers as Pronouns Choose the correct pronoun to complete each conversation. Then practice with a partner. `4.9 D`

1. A: Can I get you some cake?

   B: Sure. I'd love ___*a little*___.
   (a few / a little)

2. A: Do you have a lot of homework tonight?

   B: No, not _____.
   (many / much)

3. A: Where is the coffee?

   B: Oh, we don't have _____.
   (any / some)

4. A: Did we get a lot of phone calls?

   B: No, not _____.
   (many / much)

5. A: There were only five people there.

   B: That's not very _____.
   (many / much)

6. A: Where are all your friends?

   B: Well, _____ are at work.
   (a few / a little)

7. A: Do you want some more coffee?

   B: Sure. Just _____.
   (a few / a little)

8. A: Do you want some potato chips?

   B: OK, but I can't eat very _____.
   (many / much)

9. A: Do you have any paper?

   B: Yes, there is _____ in the bottom drawer.
   (any / some)

10. A: How many light bulbs should I get?

    B: Just _____.
    (a few / a little)

Think about It What do the underlined words above refer back to? Share ideas with your classmates.

In 1, "a little" refers back to "cake."

47 | *How Much* and *How Many* Ask and answer these questions with a partner. Use the pronouns in the box in your answers. 4.9 D

a lot	not much	a little	a few	none
some	not many	very little	very few	

IN YOUR LIFE

How much / How many . . . ?

1. homework do you have tonight

> A: *How much homework do you have tonight?*
> B: *A little. I'm going to do it after dinner.*

2. meals do you eat at home every week
3. sleep do you get every night
4. text messages do you get a day
5. friends do you have online
6. coffee or tea do you drink in the morning
7. mail do you get every day
8. days off do you have this month
9. rain have we had this month
10. people in your neighborhood do you know

48 | Error Correction Correct any errors in these sentences. (Some sentences may not have any errors.)

1. Each people brought something to eat.
2. Each seasons has different weather.
3. He has had a many exciting adventures.
4. The restaurant serves many kind of fish.
5. You can learn many thing when you travel.
6. We had a lot of funs on our way to the city.
7. He sent me many news about his trip.
8. Lot of people drive too fast.
9. I looked at every channels on TV.
10. My father has a lot of good book in his library at home.
11. If you want to get a good grade in this class, you need to study little.
12. There are a lot of difference between my brother and me.

4.10 Quantifiers with Singular Nouns

A

1 The teacher will speak with **each student** separately.
(= one student at a time)

2 There's a laptop for **every student** in the class.
(= all students in the group)

3 Take **any seat** you want.
(= It doesn't matter which seat you take.)

4 I can visit you **either week**.
(= one week or the other week)

5 **Neither person** had the answer.
(= not one person and not the other)

We can use some quantifiers with singular nouns to describe more than one thing but to talk about them one at a time.

- We use *each*, *every*, and *any* to **talk about a group of things or people**, but we use them differently. Notice the different meanings in **1 – 3**.

- We use *either* and *neither* to **talk about two things or people**, but we use them differently. Notice the different meanings in **4 – 5**.

49 | *Each, Every, Any, Either,* and *Neither* Complete the conversations with the correct word in parentheses. Then practice with a partner. **4.10 A**

1. A: Do you want to leave on Monday or Tuesday?

   B: _____*Either*_____ day is fine.
   (either / neither)

2. A: Did you finish the book?

   B: Yep. I read _____ page.
   (either / every)

3. A: What color should we paint the kitchen?

   B: _____ color but yellow.
   (any / neither)

4. A: How many people did you call?

   B: Two, but _____ person answered.
   (either / neither)

5. A: Where did you go on vacation?

   B: I spend _____ vacation with my family.
   (every / either)

6. A: What kind of ice cream do you want?

   B: _____ kind is fine with me.
   (any / neither)

7. A: How long did it take to correct _____ test?
   (each / either)

   B: About 30 minutes.

8. A: Where did you go this summer?

   B: To Mexico. We go there _____ year.
   (every / either)

9. A: Who's going to win the game?

   B: That's hard to say. _____ team is very good.
   (either / neither)

10. A: Are you going to study a foreign language?

    B: Yeah, _____ student has to take one.
    (each / every)

4.11 Measure Words

A

COMPARE QUANTIFIERS AND MEASURE WORDS

1a Don't forget to buy **some sugar**.

1b Don't forget to buy **a bag of sugar**.

MEASURE WORD + NONCOUNT NOUN

2 Can I borrow **a piece of paper**?

3 I have **two pieces of advice** for you.

4 I need **two cups of sugar** for this recipe.

MEASURE WORD + PLURAL COUNT NOUN

5 I picked up **a bunch of bananas** at the store.

6 She gave me **two boxes of books**.

7 There are **three pairs of gloves** here.

When we want to describe a specific amount of something, we can use special **measure words + of**, as in **1b**. Notice:

measure word

| a, an, one | box   cup   bunch | of | + | noncount noun / plural count noun |

Measure words allow us to "count" noncount nouns, as in **2 – 4**. We can also use them with plural count nouns, as in **5 – 7**.

When we talk about two or more, the measure word is plural, as in **3 – 4** and **6 – 7**. Notice:

measure word + -s

| two, etc. | boxes   cups   bunches | of |

For a list of common measure words, see Activity 50, p. 149.

B

CORRECT THE COMMON ERRORS (See page R-19.)

8 ✗ I would like two cup of coffee, please.

9 ✗ He drank two bottle of milks!

10 ✗ Can you get me three boxes of cracker?

11 ✗ My teacher gave us bunch of test.

50 | Learning Measure Words We use certain measure words with certain nouns. Listen to each sentence. What noun do you hear after these measure words? Add it to the chart. `4.11 A`

Measure word	+ *of*	+ noun
1. bit/bits	of	advice, _____ , money, news, time, trouble
2. bottle/bottles	of	perfume, pills, shampoo, soda, _____
3. box/boxes	of	books, _____, cereal, clothes, cookies, food, paper
4. bowl/bowls	of	cereal, food, fruit, rice, _____
5. bunch/bunches	of	bananas, carrots, emails, _____ , grapes, people, things
6. cup/cups	of	coffee, soup, sugar, _____
7. glass/glasses	of	ice, juice, milk, _____
8. loaf/loaves	of	_____
9. pair/pairs	of	eyes, glasses, gloves, pants, scissors, shoes, _____
10. piece/pieces	of	advice, cake, equipment, fruit, _____ , information, paper
11. pile/piles	of	books, _____ , dirt, mail, money, papers
12. slice/slices	of	_____ , cake, cheese, pizza

Write about It Choose five measure words above. Write true sentences about yourself using them.

I need a bit of advice.

51 | Listening for Measure Words Listen and write the missing measure words + *of*. `4.11 A`

1. I just put three ___*bottles of*___ water on the table. Is that enough?
2. Could you please move this _____ papers?
3. Do you want another _____ cake?
4. Can I borrow a few _____ paper?
5. May I offer a _____ advice?
6. There are several _____ books on the floor.
7. I have some useful _____ information for you.
8. What are you going to do with this _____ clothes?
9. Could you get me a _____ cereal?
10. Please help yourself to the _____ fruit on the table.
11. I have a _____ emails to read.
12. How many _____ bread do you need?
13. I need two _____ sugar for this recipe.

> **FYI**
>
> We can use more than one measure word with some nouns. The choice depends on the meaning and the context. Compare:
>
> Could you get me **a loaf of bread** at the store?
>
> Do you want **a slice of bread** with your dinner?

Think about It What other measure word could you use in each sentence above? Compare ideas with your classmates.

"I just put three glasses of water on the table."

52 | Using Measure Words Make these sentences more specific. Replace the **bold** words with *a* + a measure word + *of*. (More than one measure word may be possible.) `4.11 A`

a cup of
1. Could I have ~~some~~ coffee?

2. I need **some** information.

3. I gave her **some** perfume.

4. I have **a little** advice for you.

5. Would you like **a little** cake?

6. Can you get me **some** shoes?

7. I'd love **some** pizza.

8. Do you have **some** scissors at home?

9. We need **some** furniture for the bedroom.

10. Why don't you cook **some** rice?

11. My sister gave us **some** flowers.

12. Do you want **some** good news?

Write about It Rewrite each statement above. Use a plural measure word.

Could I have two cups of coffee?

53 | Error Correction Correct any errors in these sentences. (Some sentences may not have any errors.)

1. Could I have cup of tea?

2. I wrote everything on a piece of papers.

3. You should eat at least three piece of fruit every day.

4. You need two slice of bread to make a sandwich.

5. They always sent us box of food for the holiday.

6. These bunch of bananas isn't ripe.

7. I drank some bottle of water.

8. I think we need three loafs of bread.

4.12 Quantifiers for Comparing Amounts

A
1 It's very dry here. We really need **more** rain.

2 There are **more** people in class today.

3 There were **fewer** storms this year than last year.

4 I had **fewer** problems in school this semester.

5 You can lose weight by eating **less** food.

6 I should drink **less** coffee.

We use the quantifiers *more*, *fewer*, and *less* to compare different amounts or numbers, as in **1 – 6**. We can use:

| more | + a plural noun or a noncount noun |

| fewer | + a plural noun |

| less | + a noncount noun |

B
7 There are **too many** people in New York City.

8 There are **too few** days in the week.

9 I have **too much** work. I'll never finish it.

10 I have **too little** time to finish this.

We can use *too* + some quantifiers, as in **7 – 10**. Notice the different meanings and uses:

more than you want	less than you want	
too many	too few	+ a plural noun
too much	too little	+ a noncount noun

C
11 A: Are you going to buy this?
B: Yeah, I think I have **enough** money.

12 A: Did you finish the test?
B: No, I didn't have **enough** time.

We can use the quantifier *enough* + a plural count noun or a noncount noun, as in **11 – 12**. Notice:

• *enough* = No more is needed.

• *not enough* = More is needed.

54 | Understanding *More, Fewer,* and *Less* Study the chart and then read the sentences below. Check (✓) *True* or *False*. `4.12 A`

Food	Number of Calories	Amount of Sugar	Amount of Salt
1 banana	105	14.43 grams	1 mg
1 apple	72	14.34 grams	1 mg
1 hamburger (with bun)	270	3.39 grams	369 mg
7 walnuts	185	0.74 gram	1 mg
1 cup of cooked pinto beans	236	0	0
2 slices of white bread	133	2.16 grams	340 mg
1 cup of vanilla ice cream	290	15.28 grams	116 mg

data from www.fatsecret.com

	TRUE	FALSE
1. A banana has more calories than an apple.	☐	☐
2. An apple has fewer grams of sugar than a banana.	☐	☐
3. A banana has less salt than an apple.	☐	☐
4. A hamburger has more calories than a banana and an apple together.	☐	☐
5. Seven walnuts have less sugar than one hamburger.	☐	☐
6. Two slices of white bread have more salt than a hamburger with a bun.	☐	☐
7. A banana has less sugar than an apple.	☐	☐
8. A cup of beans has fewer calories than a cup of ice cream.	☐	☐

Write about It Write four true or false sentences comparing the foods in the chart above. Then read your sentences to your classmates. Ask your classmates if your sentences are true or false.

55 | Using *More, Fewer,* and *Less* Complete each statement with *more, fewer,* or *less*. `4.12 A`

FACT BOOK

1. There are _____*more*_____ sheep in New Zealand than people.

2. There were _____ cars on the road 100 years ago.

3. Warm climates get _____ snow than cold climates.

4. An adult has _____ bones than a baby. An adult has 205 bones, but a baby has over 300.

5. When you wear a seat belt in a car, there is _____ chance you will get injured.

6. Because it's efficient, a refrigerator uses _____ energy than a washing machine or a clothes dryer.

7. There are _____ countries in Africa than in Asia. Asia has 48 countries, while Africa has 54.

8. Researchers say that happy people spend _____ time alone.

9. Most people want to earn _____ money, not less.

10. There are _____ people in New Zealand than in Japan. Japan has the tenth largest population in the world.

Write about It Choose two cities or two countries. Complete these sentences.

____ *has more* ____ *than* ____.   ____ *has fewer* ____ *than* ____.   ____ *has less* ____ *than* ____.

56 | Using *Too* + Quantifier Complete the sentences with *too much, too many, too little,* or *too few.* `4.12 B`

HEALTH PROBLEMS

1. _____ sun is bad for your skin.

2. Most people get _____ sleep. This can affect your health.

3. Your skin can turn orange from eating _____ carrots.

4. Many people eat _____ salt.

5. _____ exercise can lead to depression.

6. You may not sleep well if you drink _____ cups of coffee.

7. If you drink _____ water during the day, you may feel tired.

8. In many parts of the world, there are _____ doctors.

Write about It Describe four more health problems. Use *too much, too many, too little,* or *too few.*

57 | Understanding *Too Much/Too Many* vs. *Enough* Complete these conversations with *too much, too many,* or *enough.* Then practice with a partner. `4.12 B-C`

1. A: Do you want to go out tonight?

   B: I can't. I have _____ homework.

2. A: Why are you studying down here?

   B: There's _____ noise upstairs.

3. A: Let's go. There're _____ people here.

   B: Yeah, it's really crowded.

4. A: Do you want to watch *2001: A Space Odyssey*?

   B: No, thanks. I've seen it _____ times.

5. A: Why are you so hungry?

   B: Because I didn't eat _____ for lunch.

6. A: Why did you walk home?

   B: Because I didn't have _____ money for the bus.

7. A: Can we stop for a cold drink?

   B: There isn't _____ time. The bus leaves in ten minutes.

8. A: Do you want to do something tomorrow?

   B: Sorry, I can't. I have _____ things to do this weekend.

9. A: Does the car need gas?

   B: No, I think there's _____ for you to get to work.

10. A: You look terrible. Are you OK?

    B: Yeah, I just didn't get _____ sleep last night.

11. A: Can you help me bring in the groceries?

    B: Ten bags! I think you bought _____ things.

> **F Y I**
>
> We can use words like *more, fewer, less, much, many,* and *enough* as either determiners or pronouns.
>
> We didn't have **enough money**.
>
> We saved a lot of **money**, but it wasn't **enough** to buy a house.

Talk about It Ask a partner the questions above again. Use your own ideas to answer.

A: Do you want to go out tonight?
B: Sure. I don't have much to do.

4.13 Using Pronouns and Determiners in Speaking

A	***YOU* AND *THEY* FOR PEOPLE IN GENERAL** **1** How do **you** get to the airport? (In general, how does a person do this?) **2** **They** say prices are going up. (In general, people say this.)	We sometimes use **you** and **they** to talk about a person or people in general, as in **1** – **2**. • *You* means "any person in general." • *They* means "other people in general."
B	**EXPRESSIONS WITH *IT*** **3** Lisa wouldn't stop teasing me, so I finally told her to **cut it out!** (= Stop doing that.) **4** A: I'm still mad at you for being late. B: Can you just **drop it!** (= Stop talking about that.)	We use the pronoun **it** in many informal expressions, as in **3** – **4**. In these cases, it often refers to an action or behavior.
C	**REFERRING BACK WITH *THAT*** **5** A: You're always late. B: **That's** not true. **6** A: I don't want to eat anything today. B: **That's** crazy.	In conversation, we often use **that** to refer to something the speaker has just said, as in **5** – **6**.
D	***ME TOO* AND *ME NEITHER*** **7** A: I'm hungry. B: **Me too.** (= I'm hungry too.) **8** A: I don't want to leave. B: **Me neither.** (= I don't want to leave either.)	In conversation, we sometimes use the expressions *Me too* and *Me neither* to agree with someone, as in **7** – **8**.

58 | Understanding *You* and *They* Do the **bold** words refer to specific people or people in general? Circle your answers. Then practice with a partner. 4.13 A

1. A: Do **you** want to watch a movie tonight?
   B: Sure. That would be fun.

2. A: Should we take a taxi?
   B: No, **you** can't get one at this hour.

3. A: I hope we get a lot of snow this year.
   B: **You** never know.

4. A: Did **you** send the package?
   B: Yes. I sent it yesterday.

5. A: This is a nice neighborhood.
   B: Yeah, **you** need a lot of money to live here.

6. A: **They** say it's going to be cold this winter.
   B: That's OK. I love winter.

7. A: Where did your brothers go?
   B: I don't know. **They** didn't tell me.

8. A: I can't believe my car needs a new engine.
   B: Yeah, **they** don't build very good cars anymore.

1. (a specific person) / any person in general

2. a specific person / any person in general

3. a specific person / any person in general

4. a specific person / any person in general

5. a specific person / any person in general

6. specific people / other people in general

7. specific people / other people in general

8. specific people / other people in general

Talk about It Work with a partner. Create a short conversation using *you* or *they* to talk about people in general. Present your conversation to the class.

59 | Using Expressions with *It* Listen and write the missing words. Then match each completed expression with a meaning below. Practice the conversations with a partner. `4.13 B`

1. A: I'm leaving.

   B: _____*Hold*_____ **it** for a minute. I need to show you something.

2. A: Dad, this can't be true.

   B: _____ **my word for it**, Ben. It's true.

3. A: I'm sorry I couldn't finish this today.

   B: Don't worry about it. You can _____ **it up** tomorrow.

4. A: Can I go to the movies tonight, Mom?

   B: Absolutely not. You are going to stay here and do your homework. _____ **it**?

5. A: I don't have time to cook dinner tonight.

   B: No problem. _____ **it to me**.

6. A: _____ **it**! There's a car coming.

   B: Thanks. I didn't see it.

7. A: It's five o'clock, and I'm tired.

   B: Me too. **Let's** _____ **it a day**.

   A: Good idea.

8. A: _____ **it off**, kids. You're making too much noise.

   B: OK, Dad.

MEANINGS

____ Stop doing that.   ____ Be careful.   ____ Believe me.   _1_ Wait.

____ Stop working.   ____ I'll do it.   ____ Finish it.   ____ Do you understand?

Talk about It Work with a partner. Choose one of the expressions above and use it to create a short conversation. Present your conversation to the class.

60 | Using *That* to Refer Back Give a response for each statement. Use ideas from the box. (Many different responses may be possible.) `4.13 C`

STATEMENTS

1. A: We never have any homework.   B: _____

2. A: We have class tomorrow at nine.   B: _____

3. A: I saw your brother yesterday.   B: _____

4. A: I have some money for you.   B: _____

5. A: I'm getting married tomorrow.   B: _____

6. A: It's almost three o'clock.   B: _____

7. A: It's snowing outside.   B: _____

8. A: The sun rises in the west.   B: _____

9. A: Men aren't smarter than women.   B: _____

10. A: Are you still cooking dinner for the class tomorrow?   B: _____

RESPONSES

That's great.
That's fine.
That's interesting.
That's crazy.
That's impossible.
Wait a second. I never said that.
That's nice.
That's true.
That's not true.
That's awful!

Talk about It Work with a partner. One person reads a statement above. The other person gives a response. Then think of your own statements and responses.

A: We never have any homework.
B: That's not true. We had homework yesterday.

61 | Using *Me Too* and *Me Neither* Work with a partner. One person reads a sentence. The other person agrees by saying *Me too* or *Me neither*. **4.13 D**

1. I want to take a vacation.

   A: I want to take a vacation.
   B: Me too.

2. I had a good time yesterday.

3. I don't like fried food.

4. I have a lot of friends.

5. I didn't do my homework.

6. I'm tired.

7. I don't have any money.

8. I'm not very hungry.

9. I have a headache.

Talk about It Write five statements you think your partner will agree with. Then read your statements aloud and see if your partner agrees.

A: I really like ice cream.
B: Me too. / Oh, I don't.
A: I don't like classical music.
B: Me neither. / That's interesting.

4.14 Using Pronouns and Determiners in Writing

A

COMPARE

1a **Dikembe Mutombo** came to the U.S. to study. **Mutombo** wanted to be a doctor, but instead **Mutombo** became a famous basketball player. **Mutombo** wanted to help the people in **Mutombo's** native country, so **Mutombo** helped to build a hospital there.

1b **Dikembe Mutombo** came to the U.S. to study. **He** wanted to be a doctor, but instead **he** became a famous basketball player. **Mutombo** wanted to help the people in **his** native country, so **he** helped to build a hospital there.

Writers often use **pronouns** and **possessive determiners** (such as *his*) in place of nouns and noun phrases, as in **1b**. This makes a piece of writing less repetitious.

It's sometimes necessary to repeat a **noun** or **noun phrase** later in a paragraph, as in **1b**. This helps to make the writing clear for the reader.

GRAMMAR TERM: Clearly connecting sentences to each other in writing is called **cohesion**.

B

FIRST PERSON

2 | **My** grandfather was very important to **me**. **My** first memory of him was when I was just three years old. . . .

SECOND PERSON

3 | People go on vacation to relax. If **you** don't plan carefully, however, **your** vacation can be a disaster. **You** need to pack carefully. . . .

THIRD PERSON

4 | The city of Masdar is in the United Arab Emirates. **It's** a special city because **it** doesn't use any oil. Instead, the city uses solar power. . . .

When we write a story about our own experiences, we usually use the words *I, me, my, we, us,* and *our,* as in **2**. This is called "first person."

When we write advice or instructions, we often use the words *you* and *your,* as in **3**. It's like speaking directly to the reader. This is called "second person."

For a report or a description, we often use the words *he, him, his, she, her, it, they,* and *them,* as in **4**. It's like being an observer. This is called "third person."

62 | Using Pronouns to Reduce Repetition Read the article. Add the missing pronouns and possessive determiners. **4.14 A**

BLAKE MYCOSKIE

Blake Mycoskie is not an ordinary businessman. _____'s a
                                                                                    1
businessman with a cause[11]. Mycoskie is the owner of TOMS: Shoes for

Tomorrow. _____ cause is making sure that poor children have
                             2
shoes. Every time _____ company sells a pair of shoes, a child
                                 3
somewhere gets a free pair. People told _____ that _____
                                                                       4   5
would never succeed, but Mycoskie recently gave away _____
                                                                                                6
millionth pair of shoes.

   Mycoskie got the idea for _____ company while _____
                                                  7   8
was traveling. _____ saw many children without shoes. Because
                             9
_____ didn't have shoes, _____ weren't allowed to go to
        10   11
school. Mycoskie owned a different company at the time. _____
                                                                                          12
sold it to get the money to start _____ shoe company. People like
                                                        13
_____ shoes because _____ are comfortable and _____
        14   15   16
look cool[12]. In addition to this, when _____ buy a pair of
                                                              17
Mycoskie's shoes, _____ are also helping a child live better.
                               18

Think about It Answer these questions.

1. How many times did the writer repeat the name *Mycoskie* in each paragraph above? _____

2. How many times did the writer use *he, him,* or *his* instead? _____

3. What does *they* refer to each time it is used?

   _____

   _____

   _____

   _____

   _____

   _____

---

[11] **a cause:** something a person cares about and wants to help   [12] **cool:** fashionable; attractive

63 | Using Pronouns in Writing Rewrite these paragraphs. Change some (but not all) of the **bold** nouns to pronouns or possessive determiners. `4.14 A`

CHINUA ACHEBE

The writer Chinua Achebe was born in Nigeria in 1930. **Achebe** wrote novels, essays, poetry, and children's stories. **Achebe** learned English at a young age. **Achebe** enjoyed English literature, but **Achebe** felt that English writers wrote inaccurately[13] about African culture. So **Achebe** wrote about **Achebe's** culture—the Igbo culture into which **Achebe** was born.

Even though **Achebe** spoke Igbo, **Achebe** often wrote **Achebe's** stories in English. **Achebe** believed that storytelling helped people understand themselves and where **people** came from. Unfortunately, **Achebe** was injured in a car accident in 1990. **Achebe** was in a wheelchair after the accident, but **Achebe** continued to write and teach. **Achebe** died in 2013.

Write about It Write a paragraph telling your classmates about a famous person of your choice. Include information that you think will be interesting to your classmates.

64 | Choosing a Point of View Which point of view would you choose for each of these writing topics? Check (✓) your answers. Then compare ideas with your classmates. `4.14 B`

WRITING TOPICS	FIRST PERSON	SECOND PERSON	THIRD PERSON
1. Explain how to buy a plane ticket.	☐	☐	☐
2. Write about an experience that changed your life in some way.	☐	☐	☐
3. Describe a movie you saw last year.	☐	☐	☐
4. Describe the greeting customs in another country.	☐	☐	☐
5. Write instructions for making a cup of coffee.	☐	☐	☐
6. Describe your worst experience in school.	☐	☐	☐
7. Explain how the Internet changed the way people communicate.	☐	☐	☐
8. Your friends plan to visit your favorite city. Suggest what they should do there.	☐	☐	☐

[13]**inaccurately:** incorrectly

A | DISCUSSION Choose one of these questions. In a group, come up with five or more answers. Then share the results of your discussion with the class.

QUESTIONS

1. What's important in a good relationship between friends?
2. What's important in a good employer-employee relationship?
3. What's important in a good father-son relationship?
4. What's important in a good mother-daughter relationship?
5. What's important in a good doctor-patient relationship?

A: What's important in a good relationship between friends?
B: I think friends should be honest with each other.
C: And friends should support each other when they are in trouble.

B | DEMONSTRATION Choose a simple device that you use often. Bring the device to class and explain how to use it.

"I think a stapler is a very useful device. You just put some papers together and then slide them between the two parts of the stapler. Then you press down on the stapler, and a staple goes into your papers. Now you can't lose your papers."

C | SURVEY Choose one of these questions or think of your own. Then ask your classmates the question and record their answers. Report the results of your survey to the class.

QUESTIONS

1. Do you think we get too much homework or too little homework?
2. Do you think university students pay too much, too little, or just enough for their classes?
3. Do you think we take too many tests or too few tests?
4. How important is it for children to study art and music in school?
5. Should girls and boys study together or apart?

A few people said . . .	Some people . . .	Three people think . . .
Everybody thinks . . .	No one . . .	

"I asked the question, 'Do you think we get too much homework or too little homework?' No one said we get too little homework, but a few people said we get too much homework. A few people also said we have too many long reading assignments. Everybody else said we get the right amount of homework."

D | PRESENTATION What should a visitor to your country or city see and do? Think of four or five interesting things. Plan your ideas and make a presentation to the class.

"If you visit my hometown, Tokyo, you should definitely go to the fish market at Tsukiji. If you can't sleep after traveling, you can get up early (around 5:30 a.m.) and see the fish buyers there. Then you can go have some fresh sushi for breakfast."

4.15 Summary of Pronouns and Determiners

PRONOUNS   **PRONOUN / DETERMINER**

						Pronoun	Determiner
Subject Pronouns	I	you	he	she	it	✓	—
	we	you		they			
Object Pronouns	me	you	him	her	it	✓	—
	us	you		them			
Possessive Pronouns	mine	yours	his	hers	—	✓	—
	ours	yours		theirs			
Reflexive Pronouns	myself	yourself	himself	herself	itself	✓	—
	ourselves	yourselves		themselves			
Reciprocal Pronouns						✓	—
	each other		one another				

		Pronoun	Determiner
One/Ones	one ones	✓	—
Indefinite Pronouns	someone somebody something	everyone everybody everything	anyone anybody anything	no one nobody nothing	✓	—

DETERMINERS   **PRONOUN / DETERMINER**

						Pronoun	Determiner
Possessive Determiners	my	your	his	her	its	—	✓
	our	your		their			
Measure Words	with plural count nouns a **box** of books a **bunch** of people a **pair** of shoes		with noncount nouns a **bit** of help a **cup** of coffee a **piece** of advice			—	✓

PRONOUN OR DETERMINER   **PRONOUN / DETERMINER**

				Pronoun	Determiner
Demonstratives	with singular count nouns this that	with plural count nouns these those	with noncount nouns this that	✓	✓
Quantifiers	with singular count nouns each every* either neither any	with plural count nouns a few some many a lot (of) any	with noncount nouns a little some much a lot (of) any	✓	✓
Quantifiers for Comparing Amounts		with plural count nouns more fewer too many too few enough	with noncount nouns more less too much too little enough	✓	✓

* We don't use *every* as a pronoun.

Future Forms

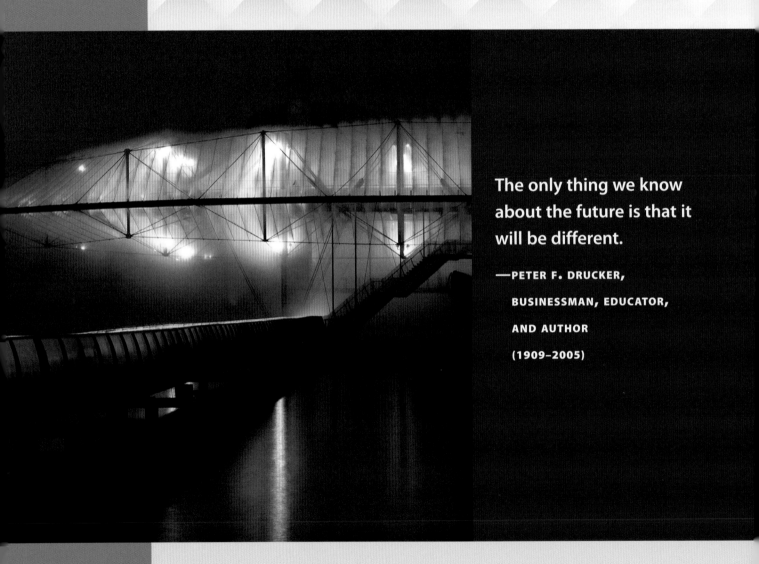

The only thing we know about the future is that it will be different.

—PETER F. DRUCKER,
BUSINESSMAN, EDUCATOR,
AND AUTHOR
(1909–2005)

Talk about It Do you agree or disagree with the quotation above? Why?

WARM-UP

A | Read these sentences and check (✓) *True* or *False*. Then compare answers with your classmates. For each statement, how many people said *true* and how many said *false*?

Your Class

	TRUE	FALSE
1. I'm going to work hard in this class in the future.	☐	☐
2. I'm not going to miss any classes next week.	☐	☐
3. I think I'll learn a lot in this class.	☐	☐
4. We won't have any tests in this class.	☐	☐
5. I'm probably going to pass this class.	☐	☐
6. We aren't going to have class tomorrow.	☐	☐
7. This class is going to be easy.	☐	☐
8. This class finishes in two months.	☐	☐

B | Answer these questions about the sentences above.

1. Which are about a future action or event?

2. Which are predictions?

3. Which are descriptions of plans?

4. What verb forms can we use to talk about the future?

C | Look back at the quotation on page 160. Identify any future verb forms.

We use several different verb forms to talk about the future in English. One common form is **be going to**.

To form statements, we use *am / is / are* (+ *not*) + *going to* + the **base form of a main verb**, as in **1 – 6**. In conversation, we often use contractions.

A

POSITIVE STATEMENTS

		be	going to	base form
1	I	am / 'm	going to	laugh.
2	We / You / They	are / 're	going to	leave.
3	He / She / It	is / 's	going to	work.

NEGATIVE STATEMENTS

		be + not	going to	base form
4	I	am not / 'm not	going to	cry.
5	We / You / They	are not / 're not / aren't	going to	stay.
6	He / She / It	is not / 's not / isn't	going to	stop.

Notice: The verb *be* is a helping verb in the *be going to* form.

B

PREDICTIONS

7 The economy **is going to get** better soon.

8 My stomach hurts. I think I'm **going to be** sick.
(evidence = a stomachache)

9 A: The sky is getting dark.
B: Yeah, I think it's **going to rain**. (evidence = dark sky)

We often use *be going to* when we make a prediction, as in **7 – 9**.

When we have clear evidence or information that something is going to happen, we usually use *be going to*, as in **8 – 9**.

C

PLANS

10 We're **going to spend** a week in California next summer.

11 My daughter bought a big house with a room for me. I'm **going to move** in with her.

12 Don't be late for dinner. We're **going to eat** at 7 tonight.

We often use *be going to* when we talk about future plans that we made earlier, as in **10 – 12**.

GO ONLINE

1 | Forming Statements with *Be Going To* Complete these sentences with the correct form of *be going to* and the word(s) in parentheses. Use contractions where possible. **5.1 A**

TALKING ABOUT WHAT TO EXPECT

1. An important package _____*is going to arrive*_____ tomorrow. Let me know when it's here. (arrive)

2. I have some big news to share, but you _____ it. (not/like)

3. Be careful with your money next month. You _____ some extra cash for books. (need)

4. I don't think anything special _____ this week. (happen)

5. Your boss _____ you an interesting offer next week. Think carefully before you make a decision. (make)

6. I don't think you _____ the answer to your question soon. Maybe next week. (get)

7. The quiz _____ difficult this week, but don't worry. You _____. (be) (not/fail)

8. We _____ early tomorrow. Traffic _____ pretty bad. (leave) (be)

9. My brother probably _____ me move. He has to work. (not/help)

10. One of your best friends _____ you a big secret. (tell)

11. Don't lie. He _____ the truth sooner or later. (find out)

12. I _____ my parents soon. I think they miss me. (visit)

2 | Making Predictions with *Be Going To* Match the situations with the predictions. (More than one answer may be possible.) Then compare with a partner. **5.1 B**

SITUATIONS

1. I don't feel well. _j_

2. I studied hard all week. ____

3. The traffic is terrible today. ____

4. I didn't eat breakfast this morning. ____

5. It's only 6 a.m. and it's already 80 degrees. ____

6. The food smells delicious. ____

7. It's a pretty cloudy day. ____

8. My brother failed his final exam. ____

9. This movie has some great actors in it. ____

10. My sister hates her new job. ____

PREDICTIONS

a. This is going to be a great meal.

b. I think it's going to rain.

c. We're going to be late to the meeting.

d. I think I'm going to pass the test tomorrow.

e. I'm going to be really hungry by lunchtime.

f. I think it's going to be really good.

g. It's going to be really hot today.

h. She's probably going to quit soon.

i. Our father is going to be really upset.

j. I think I'm going to faint[1].

Talk about It Work with a partner. Choose three situations above and write a new prediction for each one. Use *be going to.*

"I don't feel well. I think I'm going to be sick."

3 | Describing Future Plans with *Be Going To* Complete these conversations with the correct form of *be going to* and the word(s) in parentheses. Use contractions. Then practice with a partner. **5.1 C**

1. A: Is Ben going to be here for dinner?

   B: No, he _'s going to work_ late tonight. (work)

2. A: How are you going to get home?

   B: I _____ a taxi. (call)

3. A: Are you doing anything special tomorrow?

   B: Yeah. We _____ the children to see a movie. (take)

4. A: What do you want for dinner tonight?

   B: I _____ tonight. Something is bothering my stomach. (not/eat)

5. A: Is Pam still angry at Janet?

   B: Yeah, really angry. She says she _____ to Janet ever again. (not/speak)

6. A: Your father sure looks happy these days.

   B: Yeah. He _____ soon. You can tell he's looking forward to it. (retire)

> **RESEARCH SAYS...**
>
> We often use *be going to* in conversation, but we rarely use it in writing. The most common use of *be going to* is to describe personal plans or intentions.
>
> CORPUS

[1] **faint:** to suddenly become unconscious for a short time, for example because you are weak or sick

7. A: When's the meeting tonight?

   B: Eight o'clock, but I _____. I'm too tired. (not/go)

8. A: Why are we getting off the highway?

   B: I _____ some gas. The gas tank is almost empty. (get)

9. A: Are your friends still coming over?

   B: Yes, but they _____ dinner first. (have)

10. A: Are you still working on your paper?

   B: Yeah, and I _____. I need another day. (not/finish)

Talk about It Do you have plans for next weekend? Tell a classmate about them.

4 | Making Predictions with *Be Going To* Use the information in each picture below to write one or more predictions. Use *be going to* and a verb or phrase from the box. (Many different sentences are possible.) `5.1 B`

fall	get burned	have (an accident)	run into
flood (the room)	get hurt	land (on the ground)	tip over

ACCIDENTS WAITING TO HAPPEN

1. _____*He's going to get hurt.*_____   2. _____   3. _____

4. _____   5. _____   6. _____

Talk about It Work with a partner and role-play the situations above. One person gives a warning to the other person.

"Be careful! You're going to get hurt."

FYI

We often use *be going to* when we give a warning.

Be careful! That tree **is going to fall**.
Watch out! You **are going to get** hurt.

164

5.2 Questions with *Be Going To*

To form *yes/no* questions with **be going to**, we put *am / is / are* before the subject, as in **1 – 2**.
We can give short answers to *yes/no* questions with *am / is / are*, as in **3 – 6**.
In negative short answers, we often use contractions, as in **5 – 6**.

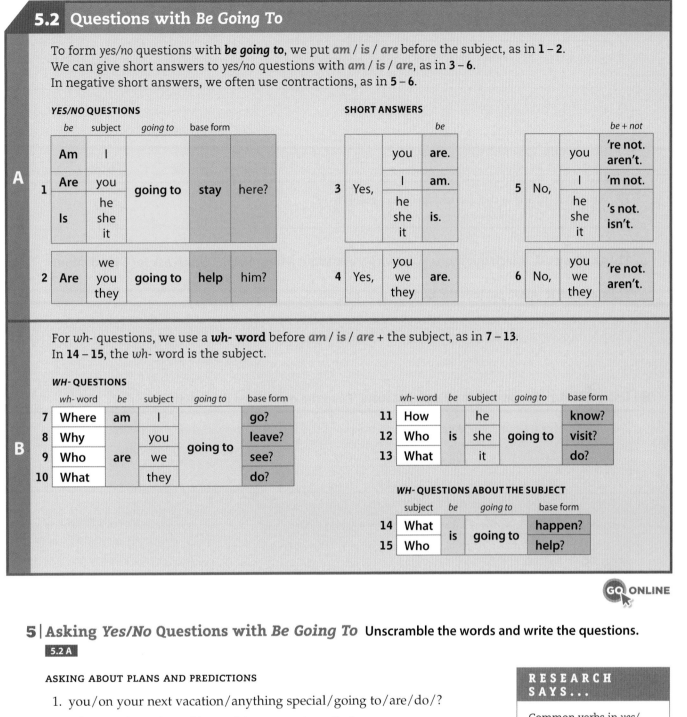

YES/NO QUESTIONS

	be	subject	*going to*	base form	
1	Am	I	going to	stay	here?
	Are	you			
	Is	he she it			
2	Are	we you they	going to	help	him?

SHORT ANSWERS

			be
3	Yes,	you	are.
		I	am.
		he she it	is.

			be + not
5	No,	you	're not. aren't.
		I	'm not.
		he she it	's not. isn't.

			be
4	Yes,	you we they	are.

			be + not
6	No,	you we they	're not. aren't.

For *wh-* questions, we use a **wh- word** before *am / is / are* + the subject, as in **7 – 13**.
In **14 – 15**, the *wh-* word is the subject.

WH- QUESTIONS

	wh- word	be	subject	*going to*	base form
7	Where	am	I	going to	go?
8	Why		you		leave?
9	Who	are	we		see?
10	What		they		do?

	wh- word	be	subject	*going to*	base form
11	How		he		know?
12	Who	is	she	going to	visit?
13	What		it		do?

WH- QUESTIONS ABOUT THE SUBJECT

	subject	be	*going to*	base form
14	What	is	going to	happen?
15	Who			help?

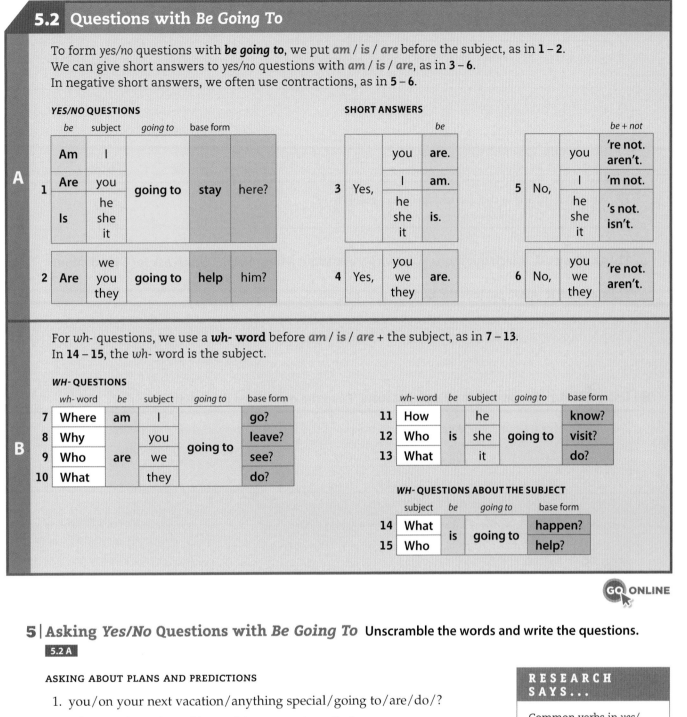

GO ONLINE

5 | Asking *Yes/No* Questions with *Be Going To*   Unscramble the words and write the questions.

5.2 A

ASKING ABOUT PLANS AND PREDICTIONS

1. you/on your next vacation/anything special/going to/are/do/?

   Are you going to do anything special on your next vacation?

2. go/going to/to school/tomorrow/you/are/?

   _____

3. tomorrow/it/rain/is/going to/?

   _____

4. going to/our next exam/be/is/difficult/?

   _____

5. warmer/it/be/anytime soon/is/going to/?

   _____

RESEARCH SAYS...

Common verbs in *yes/ no* questions with *be going to* include:

be	go	say
do	have	take
get	make	

CORPUS

6. offer/English courses/going to/your school/is/next year/?

_____

7. going to/is/soon/anyone in your family/get married/?

_____

8. go/after class/you/going to/shopping/are/?

_____

9. have/in the next few weeks/you/are/going to/any visitors/?

_____

10. we/have/peace in the world/are/ever/going to/?

_____

Think about It Which questions in Activity 5 ask about a future plan? Which ask for a prediction?

Talk about It Ask a partner the questions in Activity 5.

A: *Are you going to do anything special on your next vacation?*
B: *Yes. I'm going to visit my parents.*

6 | Usage Note: Future Time Expressions Read the note. Then do Activity 7.

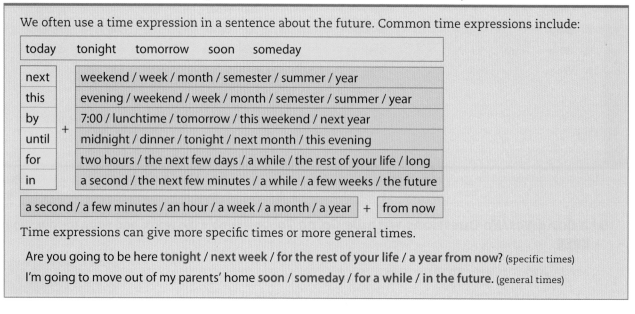

We often use a time expression in a sentence about the future. Common time expressions include:

today	tonight	tomorrow	soon	someday

next	weekend / week / month / semester / summer / year
this	evening / weekend / week / month / semester / summer / year
by	7:00 / lunchtime / tomorrow / this weekend / next year
until	midnight / dinner / tonight / next month / this evening
for	two hours / the next few days / a while / the rest of your life / long
in	a second / the next few minutes / a while / a few weeks / the future

(+)

a second / a few minutes / an hour / a week / a month / a year	+	from now

Time expressions can give more specific times or more general times.

Are you going to be here **tonight / next week / for the rest of your life / a year from now?** (specific times)

I'm going to move out of my parents' home **soon / someday / for a while / in the future.** (general times)

7 | Using Time Expressions Circle the most logical time expression to make meaningful questions.
`5.2 A–B`

ASKING ABOUT FUTURE PLANS

1. Are you going to live here (for the rest of your life) / an hour from now / this weekend)?

2. Are you going to be in this room (someday / for a while / soon)?

3. Where are you going to be (tomorrow / for the rest of your life / by 7:00)?

4. Where are you going to be (for long / someday / 50 years from now)?

5. Are you going to buy a house (an hour from now / tomorrow / someday)?

6. Are you going to graduate (by your next birthday / in a while / ten minutes from now)?

7. Is anything surprising going to happen (in the near future / for long / until tomorrow)?

8. Are you going to go anywhere special (this month / for the next few minutes / in a while)?

9. Are you going to have a job (next year / tonight / this weekend)?

10. Is this class going to continue (soon / someday / until next month)?

Talk about It Ask a partner the questions in Activity 7. Then tell your classmates something interesting you learned about your partner.

8 | Pronunciation Note: "Gonna" Listen to the note. Then do Activity 9.

In everyday conversation, we often reduce the words *going to*. We say "**gonna**" instead.

WRITTEN FORM	SPOKEN FORM
1 Are they going to leave soon?	"Are they **gonna** leave soon?"
2 Who is going to tell him?	"Who's **gonna** tell him?"
3 What is going to happen?	"What's **gonna** happen?"
4 I am going to stay here.	"I'm **gonna** stay here."
5 Somebody is going to find out.	"Somebody's **gonna** find out."

WARNING! We don't normally use "gonna" in writing.

9 | Listening for Reduced Words Listen and repeat the spoken form of these questions. `5.2 A–B`

1. Are you going to do anything special tomorrow?
2. Is it going to rain tomorrow?
3. Are you going to be here in an hour?
4. Are the stores going to be open tomorrow?
5. Are you going to stay up late tonight?
6. What are you going to do tonight?
7. Where are you going to go on your next trip?
8. When are you going to get up tomorrow?
9. How long are you going to stay at school today?
10. How much longer are you going to be here?

Talk about It Choose one of the questions above and interview five classmates. Report the results to the class.

"I asked the question, 'Where are you going to go on your next trip?' Three people are going to visit relatives. One person doesn't know, and one person is going to go someplace warm."

10 | Asking Questions with *Be Going To* Complete these conversations with the correct form of *be going to* and the word(s) in parentheses. Use contractions where possible. `5.2 A–B`

1. A: Do you have plans for the weekend?

    B: Yeah. Josh and I _____*are going to drive*_____ to New York. (drive)

    A: Where _____? (you/stay)

    B: With Josh's friends.

    A: Sounds like fun. _____ a play? (you/see)

    B: Yeah, we have tickets for *Once*.

2. A: Are all these books yours?

    B: Uh-huh.

    A: What _____ with them when you move?

    (you/do)

    B: I _____ them with me. (take)

    A: That _____ expensive. (be)

    B: I know.

3. A: _____ the president's speech tonight?

    (you/watch)

    B: I don't think so. I mean, what _____ that's new?

    (she/say)

    A: Yeah, but it _____ a very long speech. (not/be)

    B: OK, maybe.

4. A: Where is everybody?

    B: They're still at work. It _____ a long night

    for them. (be)

    A: Why do you say that?

    B: Because they have a lot of work to do for the meeting tomorrow.

    A: _____ enough time? (they/have)

    B: I think so.

5. A: _____ a new car? (Anne/really/get)

    B: Yeah, a BMW.

    A: That _____ a lot. (cost)

    B: I know.

    A: Where _____ the money from? (she/get)

    B: I have no idea².

6. A: _____ the project? (they/ever/finish)

    B: I don't know. I think it _____ years. (take)

    A: Years? Really?

    B: Uh-huh. And they _____ a lot of extra help. (need)

> **F Y I**
>
> We sometimes use an adverb in a sentence with *be going to*. Notice the placement of the adverb.
>
> Is Tom **really** going to go?
>
> Are we **ever** going to get there?
>
> Are they **still** going to come?
>
> She is **never** going to be happy.

Talk about It Practice the conversations above with a partner. Practice saying *gonna* instead of *going to*.

² **have no idea:** don't know

11 | Error Correction Correct any errors in these sentences. (Some sentences may not have any errors.)

1. Is they going to buy a new car?
2. What you going to do tomorrow?
3. How am I gonna do it?
4. What I am going to tell him?
5. What you gonna do?
6. My youngest brother going to college next year.
7. My parents are going to come, but they not going to have dinner with us.
8. Are you going to see your family while you are there?
9. Who are going to be there tomorrow?

5.3 The Future with *Will*

A

POSITIVE AND NEGATIVE STATEMENTS

	will (+ *not*)	base form	
I		**have**	time tomorrow.
We You They	**will** **'ll**	**wait** **find out** **know**	for you. today. the answer.
1			
He She It	**will not** **won't**	**finish** **get** **work.**	soon. home before me.

Another form we use to talk about the future is **will**. (*Will* is a type of helping verb called a **modal**.) We use the same form of *will* with all subjects.

To form statements, we use **will** (+ **not**) + the **base form of a main verb**, as in **1**. In conversation, we often use contractions.

won't = will not

YES/NO QUESTIONS AND SHORT ANSWERS

	will	subject	base form	
2	**Will**	I / you / he / she / it / we / they	**be**	late?

			will
3	Yes,	I / you / he / she / it / we / they	**will.**
	No,		**won't.**

To form *yes/no* questions, we put **will** before the subject, as in **2**. We can give short answers to *yes/no* questions with **will** and **won't**, as in **3**.

WH- QUESTIONS

	wh- word	*will*	subject	base form	
4	**How**	**will**	**I**	**know?**	

	subject	*will*	base form	
5	**What**	**will**	**happen**	next?

For *wh-* questions, we use a *wh-* word before **will**, as in **4 – 5**.

For more information on modals, see Units 6 and 9.

B

PREDICTIONS

6 Many people think the economy **will get** better soon.
(= Many people think the economy is going to get better soon.)

7 In the future, cars **will be** much smaller.

We can use *will* to make a prediction, as in **6 – 7**. It is often similar in meaning to **be going to**.

C

PLANS, PROMISES, OFFERS, AND REQUESTS

8 I'm tired. I think I**'ll go** home.

9 I**'ll see** you tomorrow.

10 Thanks for the money. I**'ll pay** you back tomorrow.

11 I promise I **won't be** late.

12 You rest. I**'ll fix** dinner for everyone.

13 A: Where's my purse?
B: It's on your desk. I**'ll get** it for you.

14 I need to know. **Will** you please **tell** me the truth?

15 **Will** you **do** me a favor?

We can also use *will* for:

• a plan or decision that we make at the moment of speaking, as in **8 – 9**

• a promise, as in **10 – 11**

• an offer of help, as in **12 – 13**

• a request, as in **14 – 15**

GO ONLINE

12 | Noticing _Will_ Read this text. Underline the uses of _will_ + a verb. Do you think these are predictions or plans? Why? `5.3 A`

Dreaming for a Better World

We are a second-grade class at Brown Elementary School in Natick. We have been learning about the work of Martin Luther King, Jr. and his dreams. As a class we made a list of our dreams to make the world a better place to live. We have a dream that:

There <u>will be</u> peace.

People will stop smoking.

No one will litter.

There will be no such things as weapons or guns.

Everyone will help each other and get along[3].

There will be no bad guys.

People won't pollute the ocean.

There will be no more violence, swearing[4], stealing, name calling, or mischief[5].

Houses will not burn down.

People will play nicely.

More people will have smiles on their faces.

We hope that our dreams come true.

F Y I

We can use _will be_ or _is/are going to be_ after _there_.

There will be peace.
There is going to be peace.

13 | Making Predictions with _Will_ How will things change by 2050? Complete the predictions below with _will_ or _won't_ and a verb from the box. (You can use a verb more than once.) `5.3 A–B`

be	design	do	have	live	stay	take	use

By the Year 2050

1. Robots _____will do_____ most household chores.

2. There _____ only one language in the world.

3. People _____ cars to get around.

4. Students _____ in school until the age of 30.

5. There _____ fewer countries in the world.

6. Most people _____ more than 100 years.

7. People _____ their own clothes.

8. Students _____ all their classes from their homes.

9. Television _____ very different.

---

[3] **get along:** to be friendly
[4] **swearing:** using bad language

[5] **mischief:** activities that cause trouble or harm

10. Self-driving cars _____ commercially available.

11. The world _____ warmer.

12. We _____ enough food for everyone on earth.

Think about It Could you use *be going to* instead of *will* in the sentences in Activity 13?

Talk about It How likely is each prediction in Activity 13? Tell your classmates your ideas.

14 | Pronunciation Note: Contractions with *Will* Listen to the note. Then do Activities 15 and 16.

We often pronounce *will* like 'll after pronouns, nouns, question words, and the word *there*.

WRITTEN FORM	**SPOKEN FORM**
1 I**'ll** call him.	I'll call him.
2 The store **will** open at 10.	The store['ll] open at 10.
3 Where **will** he be?	Where['ll] he be?
4 There **will** be plenty to do.	There['ll] be plenty to do.

WARNING! We can write the contraction 'll with subject pronouns (*I, you, he, she, it, we,* or *they*). However, we don't usually write 'll with other subjects. We write the full form *will* instead.

The contraction **'ll** is usually easy to hear before a **vowel sound** because the /l/ sound connects with the vowel sound.

5 I'll **o**pen the window.
6 My parents['ll] **u**nderstand.
7 Who['ll] **a**sk him?

The contraction **'ll** is often harder to hear before a **consonant sound** because we don't usually pronounce the /l/ sound clearly.

8 She'll **h**elp you.
9 Dinner['ll] **b**e late.
10 Things['ll] **g**et better.

15 | Listening for Contractions Listen and check (✓) the sentence you hear. [5.3 A–C]

1. ☑ a. I drink coffee.
   ☐ b. I'll drink coffee.

2. ☐ a. I do a good job.
   ☐ b. I'll do a good job.

3. ☐ a. We have time.
   ☐ b. We'll have time.

4. ☐ a. They want it.
   ☐ b. They'll want it.

5. ☐ a. You love it.
   ☐ b. You'll love it.

6. ☐ a. I have a salad.
   ☐ b. I'll have a salad.

7. ☐ a. The students get there on time.
   ☐ b. The students['ll] get there on time.

8. ☐ a. People like you better.
   ☐ b. People['ll] like you better.

9. ☐ a. They worry about it.
   ☐ b. They'll worry about it.

10. ☐ a. They show you.
    ☐ b. They'll show you.

11. ☐ a. I put it there.
    ☐ b. I'll put it there.

12. ☐ a. My parents take him to school.
    ☐ b. My parents['ll] take him to school.

13. ☐ a. I come here often.
    ☐ b. I'll come here often.

14. ☐ a. We work hard.
    ☐ b. We'll work hard.

15. ☐ a. Things change.
    ☐ b. Things['ll] change.

16. ☐ a. I try to be nice.
    ☐ b. I'll try to be nice.

Talk about It Work with a partner. Read a sentence in each pair in Activity 15. Ask your partner to say "Sentence A" or "Sentence B."

🔊 **16 | Listening for Contractions** Listen and write the full (uncontracted) form of the missing words. `5.3 A–C`

1. _____*Everything will*_____ be OK.
2. _____ we get there?
3. _____ be a lot of people there.
4. _____ help you.
5. _____ see.
6. _____ be ready soon.

7. _____ you do there?
8. _____ be a great day.
9. _____ be surprised.
10. _____ do it.
11. _____ you know there?
12. _____ be snow tomorrow.

Talk about It Work with a partner. Choose three of the sentences above and use them to create short conversations. Present one conversation to the class. Say *'ll* where appropriate.

A: Oh, no! I can't find my cell phone.
B: Don't worry. Everything['ll] be OK! I'll help you look for it.

17 | Using *Will* for Promises Complete these promises with *'ll* or *won't*. `5.3 C`

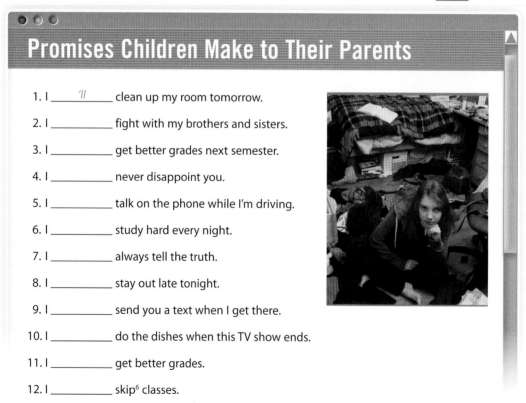

Promises Children Make to Their Parents

1. I _____*'ll*_____ clean up my room tomorrow.
2. I _____ fight with my brothers and sisters.
3. I _____ get better grades next semester.
4. I _____ never disappoint you.
5. I _____ talk on the phone while I'm driving.
6. I _____ study hard every night.
7. I _____ always tell the truth.
8. I _____ stay out late tonight.
9. I _____ send you a text when I get there.
10. I _____ do the dishes when this TV show ends.
11. I _____ get better grades.
12. I _____ skip[6] classes.

Write about It What are some promises that parents make to their children? Write five sentences. Then read your sentences to a classmate.

[6] **skip:** to not attend

18 | Talking about the Future with *Will* Complete the sentences below with *will* or *'ll* and a verb from the box. Then identify how the speaker is using *will*. Write *prediction, plan, promise, offer of help,* or *request.* `5.3 B-C`

bring	forget	get	go	help	join	pay	put	see	take

PREDICTION, PLAN, PROMISE, OFFER OF HELP, OR REQUEST?

1. A: Are you coming to lunch with us?

   B: Not today. I don't have time for lunch.

   A: I _____*'ll bring*_____ you a sandwich. How about that?

   B: Thanks. I _____ you back tomorrow.

   > 1A. *offer of help*
   >
   > 1B.

2. A: Are you ready to leave?

   B: Not yet. I still have to copy these articles.

   A: I _____ you with that.

   B: Thanks. It _____ faster with two people.

   > 2A.
   >
   > 2B.

3. A: Is that new pizza place any good?

   B: We like it. We're going to eat there again tonight.

   A: Maybe we _____ you.

   > 3.

4. A: It's getting late. I don't think you're going to finish it.

   B: Don't worry. We _____ it done.

   > 4.

5. A: Hey, John, can you help me?

   B: Sorry, I'm busy.

   A: But it _____ only _____ ten minutes.

   B: OK, OK.

   > 5.

6. A: Time is up. _____ you please _____ your pencils down?

   > 6.

7. A: Did you have a good trip?

   B: Yeah, I _____ never _____ it.

   > 7.

8. A: Are you leaving now?

   B: Yeah, but I _____ you tomorrow.

   > 8.

Talk about It Practice the conversations above with a partner.

5.4 Be Going To vs. Will

A	**PREDICTIONS**

A

PREDICTIONS

1 The economy **is going to get** better. I'm sure of it.

2 I think the economy **will get** better.

3 Watch out! That tree **is going to fall**.
(NOT: ~~I think it will fall.~~)

4 What's wrong with Sarah? She looks like she**'s going to cry.** (NOT: ~~She looks like she will cry.~~)

5 The first step in finding a job is to write a resume or complete a job application. In most cases, you **will need** a resume to apply for professional job opportunities. For other types of jobs, you **will complete** an application for employment.

We can often use either **be going to** or **will** to make predictions, as in **1 – 2**. However, different things can affect our choice. For example:

• When we have evidence or information that something is going to happen, we usually use *be going to*, as in **3 – 4**.

• When we make predictions in writing, *will* is much more common than *be going to*, as in **5**.

B

PLANS

6 A: Do you have your plane tickets yet?
B: Yeah, we**'re going to leave** on the 5th.

7 Did you hear? Jill**'s not going to take** that job. She**'s going to go** back to school instead.

8 A: What do you want to do tonight?
B: Oh, I'll probably **go** home.

9 A: Can I tell you a secret?
B: Sure. I **won't tell** anyone.

10 A: I'm too tired to cook tonight.
B: That's OK. I**'ll do** it.

11 The library **will be** closed on September 8.

We use both **be going to** and **will** when we talk about future plans, but we use them in different ways.

We often use *be going to* when we talk about a plan made earlier, as in **6 – 7**.

We often use *will* when we make a decision at the moment of speaking, as in **8 – 10**. Using *will* suggests willingness. The speaker is choosing to do something. *Be going to* does not have this meaning.

> A decision made at the moment of speaking might be a plan, a promise, or an offer of help.

When we write about future plans, *will* is much more common than *be going to*, as in **11**.

 GO ONLINE

19 | Making Predictions Which future forms can you use in these sentences? Circle one or both forms.
5.4 A

1. Everything (**will**) / (**is going to**) be fine.

2. I'm not saying it **'ll** / **'s going to** be easy.

3. It **'ll** / **'s going to** take years to do this.

4. Could you hand me a tissue? I think I **'ll** / **'m going to** sneeze.

5. I **'ll** / **'m going to** be OK. I **'ll** / **'m going to** find a new job soon.

6. Watch out! That bookcase **will** / **is going to** fall over.

7. According to a recent poll, 57 percent of people believe that ordinary individuals **will** / **are going to** travel in space by 2050.

8. An enemy **will** / **is going to** agree with you, but a friend **will** / **is going to** argue. (*Russian proverb*)

Think about It In which sentences above is *be going to* a better choice? Why? In which sentences is *will* a better choice? Why?

20 | Identifying Uses of Future Forms Read these conversations and underline the examples of *be going to* and *will*. Then check (✓) why you think the speaker chose each form. 5.4 A–B

	PREDICTION	PLAN	PROMISE	OFFER
1. A: Where's Tom? B: He'll be here any minute.	✓	☐	☐	☐
2. A: Where are you going? B: To Jim's house, but I'll be home early.	☐	☐	☐	☐
3. A: I'm worried about Sarah. B: Really? I think she's going to be OK.	☐	☐	☐	☐
4. A: Tonight's going to be a good night. B: Why do you say that?	☐	☐	☐	☐

5. A: How did you dent the car?
   B: I ran into the side of the garage.
   A: Too bad. Dad's going to be really upset.
	☐	☐	☐	☐

6. A: I think I need a ride to the meeting. B: No problem. I'll drive you.	☐	☐	☐	☐
7. A: Do you need a ride to the meeting? B: No, I'll drive myself.	☐	☐	☐	☐

8. A: Are you busy?
   B: Yeah, I have to finish this paper.
   A: OK. I'll come back at a better time.
	☐	☐	☐	☐

9. A: Where are my glasses? B: I'll get them for you.	☐	☐	☐	☐
10. A: This room is a mess. B: Yeah, it's going to take us all day to clean it.	☐	☐	☐	☐
11. A: Why are you so excited? B: I just got a new job! I'm going to move to California!	☐	☐	☐	☐
12. A: Mom's expecting you for dinner tonight. B: Don't worry. I'll be there.	☐	☐	☐	☐

Think about It In which conversations above does the speaker talk about a plan? Is it a plan made earlier or a plan made at the moment of speaking? How do you know?

Talk about It Practice the conversations above with a partner.

21 | Using *Be Going To* and *Will* Read about each situation. Then work with a partner to write answers to the questions. 5.4 A–B

1. Your doctor's appointment is in 10 minutes, but you are 20 minutes away. You call the doctor's office.

   What do you say to the receptionist?

   "This is Roger Smith calling. My appointment is in 10 minutes, but I'm going to be 10 minutes late."

2. You are on your way to the supermarket. Your aunt tells you that she needs some eggs.

   What do you say?

   _____

3. There is a pile of books on your teacher's desk. He needs someone to hand out one book to each student. What do you say to him?

_____

4. Your friend asks about your plans for tonight. You haven't thought about it before now. What do you say?

_____

5. A friend tells you a secret. She doesn't want you to tell it to anyone else. What do you say to her?

_____

6. Your brother sees you wearing fancy evening clothes. He asks why you are wearing these clothes. What do you say?

_____

7. A child is walking out on a frozen lake. You know the ice on the lake is very thin. What do you yell?

_____

8. Your friend is going to go an office supply store this afternoon. You want your friend to get some printer paper for you. What do you say to your friend?

_____

Talk about It Choose one situation in Activity 21 to role-play for your classmates.

A: Hello. Dr. Brown's office. How can I help you?
B: This is Roger Smith calling. My appointment is in 10 minutes, but I'm going to be 10 minutes late.
A: No problem, Mr. Smith. I'll tell the doctor.

5.5 Using Present Forms to Talk about the Future

A

SCHEDULED EVENTS	
1 The movie **starts in five minutes**.	We sometimes use the **simple present** to talk about a previously scheduled event in the future, as in **1 – 3**. This is especially true when we are talking about timetables and official schedules.
2 Jen's flight **arrives at ten tomorrow**.	
3 My first exam **is next Monday**.	Common verbs used with the simple present to talk about the future include:

arrive	begin	end	leave	start
be	close	finish	open	stop

We usually use a time expression to show that we are talking about the future, as in **1 – 3**.

B

PERSONAL PLANS AND ARRANGEMENTS	
4 I'm **leaving at noon tomorrow**.	We sometimes use the **present progressive** instead of *be going to* when we talk about personal plans and arrangements, as in **4 – 5**.
(= I'm going to leave at noon tomorrow.)	
5 A: What **are you doing this weekend**?	
B: I'm **taking** my brother to the beach.	

6 It's going to rain tomorrow.	We do not use the present progressive to make predictions, as in **6**.
(NOT: ~~It's raining tomorrow.~~)	

22 | Talking about Scheduled Events Read these sentences and check (✓) *True* or *False* based on the schedules. Then correct the false statements. `5.5 A`

SCHEDULED EVENTS

Flight Departures

Flight Number	Destination	Time	Gate
3988	London	3:52 p.m.	8
3417	Paris	5:15 p.m.	24
315	Cairo	7:35 p.m.	32

	TRUE	FALSE
1. Flight 3988 arrives at ~~3:25~~ *3:52* this afternoon.	☐	✓
2. Flight 3417 leaves from Gate 32.	☐	☐
3. Flight 3417 and Flight 315 depart at the same time.	☐	☐

Fall Term

September 10	Classes begin.
November 13	Classes end.
November 16	Final examination period begins.
November 20	Final examination period ends.

	TRUE	FALSE
4. The fall term ends in September this year.	☐	☐
5. The fall term lasts for about two months.	☐	☐
6. Students finish their final exams on November 16.	☐	☐
7. Classes end two weeks before the final exam period.	☐	☐

Parks and Recreation, Town of Franklin

The Franklin Parks and Recreation Department announces an evening with humorist Tim Widener on Sunday, October 27, at Franklin High School. The event begins at 7 p.m. and doors open at 6 p.m. This is an all-age, family-friendly show.

	TRUE	FALSE
8. The program with Tim Widener takes place on October 27.	☐	☐
9. The doors close at 6 p.m.	☐	☐
10. This program is for adults only.	☐	☐

Talk about It What is on your school schedule for the next few months? Share ideas with your classmates.

23 | Talking about the Future with Present Forms Complete this conversation with the simple present or present progressive form of the verb in parentheses. (In some sentences, either form may be possible.) `5.5 A–B`

A: Do you want to get together sometime next week?

B: I can't next week. I _____ to California.
   (1. go)

A: _____ from Boston?
   (2. you / fly)

B: Yeah, my plane _____ at 7 tomorrow morning.
   (3. leave)

A: How long a trip is it?

B: I _____ planes in Denver, so I don't get to
   (4. change)
   Los Angeles until 4.

A: Long day.

Flight Confirmation

Passenger(s)

Anita Erickson
Jill Erickson

Date	Flight	Departure/Arrival
Nov. 10	1228	7:05 a.m. Depart Boston
		10:05 a.m. Arrive Denver
	2224	2:40 p.m. Depart Denver
		4:00 p.m. Arrive Los Angeles

B: Yeah, but I _____ a good book, and my sister _____ with me.
    (5. take)   (6. come)

A: So it's not a work trip?

B: No, we _____ relatives.
    (7. visit)

A: Where _____?
    (8. you / stay)

B: With our relatives. They live in Pasadena.

A: Well, have fun and call me when you get back.

Think about It In which sentences in Activity 23 is either form possible? Why?

24 | Future or Present Time? Underline the simple present and present progressive verbs in these sentences. Then write *F* over the verbs that refer to the future. `5.5 A–B`

1. Our school football team <u>is traveling</u> all over the country this winter.
   F

   I <u>like</u> to watch them play, so I'<u>m planning</u> to go to a few games.

2. Jon leaves for Peru in three days. His mother is really sad about that.

3. The school is having a job fair in the spring. I'm getting my resume

   ready now.

4. In two weeks, I have an appointment with my career counselor. He's

   always very helpful.

5. We usually work from 9 to 5, but tomorrow we are only working until 1.

6. Julia's meeting begins early next Monday, so I'm driving the kids

   to school.

7. Tomorrow is a holiday, so the stores close at 6 p.m.

8. The concert doesn't end until midnight tonight. Do you still want to go?

9. I'm already at the airport, but my brother's plane doesn't arrive for three

   more hours.

10. The train is leaving now, but there's another one in 20 minutes.

W A R N I N G !

We don't use the present progressive to talk about the future when the verb has a non-action meaning.

Present Time

I **have** a doctor's appointment tomorrow. (have = possess)

Future Time

We **are having** a picnic tomorrow. (have = organize)

Think about It Circle the time expressions in the sentences above. Then group them in this chart.

Present time expressions	Future time expressions
	in three days

25 | Error Correction Correct any errors in these conversations. (Some conversations may not have any errors.)

1. A: What are you going to do in Paris?
   B: I'll go to the museums.
2. A: How are you going to get home tonight?
   B: I'm going to take the train.
3. A: Do you think you'll do OK on the test tomorrow?
   B: No, I think I'm failing.
4. A: Do you cook dinner tonight?
   B: No, it's Jill's turn.
5. A: How are you getting to school tomorrow?
   B: My brother takes me.
6. A: Is Sue still here?
   B: Yes, but she leaves soon.
7. A: Do you think Tom will get here on time?
   B: No, I think he's getting here late.
8. A: Is there a movie at 7 tonight?
   B: Yes, I think so.
9. A: Is it snowing tomorrow?
   B: I hope not.

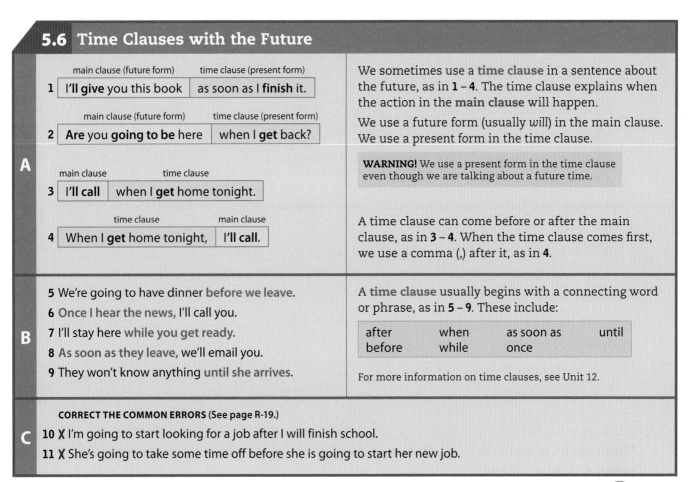

5.6 Time Clauses with the Future

A

	main clause (future form)	time clause (present form)
1	I'll **give** you this book	as soon as I **finish** it.

	main clause (future form)	time clause (present form)
2	**Are** you **going to be** here	when I **get** back?

	main clause	time clause
3	I'll **call**	when I **get** home tonight.

	time clause	main clause
4	When I **get** home tonight,	I'll **call**.

We sometimes use a **time clause** in a sentence about the future, as in **1 – 4**. The time clause explains when the action in the **main clause** will happen.

We use a future form (usually *will*) in the main clause. We use a present form in the time clause.

WARNING! We use a present form in the time clause even though we are talking about a future time.

A time clause can come before or after the main clause, as in **3 – 4**. When the time clause comes first, we use a comma (,) after it, as in **4**.

B

5 We're going to have dinner **before we leave**.

6 **Once I hear the news,** I'll call you.

7 I'll stay here **while you get ready**.

8 **As soon as they leave,** we'll email you.

9 They won't know anything **until she arrives**.

A **time clause** usually begins with a connecting word or phrase, as in **5 – 9**. These include:

after	when	as soon as	until
before	while	once	

For more information on time clauses, see Unit 12.

C

CORRECT THE COMMON ERRORS (See page R-19.)

10 ✗ I'm going to start looking for a job after I will finish school.

11 ✗ She's going to take some time off before she is going to start her new job.

26 | Noticing Time Clauses Underline the time clauses in these sentences and circle the connecting word. Then check (✓) *True* or *False* and compare answers with a partner. `5.6 A–B`

	TRUE	FALSE
1. (When) we have our next test, I'll probably do well.	☐	☐
2. I'll probably be tired when this class is over.	☐	☐
3. As soon as the bell rings, I'm going to run out of this room.	☐	☐
4. It won't be dark when I get home tonight.	☐	☐
5. When I get home today, I'll probably study for a while.	☐	☐
6. I will probably have dinner before I do any homework tonight.	☐	☐
7. My parents won't come to visit me until I have a bigger apartment.	☐	☐
8. Once I finish this course, I'm going to look for a job.	☐	☐

27 | Using Time Clauses Complete these conversations with a present or future form of the verb(s) in parentheses. (More than one form may be possible.) Then practice with a partner. `5.6 A–B`

1. A: Are you going to be here late?

   B: Yeah, I'll probably be here until they _____ *lock* _____ the doors. (lock)

2. A: Did you buy that book Pat wanted?

   B: Not yet. I _____ it when I go to the bookstore. (get)

3. A: What are your plans for the holiday?

   B: I _____ for Florida as soon as classes end. (leave)

4. A: What are we going to do in the city?

   B: We'll figure it out when we _____ there. (get)

5. A: Can I use your laptop?

   B: Can you wait a few minutes? I _____ you use it as soon as I finish this. (let)

6. A: How long are you going to be in London?

   B: Hard to say. I'll just stay there until my grandmother _____ better. (feel)

7. A: Did you make dinner?

   B: No, not yet. I _____ it when this program is over. (make)

8. A: Can you check this paper for me?

   B: Sure. Just put it over there. I _____ it as soon as I _____ some free time. (do/have)

9. A: Do we have any milk?

   B: No, but Tom _____ some when he _____ to the store.
   (buy/go)

10. A: When are we meeting tomorrow?

    B: I don't know, but I _____ you as soon as I _____.
    (call/find out)

Think about It We usually use *will* when we make a promise. In which of the conversations above is someone making a promise?

28 | Completing Clauses Complete these sentences with your own ideas about the future. (Many different answers are possible.) `5.6 A–B`

TIME CLAUSES

1. I'll probably have dinner before *I go to work tonight* _____.
2. I'm not going to stop studying English until _____.
3. Things will get better in the world once _____.
4. I'll probably live here until _____.
5. I'm going to leave school today as soon as _____.
6. I'll be happy when _____.
7. After _____, I'll have some money.
8. I'm going to be sad when _____.

MAIN CLAUSES

9. *I'm going to take a nap* _____ as soon as I get home today.
10. When I have some free time, _____.
11. _____ when we have our next test.
12. _____ until I go on my next vacation.
13. Once this class is over, _____.
14. _____ when I talk to my parents.
15. Before I do any homework, _____.
16. _____ when the weather changes.

Talk about It Read five of your sentences above to a partner and ask your partner to respond.

A: *I'll probably have dinner before I go to work tonight. What about you?*
B: *I don't work at night. But I'll have dinner before I do my homework.*

B: *I'm going to take a nap as soon as I get home today. What about you?*
A: *Me too. I need a nap after a long day.*

29 | Error Correction Correct any errors in these sentences. (Some sentences may not have any errors.)

1. I will study hard until I will graduate from this university.
2. When I get older, I look back on this time and laugh.
3. When my daughter will learn to walk, I will be very excited.
4. When I am in a bad mood, my friends will make me happy.
5. My parents know I will call them when I have a problem.
6. After the exam period will be over, I feel much better.
7. Once my brother is going to get a job, he will get married.

5.7 Using Future Forms in Speaking

A

USING CONTRACTIONS AND FULL FORMS

1 I**'ll see** you later.

2 Please have a seat. The president **will be** here very soon.

3 A: Why won't you help me?
   B: But I **will help** you.

In conversation, we usually use the contracted form *'ll* instead of the full form *will*, as in **1**. Using *will* sounds very formal, as in **2**.

However, we sometimes use the full form *will* to emphasize information or to contradict someone, as in **3**.

B

OMITTING WORDS

4 Talk to you later. (= **I'll** talk to you later.)

5 See you tomorrow? (= **Will we** see you tomorrow?)

6 You going to help me next week?
   (= **Are** you going to help me next week?)

7 You doing anything tomorrow?
   (= **Are** you doing anything tomorrow?)

8 Going home soon? (= **Are you** going home soon?)

In casual conversation, we sometimes omit words in:

• statements with *I'll* or *We'll*, as in **4**

• questions with *Will I* or *Will we*, as in **5**

We sometimes omit words in yes/no questions with *be going to* or the present progressive when the subject is *you*, as in **6 – 8**.

C

YES/NO QUESTIONS

9 **Will** you **get** me a dictionary, please?
   (= A request: Are you willing?)

10 **Are** you **going to get** me a dictionary?
   (= Asking for information: What's your plan?)

11 It's getting late. **Are** you **going to help** me or not?
   (The speaker is annoyed.)

We often use *will* in a yes/no question to make a request, as in **9**. We use *be going to* when we ask for information about a person's plans or intentions, as in **10 – 11**.

WARNING! Using *be going to* in a question can sometimes suggest that the speaker is annoyed, as in **11**.

30 | 'll or Will? Listen to each conversation. Does the speaker use the contracted form *'ll* or the full form *will*? Circle your answer. Then practice with a partner. `5.7 A`

1. A: Do you want to watch this movie tonight?
   B: No, I don't think so.
   A: But you **'ll** / **will** like it.

2. A: Can you get me a ticket for Saturday?
   B: There aren't any left for this Saturday, but they **'ll** / **will** have some for next Saturday.

3. A: Do you want to meet on Monday?
   B: I'm not coming in on Monday, but I **'ll** / **will** be there on Tuesday.

4. A: Did you call Jessica?
   B: No, I **'ll** / **will** call her tomorrow.

5. A: You need to see a doctor.
   B: I know. I **'ll** / **will** see one—tomorrow.

6. A: Don't forget the meeting tonight.
   B: I won't.
   A: You always say that and then you forget.
   B: But I **'ll** / **will** remember tonight's meeting. I'm the main speaker.

7. A: Are you going to miss me?

   B: Of course.

   A: I'm not sure I believe you.

   B: But I 'll / **will** miss you. Honest.

8. A: Why are you so excited?

   B: I 'll / **will** tell you later.

   A: No, tell me now.

   B: Nope. I 'll / **will** tell you after dinner.

Think about It In which conversations in Activity 30 does the speaker use the full form *will*? Why?

31 | Understanding Sentences with Omitted Words Listen and complete these statements and questions. Then listen again and repeat the sentences. `5.7 B`

1. *Be with you* _____ in a minute.
2. _____ soon.
3. _____ tonight.
4. _____ you soon?
5. _____ anywhere tomorrow?

6. _____ this afternoon?
7. _____ this weekend?
8. _____ tonight?
9. _____ tomorrow?
10. _____ with us?

Think about It Rewrite the sentences above and add the omitted words.

1. *I'll be with you in a minute.*
2. _____
3. _____
4. _____
5. _____

6. _____
7. _____
8. _____
9. _____
10. _____

32 | Making a Request or Asking for Information? Listen to each conversation. Is the speaker making a request or asking for information about the other person's plans? Check (✓) your answer. `5.7 C`

	Making a request	Asking for information
1.	☐	✓
2.	☐	☐
3.	☐	☐
4.	☐	☐
5.	☐	☐
6.	☐	☐
7.	☐	☐
8.	☐	☐

Think about It Listen to the conversations again. Does the speaker sound annoyed in any of the conversations? Which ones?

5.8 Using Future Forms in Writing

<table>
<tr>
<td rowspan="2">A</td>
<td>

USING _WILL_ IN WRITING

1 Berries are a great source of vitamins. Including berries in your diet **will help prevent** illness and **keep** you healthy. (magazine article)

2 By 18 months, most children **will have** a vocabulary of about 5 to 20 words. By 24 months, their vocabulary **will include** 150 to 300 words. By 36 months, most children **will know** how to use pronouns correctly. (web article)

</td>
<td>

Will is much more common than _be going to_ in writing, as in **1 – 2**. This use of _will_ expresses a strong prediction or expectation.

Remember: When we use more than one verb after _will_, it's not necessary to repeat _will_, as in **1**.

</td>
</tr>
</table>

<table>
<tr>
<td rowspan="2">B</td>
<td>

INTRODUCING IDEAS

3 This course **will feature** many hands-on activities; students are encouraged to raise questions and issues relevant to the topics covered in class. (from a course syllabus)

4 Each chapter in this book **will** first **present** the key points of a topic. (from a book introduction)

5 This essay **will discuss** the main causes of pollution in Los Angeles. (from an introduction to an essay)

</td>
<td>

In formal writing, writers sometimes tell their readers what is coming later in an essay, chapter, or book. They usually use _will_ to do this, as in **3 – 5**.

When writers identify the goals of a piece of writing, they often use these verbs:

will describe	will explore
will discuss	will present
will examine	

</td>
</tr>
</table>

 ONLINE

33 | Noticing Future Forms in a Magazine Article Which verbs in this article refer to the future? Underline them. **5.8 A**

ADVICE FOR PARENTS WITH YOUNG CHILDREN

As the school year begins, you can help your child reach her goals in the classroom, stay healthy, and feel good about herself. Model these behaviors now to help your child do her best at school.

Eat breakfast. Get a healthy start to each day by eating breakfast together. It will give your whole family fuel for the day ahead.

Get plenty of sleep. This will help your family start the day alert and refreshed. It also will encourage a positive attitude through the day.

Plan ahead. By getting organized, you and your child can find the right balance of work and play. Your child will learn to manage her time better, and so will you.

Make a schedule. Sit down to plan your activities together. This will help you and your child stay involved in each other's lives.

Think about It Why do you think the writer uses _will_ instead of _be going to_ above?

Think about It The **bold** sentences above give advice. What do the sentences with the future form do?

34 | Giving Advice and Explanations Choose one of these topics. Write several sentences giving advice. Use a future form to give the reasons for your advice. `5.8 A`

☐ Advice for a New Student at College   ☐ Advice for Saving Money

☐ Advice for Someone in a New Country   ☐ Advice for Getting Good Grades

☐ How to Take Public Transportation   ☐ How to Run a Successful Business

Example: Advice for a New Student at College
Advice: Get a map of the campus and go exploring.   *Reason: This will introduce you to new places at school.*

Advice	Reasons to follow this advice

Write about It Develop your ideas above into a paragraph. Look back at Activity 33 for a model.

35 | Noticing Future Forms in an Essay Circle the future forms in this essay. Underline the time clauses. Then answer the questions below. `5.8 A`

Essay Prompt: What do you hope to accomplish[5] in the next ten years? Explain.

I want to accomplish a lot of things in the next ten years. I think that this will be a very busy time for me. The first thing I will do is complete my education. I will go to college and study to become a teacher. Getting my degree will be hard work, but it is very important to me. After I get my teaching degree, I will try to find a job in a public school. I think it will be fun to have my own students, and I will work hard to be a very good teacher. Once I have a teaching job, I will think about getting married. Hopefully my partner won't be too hard to find.

FYI

We can also use the simple present form of verbs such as *want*, *hope*, and *plan* to talk about the future.

I **hope** to go to France next year.

I **want** to run my own business in the future.

QUESTIONS

1. Why do you think the writer uses *will* instead of *be going to* in this essay?
2. Why do you think the writer uses the time clauses? What purpose do they serve?

Write about It What do you hope to accomplish in the next ten years? Write several sentences. Try to use a time clause in your answer.

[5] **accomplish:** to do; to complete

36 | Identifying the Goals of an Essay Complete these essay outlines with your own ideas. 5.8 B

Topic: How can students save money while they are going to school?

Overview Statement: This essay will present several ways that students can live cheaply while they are going to school.

The first section will _discuss several ways to save money on food._ _____

_____

The second section will _____

_____

The third section will _____

_____

Topic: What are the problems and concerns of foreign students at universities in this country?

Overview Statement: This essay will _____

_____

The first section will _____

_____

The second section will _____

_____

The third section will _____

_____

WRAP-UP Demonstrate Your Knowledge

A | DISCUSS AND REPORT Work with a partner. Write one or two sentences to answer each question in the chart. Then read your ideas to the class.

How will communication be different in the future?	How will education be different in the future?	How will transportation be different in the future?

"In the future, people will have communication devices inside their heads. We won't need telephones or email."

B | WEB SEARCH Choose a topic from the box and do a web search about how it will be in the future. List five interesting things that you learn.

IN THE FUTURE

cars   cities   computers   fashion   houses   schools

C | PLAN AND REPORT Design a holiday weekend for you and your classmates. Choose a place and make a plan for each morning, afternoon, and evening. Take notes in the chart below.

PLACE _____

	Saturday	Sunday
Morning		
Afternoon		
Evening		

Describe your plan above to your classmates. Your class can then choose the best weekend plan.

"For my holiday weekend, we are going to go to Los Angeles, California.
On Saturday morning, we're going to drive to Venice Beach...."

5.9 Summary of Future Forms

PREDICTIONS	*will +* base form	You'll **have** a great time. Everything **will be** fine.	
	be going to + base form	You**'re going to have** a great time. Everything **is going to be** fine.	
	be going to + base form	The weather report says it**'s going to rain** soon.	with clear evidence
		Watch out! You**'re going to fall**.	Person can't control what happens.
PLANS, PROMISES, OFFERS, AND REQUEST	*be going to* + base form	I**'m going to leave** early to pick up my children at school.	plans made in advance
	will + base form	I**'ll be** there in a minute. I just need to finish.	plans made at the moment of speaking
		I **won't be** late. I know you need me.	promises
		I**'ll come** over tonight to help.	offers of help
		Will you **wait** for me?	requests
	present progressive	We**'re leaving** in an hour.	personal plans and arrangements
	simple present	The train **arrives** at 7 tonight.	scheduled events or fixed plans

6 Modals

We must learn to live together as brothers or perish[1] together as fools[2].

—MARTIN LUTHER KING, JR., LEADER IN THE AFRICAN-AMERICAN CIVIL RIGHTS MOVEMENT (1929–1968)

Talk about It What does the quotation above mean? Do you agree or disagree?

[1] **perish:** to die

[2] **fools:** people who do silly things

WARM-UP

A | Read these conversations. Where does each one take place? Tell your classmates.

Overheard Conversations

1. A: **May** I help you with something?
   B: Yeah. Where **can** I find the laundry detergent?
   A: It's in Aisle 5.
   B: **Could** you check for me? I looked, but I **can't** find it anywhere.

2. A: I'm sorry, but you **can't** bring that bag on board.
   B: OK. So what **should** I do?
   A: You **can** give it to me. I'll check it for you.

3. A: That doesn't look right on him.
   B: He **might** want to try a smaller size.
   A: **Would** you grab one for us?
   B: Of course.

B | Answer these questions about the conversations above.

1. The words in blue are modals. What verb form comes after a modal?

2. How do you form a negative statement with a modal?

3. How do you form a question with a modal?

4. Is there a different form of the modal for a third-person singular subject?

5. Are these statements about the past, present, or future?

C | Look back at the quotation on page 188. Identify any modal forms.

6.1 Overview of Modals; Statements with Modals

A

WHAT IS A MODAL?

	main verb	
1a	Maria	**swims**	at the Community Center almost every day.

	modal + main verb	
1b	Maria	**can't**	**swim**	on Sundays because the pool is closed.

	modal + main verb	
1c	I think she	**should**	**swim**	on her school swim team. She's really good.

A **modal** is a kind of helping verb. It gives us more information about a **main verb**. Compare:

- Sentence **1a** uses a main verb alone to show a statement of fact.
- Sentences **1b** and **1c** use the modals **can** and **should** to give more information about the main verb *swim*.

The simple (one-word) modals are:

can	may	must	shall	will
could	might		should	would

Most modals have more than one meaning.

GRAMMAR TERM: Helping verbs (such as modals) are also called **auxiliary verbs**.

B

POSITIVE STATEMENTS

		modal	base form
2	I You He She It We You They	**can** **should** **must**	**start.**

NEGATIVE STATEMENTS

		modal + *not*	base form
3	I You He She It We You They	**cannot** **can't** **should not** **shouldn't** **must not** **mustn't**	**start.**

To make statements with simple modals, we use a **modal** (**+ *not***) + the **base form of a main verb**, as in **2 – 3**. We use the same modal form with all subjects.

We often contract a modal and the word *not*, especially in conversation, as in **3**.

> **WARNING!** We don't use two simple modals together. (NOT: ~~You must can start.~~)

 GO ONLINE

---

1 | Noticing Modals Circle the modals in these sentences. Underline the main verb that goes with each modal. `6.1 A–B`

PROFESSOR GANTRY'S TIPS FOR IMPROVING YOUR ENGLISH

1. To expand[3] your vocabulary, you (should) read something in English every day.

2. You can keep a vocabulary notebook to help you remember new words.

3. To improve your listening ability, you should watch TV or videos in English every day.

4. You shouldn't stop practicing your English, even during vacations.

5. If you don't know many English speakers, you can meet people online and chat with them.

6. You can keep a journal for everyday writing practice.

7. Remember that you must work hard if you want to improve.

8. Most important, you mustn't get discouraged[4]!

> **FYI**
>
> We use **helping verbs** together with **main verbs**. There are many different kinds of helping verbs. For example:
>
> Tom **is studying** a lot these days.
>
> Mary **doesn't live** in New York anymore.
>
> Next month, our class **will study** earth science.
>
> Susan **can't study** on Sundays because she works.

---

[3] **expand:** to increase

[4] **discouraged:** without confidence

Talk about It How many of the suggestions in Activity 1 do you follow? Compare ideas with a partner.

A: *I read something in English almost every day.*
B: *That's good. I don't read something every day, but I watch TV in English.*

Write about It Write two or three other ways to improve your English. Share your ideas with your classmates.

2 | Error Correction Correct any errors in these sentences but do not change the modal. (Some sentences may not have any errors.) `6.1 A–B`

RULES AND REGULATIONS

1. Students must to come to class on time.

   Students must come to class on time.

2. Customers are can pay with cash or a credit card.
3. Employees don't can wear jeans to work.
4. Guests shouldn't smoking in the rooms.
5. Clerks should be polite and courteous at all times.
6. Employees not can make personal phone calls at work.
7. Students must brought a laptop to class every day.
8. A customer cannot sit in the front seat with the driver.
9. Only a customer can uses the restroom.

Think about It Based on the sentences above, check (✓) the true statements about simple modals. Then share your answers with your classmates.

TRUE

- ☐ We can use the word *to* directly after a modal.
- ☐ We can use the verb *be* before a modal.
- ☐ To make a modal negative, we use *not* after the modal.
- ☐ We can use a main verb + *-ing* directly after a modal.
- ☐ We can use a past verb form after a modal.
- ☐ We use a main verb + *-s* / *-es* after a modal after singular subjects.
- ☐ We use the same modal form with all subjects.

Talk about It Where might you see each of the rules above? Share your ideas with a partner.

A: *The first rule is "Students must come to class on time." You probably see that rule in a class syllabus.*
B: *Or maybe in a student handbook.*

6.2 Questions with Modals

A

YES/NO QUESTIONS

	modal	subject	base form
1	Can / Should	I / you / he / she / it / we / you / they	start?

SHORT ANSWERS

			modal (+ *not*)
2	Yes,	you / I / he / she / it / you / we / they	can. / should.
	No,	you / I / he / she / it / you / we / they	can't. / shouldn't.

To form *yes/no* questions with modals, we put the **modal** before the subject and use the **base form of a main verb**, as in **1**.

We can give short answers to *yes/no* questions with the modal alone, as in **2**. In negative short answers, we often use contractions.

WARNING! We don't begin modal questions with other helping verbs (such as *be* or *do*).
(NOT: ~~Do I can . . . ?~~ or ~~Are they should . . . ?~~)

B

WH- QUESTIONS

	wh- word	modal	subject	base form	
3	What	should	I	do?	
4	How	can	you	lose	the game?
5	Where	should	Tom	meet	us?
6	When	can	she	come?	
7	Why	should	people	care	about the ocean?

	subject	modal		base form	
8	Who	should		come	to the meeting?
9	What	can		go	wrong?

For *wh-* questions, we use a **wh- word** + a **modal** and the **base form of a main verb**, as in **3 – 9**.

GO ONLINE

---

3 | Identifying Questions and Statements Circle the modals and underline the main verbs in these statements and questions. Then add a period or a question mark to each one. Who says each sentence? Check (✓) your ideas. `6.2 A`

AT THE DOCTOR'S OFFICE	DOCTOR	RECEPTIONIST	PATIENT
1. (Can) you please <u>take</u> a deep breath?	✓	☐	☐
2. Patients must sign in here	☐	☐	☐
3. Should I take this medicine every day	☐	☐	☐
4. Visitors can stay until 6 p.m. on weekdays	☐	☐	☐
5. You should make your next appointment now	☐	☐	☐
6. Can I speak to the doctor	☐	☐	☐
7. Should I go back to the waiting room	☐	☐	☐
8. You can go back to work next week	☐	☐	☐

---

4 | Using *Wh-* Questions with Modals Put the words in the correct order to make *wh-* questions. `6.2 B`

ASKING FOR INFORMATION

1. should / I / when / pay / for my classes

   When should I pay for my classes?

2. I / who / should / talk to / about joining

3. I / my account balance / can / find / where

192

4. can/tickets/buy/we/when

5. what time/we/get in line/should

6. the receipt/we/how long/keep/should

7. my car/can/park/I/where

8. keep/how long/I/can/a book

9. should/what time/we/get together

10. she/where/sign up/can/for that class

11. can/who/a ride/me/give

Talk about It In what situations do people use each question in Activity 4? Share ideas with your classmates.

"The first question is 'When should I pay for my classes?' You probably ask that when you're registering for classes."

6.3 Permission with *Can* and *Could*

<table>
<tr><td rowspan="2">A</td><td>

GIVING AND DENYING PERMISSION

1 A: Alan **can watch** TV until 5. Then he needs to clean his room before dinner.
B: No problem, Mrs. Parker.

2 A: Do you want that piece of cake?
B: No, I'm full. You **can have** it.

3 A: Excuse me. You **can't use** your cell phone in here.
B: Oh, sorry! I didn't see the sign.

4 A: Is Tara here?
B: She is, but she **can't go out** until she finishes her homework.

</td><td>

In conversation, we often use sentences with **can** to give permission, as in **1 – 2**. This means that something is allowed.

We use **can't** to refuse permission or say something is not allowed, as in **3 – 4**.

Notice: The contracted form *can't* is more common than the full form *cannot*, especially in conversation.

</td></tr>
<tr><td>

ASKING FOR PERMISSION

5 A: **Can** I **have** a copy of that article?
B: Sure.

6 A: **Can** Tony **stay** for dinner?
B: Of course. He's always welcome.

7 A: **Could** I **look** at that picture again?
B: Absolutely. Here you go.

8 A: **Could** we **use** your car this afternoon?
B: Oh, sorry. I need it today.

</td><td>

To ask for permission, we usually use **can** or **could**, as in **5 – 8**. *Could* usually sounds more polite than *can*.

To respond, we usually use expressions like *Sure*, *Of course*, etc., as in **5 – 7**. To say no politely, we often use *sorry* and give a reason, as in **8**.

WARNING! When we respond to a permission question, we don't typically use *can*. (*Yes, you can* is not very common.) Don't use *could* to respond to permission questions. (NOT: ~~Yes, you could~~ or ~~No, you couldn't.~~)

</td></tr>
</table>

 ONLINE

5 | Giving and Refusing Permission with *Can* and *Can't* Complete these statements with *can* or *can't* and a verb from the box. (More than one answer may be possible.) `6.3 A`

THE PERSON IN CHARGE[5]

Bus driver to passenger

1. Please move back behind the line. You _____ *can't stand* _____ in this area.

2. Keep your transfer[6]. You _____ it again.

Boss to employee

3. You _____ home a little early today. We're not busy.

4. You _____ personal calls during work hours.

bring
buy
come
eat
go
make
park
stand
start
use

---

[5] **in charge:** responsible for someone or something

[6] **transfer:** a ticket that a passenger can use to change buses without paying again

Security guard to amusement park guest

5. This area is full right now. You _____ a new line over there along the fence.

6. I'm sorry. You _____ your food on the ride. The trash cans are over there.

Police officer to driver

7. You _____ this way. We're closing the street.

8. You _____ your car over there. See where the other cars are?

Parent to child

9. You _____ whatever you want. It's your money.

10. You _____ candy every day. It'll ruin[7] your teeth.

bring
buy
come
eat
go
make
park
stand
start
use

Write about It What other things would the people in Activity 5 say to give or deny permission? Write more sentences for three of the people in charge. Use *can* or *can't*.

Boss: I'm sorry. You can't take tomorrow off. We have too much work to do.

6 | Pronunciation Note: *Can/Can't/Could* Listen to the note. Then do Activities 7–9.

In positive statements, we don't usually stress **can**. This means we pronounce it as /kən/ or /kn/. In negative statements, however, we usually stress **can't**. We pronounce it as /kænt°/*.

POSITIVE STATEMENTS (sounds like /kən/ or /kn/)

1 You **can** EAT as many vegetables as you want.

2 You **can** CALL me after 9.

NEGATIVE STATEMENTS (sounds like /kænt°/)

3 You **CAN'T** eat dessert yet.

4 You **CAN'T** call before 9.

WARNING! If you stress the word *can* in a statement, listeners may think you said *can't*.

In yes/no questions, we don't usually stress **can** or **could**. (We usually pronounce *could* as /kʊd/ or /kd/.) It is often difficult to hear the difference between them in informal speech.

YES/NO QUESTIONS

5 A: **Can** I use this pen? (sounds like /kən/ or /kn/)
  B: Of course.

6 A: **Could** I take a piece of paper? (sounds like /kʊd/ or /kd/)
  B: Sure, no problem.

* The symbol ° means a consonant is "unreleased." For example, in the word *can't*, the final t does not make a hard t sound.

7 | Listening for *Can* and *Can't* Listen and circle the modal you hear—*can* or *can't*. 6.3 A

1. You **can** / **can't** have dessert tonight.

2. The children **can** / **can't** stay up late.

3. Students **can** / **can't** bring food to class.

4. You **can** / **can't** use your notes during the test.

5. You **can** / **can't** sell your used books.

6. Customers **can** / **can't** seat themselves.

[7] **ruin:** to damage something so that it is no longer good

7. Passengers **can** / **can't** use cell phones during the trip.

8. You **can** / **can't** enter the building anytime after 6 p.m.

9. You **can** / **can't** wear T-shirts in the office.

10. Employees **can** / **can't** park in front of the store.

Talk about It Take turns reading the sentences in Activity 7 to a partner. Use *can* or *can't*. Your partner listens and says yes if you used *can* and no if you used *can't*.

A: You can't stay in this room.
B: No.

8 | Making Statements with *Can* and *Can't* Write *can* or *can't* to make true statements about your school. Take turns reading your sentences to a partner. Discuss any differences between your answers. `6.3 A`

ON CAMPUS

1. You _____ study in the library after midnight.

2. You _____ make photocopies in the library.

3. Students _____ use the printer in the office.

4. You _____ check out library books for four weeks.

5. You _____ access Wi-Fi everywhere on campus.

6. You _____ buy pizza on campus.

7. Freshmen _____ register for classes before seniors.

8. You _____ pay your tuition with a credit card.

9. You _____ get food late at night.

10. You _____ buy T-shirts in the bookstore.

Write about It Write three more sentences with *can* or *can't* about your school.

9 | Listening for *Can* and *Could* Listen and circle the modal you hear in each question—*can* or *could*. Then listen again and complete the responses. `6.3 B`

1. A: (Can) / Could I take one of these menus?

   B: _*Of course*_____. Help yourself.

2. A: **Can** / **Could** I use your restroom?

   B: _____. It's back there.

3. A: **Can** / **Could** I call you tomorrow?

   B: _____! I'm looking forward to hearing from you.

4. A: **Can** / **Could** we sit at a table by the window?

   B: _____. There isn't one available.

5. A: **Can** / **Could** I borrow your pencil for a minute?

   B: _____. Here you go.

6. A: **Can** / **Could** I take the car tonight?

   B: _____. You need to study.

> **PRONUNCIATION**
>
> With short answers, we pronounce the full form of *can* and *can't*.
>
> A: Can I leave now?
> B: Yes, you **CAN**. But don't go far.

7. A: **Can** / **Could** I take the test tomorrow instead of today?

   B: _____. But you need to come in early.

8. A: **Can** / **Could** the children go upstairs?

   B: _____. But you need to go with them.

Think about It Which responses in Activity 9 are positive and which are negative? Write them in this chart.

Positive	Negative
Of course.	

Talk about It Practice the conversations in Activity 9 with a partner.

10 | Using *Can* and *Could* for Permission For each situation, write a short conversation using *can* or *could* for permission. Use at least two negative responses. 6.3 A–B

1. Car rental customer: You want to take the car out of the country, and you want your friend to be able to drive the car.

   Car rental clerk: Give or deny permission.

   Customer: Can I take this car out of the country?
   Clerk: Yes, but you'll have to pay for insurance.
   Customer: And can my friend drive the car?
   Clerk: I'm sorry. Only you can drive the car.

2. Tenant: You want to hang pictures on the walls and paint the bedroom.

   Landlord: Give or deny permission.

3. Patient: You want to take medicine in the morning instead of at night, and you want to keep exercising.

   Doctor: Give or deny permission.

4. Customer: You want to return a shirt and receive a refund.

   Store clerk: Give or deny permission.

5. Friend 1: You want to borrow a book and keep it for three days.

   Friend 2: Give or deny permission.

> **RESEARCH SAYS...**
>
> It is also possible to use **may** to ask for permission; however, we don't usually do this. *May* usually sounds very polite.
>
> A: Excuse me. **May I borrow** this chair?
> B: I'm sorry. Someone's using it.

Think about It Look at the conversations you wrote above. Write /kn/ over every *can* that you would pronounce without stress. Then practice your conversations and present one to the class.

6.4 Offers with *Can, Could, May,* and *'ll*

A

STATEMENTS

1 A: I **can take** you to the airport.
B: Great! Thanks!

2 A: I **could make** those calls if you want.
B: Thanks so much! I really appreciate that.

3 A: I'm going to be late for work.
B: I'**ll give** you a ride. My car is right outside.

We often use statements with *can* and *could* to make offers, as in **1 – 2**.

We also make offers with *will* using the contraction *'ll*, as in **3**.

B

QUESTIONS

4 A: **Can I open** the door for you?
B: Please!

5 A: **Could we help** you with that?
B: That's OK. I've got it.

6 A: **May I take** your jacket?
B: Thank you.

7 Store clerk: **How may I help** you?
Customer: I'm looking for a silver ring.

We also use questions with *can, could,* and *may* to make offers, as in **4 – 6**. Notice:

←	**MORE POLITE**	→
can	could	may

Store clerks often use *how* with offers of help, as in **7**.

C

POSITIVE RESPONSES	**NEGATIVE RESPONSES**
Positive responses can be less formal, as in **8 – 9**, or more formal, as in **10 – 11**.	For negative responses, it sounds impolite to just say no. Instead, we usually use an expression like the ones in **12 – 15**.

8 A: I'll lend you my notes.
B: **Thanks!**

9 A: May I help you put things away?
B: **Yes, please.**

10 A: I could come in early tomorrow.
B: **Great. It's so nice of you to offer.**

11 A: Could I get you a cup of coffee?
B: **Thanks. I really appreciate that.**

12 A: Can I take you home?
B: **That's all right.**

13 A: I can pay for the tickets.
B: **That's OK, but thanks for offering.**

14 A: Could I get you a pillow?
B: **That won't be necessary. Thanks.**

15 A: Can I call someone for you?
B: **No, but thanks anyway.**

GO ONLINE

11 | Making Offers with *Can, Could,* and *'ll* Complete the offers. Use a subject with *can, could,* or *'ll* and a verb from the box. (More than one answer is possible.) `6.4 A`

A CLASS PRESENTATION

1. A: All right. Who wants to do the research?

   B: _I can look up_ the articles and other information.

2. A: Great! And then we need someone to do the writing.

   C: _____ the script.

   A: Perfect!

3. B: _____ the script—to make sure it doesn't have any mistakes.

   A: Good idea.

create	lend	read
find	look up	take
help	proofread[8]	write

---

[8] **proofread:** to check for mistakes

4. D: I have a good camera. _____ some pictures.

A: Oh, wonderful. But we'll need images from the Web, too.

5. E: _____ some images online.

A: OK. Then someone needs to put it all together.

6. D: Send everything to me. _____ the presentation.

A: Perfect! Then, once the slides are done, we need to record⁹ the narration¹⁰.

7. D: Oh, I don't have a very good microphone on my laptop.

C: _____ you mine. _____ you with the recording, too.

D: Thanks.

8. A: Well, I think that's everything. Send it to me when it's all finished and _____ it!

create	lend	read
find	look up	take
help	proofread	write

Talk about It Work in a group of three or four. Choose an activity from this box. Plan the activity. Take turns making offers to help. Continue until everyone has made two offers.

GROUP EVENTS AND PROJECTS

| a class picnic | a field trip to a museum | a potluck lunch on campus |
| a community cleanup project | a grammar presentation | a study group meeting |

A: What do you want to bring to the picnic?
B: I'll bring a salad.
C: I can bring a tablecloth.

12 | Noticing Offers with *Can* and *Could* Listen and complete these sentences. Then add a period or a question mark to each sentence. `6.4 A–B`

OFFERS FROM HOTEL EMPLOYEES

1. _I can_____ carry your luggage.
2. _____ call you a taxi if you want
3. _____ offer you today's newspaper
4. _____ take a message for you
5. _____ take your bags to your room
6. _____ offer you some coffee
7. _____ move you to a different room
8. _____ help you find something
9. _____ charge¹¹ the bill to your room
10. _____ make a reservation for you

Talk about It Work with a partner. Choose three of the statements or questions above, and use them to create short conversations. Present one of your conversations to the class.

A: I can carry your luggage.
B: Thanks!
A: No problem.

⁹**record:** to save words or music using a machine
¹⁰**narration:** spoken words that explain what is happening

¹¹**charge:** to put money you owe on a bill that you pay later

13 | Listening for Offers with *May* Listen and write the missing words. Then decide where each conversation takes place. Write your ideas in the boxes. (More than one answer is possible.) `6.4 B`

POLITE OFFERS

WHERE?

1. A: Good morning. _May I help_____ you?

    B: Yes. I need to make an appointment.

    | 1. *a doctor's office* |

2. A: _____ your coat?

    B: Thank you.

    | 2. |

3. A: _____ you something to drink?

    B: Yes. Thank you.

    | 3. |

4. A: _____ your order?

    B: Yes, please. I'll have a small salad.

    | 4. |

5. A: _____ you to your table?

    B: Thank you.

    | 5. |

6. A: _____ you a different size?

    B: Sure.

    | 6. |

7. A: _____ you find something?

    B: Yes. I'm looking for some comfortable boots.

    | 7. |

8. A: _____ these to your car for you?

    B: That won't be necessary. Thanks.

    | 8. |

Think about It Why do the speakers use *may* in each of the conversations above?

Write about It Work with a partner. Write another conversation for one of the places above. Use offers with *may I*.

Doctor's office (on the telephone)
A: Hello. May I speak to Dr. Tam?
B: I'm sorry. He's not available. May I take a message?

14 | Usage Note: Using Several Responses Listen to the note. Then do Activities 15 and 16.

> When responding to an offer, we often use several expressions to give a longer (and more polite) response.
> A: Can I help you with that?
> B: **Thanks. I appreciate that. It's so nice of you to offer.**
>
> A: Can I help you with that?
> B: **That's all right, but thanks anyway. I'm OK.**

15 | Identifying Responses Listen to the offers and responses. Check (✓) *Yes* for positive responses and *No* for negative responses. Then listen again and write each response. Practice the conversations with a partner. `6.4 C`

	YES	NO
1. A: Can I get the door for you? B: *Thank you. That would be great.*	✓	☐
2. A: Could I help you with that? B: _____	☐	☐

	YES	NO
3. A: I'll dry the dishes.	☐	☐
B: _____		
4. A: Can I carry that for you?	☐	☐
B: _____		
5. A: I could take those to the office for you.	☐	☐
B: _____		
6. A: Can I call somebody for you?	☐	☐
B: _____		
7. A: We can pay for the supplies.	☐	☐
B: _____		
8. A: Can I bring you something to drink?	☐	☐
B: _____		

Think about It Which speakers in Activity 15 give shorter responses? Why? Discuss your ideas with a partner.

16 | Using Offers and Responses Work with a partner. Write a short conversation for each situation. Use *can*, *could*, *'ll*, and *may*. Then present your conversations to another pair. 6.4 A–C

WHEN PEOPLE NEED HELP

1. A: Your partner doesn't understand the homework. Offer to help.
   B: Accept the offer.

   A: Can I help you with that? I took that class last year.
   B: Thanks! That would be great. I really appreciate it.

2. A: Your friend forgot to bring money for lunch. Offer to pay for today's lunch.
   B: Refuse the offer.

3. A: Your partner looks lost. Offer to help.
   B: Accept the offer. Explain what you are looking for.

4. A: Your teacher is having trouble opening the door because she is holding a large box. Offer to carry the box.
   B: You are the teacher. Accept the offer.

5. A: You have just eaten dinner at your partner's house. Offer to help with the dishes.
   B: Refuse the offer.

6. A: Your partner has just arrived at your home. Offer something to eat or drink.
   B: Accept the offer.

7. A: The class is over and the whiteboard is covered with writing. Offer to help the teacher.
   B: You are the teacher. Accept the offer.

8. A: A friend is having difficulty opening a jar. Offer to help.
   B: Refuse the offer.

Think about It Did any of the conversations you heard above use *may I*? Was the choice appropriate? Why or why not?

6.5 Requests with *Can / Could / Will / Would* and *Would You Mind*

A

MAKING REQUESTS WITH *CAN / COULD / WILL / WOULD*

1 A: **Can** you **please** turn off the light?
B: Sure.

2 A: **Could** you **please** repeat the question?
B: Of course. . . . Where do you live?

3 A: **Will** you **help** me, **please**?
B: No problem. What can I do?

4 A: **Would** you **take** this outside for me?
B: I'm sorry. I hurt my back yesterday and I can't carry anything.

We use **can**, **could**, **will**, and **would** to make requests, as in **1 – 4**. *Could* and *would* usually sound more polite than *can* and *will*.

To make a request more polite, we can put **please** between the subject and the verb, as in **1 – 2**, or at the end, as in **3**.

WARNING! We don't usually use short answers to respond to requests. (NOT: ~~Yes, I can / could / will / would.~~) We usually use expressions like *Sure, Of course,* etc., as in **1 – 3**.

B

MAKING REQUESTS WITH *WOULD YOU MIND*

5 A: **Would you mind** working this Saturday?
B: Not at all. What time should I come in?

6 A: **Would you mind** moving that way a little, **please**?
B: No, of course not.

7 A: **Would you mind** closing the shop today?
B: I'm sorry. I can't. I have an appointment.

We also make polite requests with **would you mind** + the *-ing form of a verb*, as in **5 – 7**. We sometimes use **please** at the end of questions with *would you mind*, as in **6**.

Notice: To agree with a request with *would you mind*, we usually use *no* or another negative word, as in **5 – 6**. It's also possible to respond with words such as *Sure* and *OK*.

GO ONLINE

17 | Listening for *Can/Could/Will/Would* in Requests Listen and complete the requests. (Some of the requests include *please*.) Then practice with a partner. **6.5 A**

REQUESTS FOR AN ADMINISTRATIVE ASSISTANT

1. A: _Would you make_____ four copies of this, please?
   B: Of course.

2. A: _____ me the file on the Jones account?
   B: Sure. I'll be right back.

3. A: _____ Martin Garcia for me?
   B: Sure. Right now?

4. A: _____ a meeting with Jill Summers?
   B: Yes, of course.

5. A: _____ the mail, please? I left it on your desk.
   B: OK.

6. A: _____ until 5:30 tonight?
   B: I'm sorry. I can't tonight. I can come in early tomorrow, though.

7. A: _____ a copy of the report? I can't find mine.
   B: No problem.

8. A: _____ tech support to come by? My computer isn't working.
   B: Sure. I'll call them now.

◀))) 18 | Pronunciation Note: *Would You/Could You* Listen to the note. Then do Activity 19.

> In everyday conversation, we usually pronounce ***would you*** and ***could you*** as "wouldja" and "couldja."
> **1 Would you** hand me the TV remote?   *sounds like*   "Wouldja hand me the TV remote?"
> **2 Could you** open the window?   *sounds like*   "Couldja open the window?"

◀))) 19 | Listening for Reduced Questions Listen to and repeat these questions. Then ask and answer the questions with a partner. `6.5 A`

CLASSROOM FAVORS

1. Would you help me with the homework?
2. Could you lend me a pencil?
3. Could you check my paper for mistakes?
4. Would you pronounce this word for me?
5. Would you tell the teacher that I went to the office?
6. Could you hand me a dictionary?
7. Would you trade[12] seats with me?
8. Could you explain the assignment for me?

   A: Would you help me with the homework?
   B: We don't have any homework, do we?

◀))) 20 | Making Requests with *Would You Mind* Use the verb in parentheses to write a request with *would you mind*. Then listen to the conversations and write the responses. `6.5 B`

GETTING READY FOR A CELEBRATION

1. A: *Would you mind setting* _____ the table? (set)

   B: *Of course not.* _____

2. A: _____ these decorations? (put up)

   B: _____. Where do you want them?

3. A: _____ the napkins? (fold)

   B: _____. Which napkins?

4. A: _____ the glasses? (wash)

   B: _____, but I have to leave for a few minutes.

5. A: _____ some balloons? (blow up)

   B: _____. How many do you want?

6. A: _____ the candles on the cake? (put)

   B: _____

7. A: _____ some ice cream? I forgot to buy it. (pick up)

   B: _____. What kind do you want?

8. A: _____ the chairs? (set up)

   B: _____. I hurt my back.

---

[12]**trade:** to exchange something for something else

Think about It Which responses in Activity 20 are positive and which are negative? Write them in this chart.

Positive (agreeing to a request)	Negative (refusing a request)
Of course not.	

21 | Making Requests Read these requests for clarification. Rewrite each one as a question using the words in parentheses. 6.5 A–B

ASKING FOR CLARIFICATION

1. Repeat that. (can/please)

   Can you repeat that, please?

2. Spell that for me. (could/please)
3. Say that again. (would)

4. Say that more slowly. (would you mind)
5. Speak a little louder. (will/please)
6. Say that one more time. (can)
7. Repeat that. (would you mind)
8. Speak more slowly. (would/please)

Talk about It Ask a partner these questions. When your partner answers, ask for clarification using one of the questions you wrote above.

1. What's your family name?

   A: *What's your family name?*
   B: *Reynoso.*
   A: *I'm sorry. Can you repeat that, please?*

2. What street do you live on?
3. What city were you born in?

4. What's your phone number?
5. What was the name of your high school?
6. What is your date of birth?
7. Where are your parents from?
8. What's your favorite kind of music?
9. Who is your favorite actor?

22 | Making Polite Requests Read each informal situation. Then rewrite each conversation to fit the more formal situation. Use a polite form for every request and response. 6.5 A–B

INFORMAL SITUATIONS

1. Mother: Will you close the door when you leave?

   Son: Yeah, sure.

2. Father: Make sure the back door is locked before you go.

   Son: Uh-huh.

3. Friend 1: Could you move your chair? I can't see.

   Friend 2: OK.

4. Friend 1: Can you open the window? It's hot in here.

   Friend 2: That window doesn't open.

FORMAL SITUATIONS

1. Host: *Would you please close the door when you leave?*

   _____

   Houseguest: *Of course.* _____

2. Host: _____

   _____

   Houseguest: _____

3. Stranger 1: _____

   _____

   Stranger 2: _____

4. Stranger 1: _____

   _____

   Stranger 2: _____

INFORMAL SITUATIONS	FORMAL SITUATIONS
5. Friend 1: Could you help me with this? Friend 2: Sure.	5. Worker: _____ _____ Employer: _____
6. Co-worker 1: Could you hand me that paper? Co-worker 2: Here.	6. Worker: _____ _____ Employer: _____
7. Co-worker 1: Can you show me the new printers? Co-worker 2: They're over there.	7. Customer: _____ _____ Clerk: _____
8. Co-worker 1: Wait for me! I'll be done in a minute. Co-worker 2: OK.	8. Worker: _____ _____ Employer: _____

6.6 Desires and Offers with *Would Like*

A

STATING DESIRES

noun phrase

1 | I'd like | some coffee.

to- infinitive

2 | I'd like | to live | in Paris.

noun phrase   *to-* infinitive

3 | I'd like | my friend | to come | for dinner.

We can use **would like** to talk about desires (what someone wants). We can use *would like* with:

• a **noun phrase**, as in **1**
• a **to- infinitive**, as in **2**
• a **noun phrase** + to- infinitive, as in **3**

Notice the contractions with *would*:

| I'd | you'd | he'd | she'd | * | we'd | they'd |

* We don't contract *it would* in writing.

B

ASKING ABOUT DESIRES

4 A: **Would you like to live** in Europe someday?
B: Yes, I **would**. / No, I **wouldn't**.

5 A: **What would** Sara **like to study**?
B: I think she'**d like to study** medicine.

We can also use *would like* in questions to ask about desires, as in **4 – 5**.

Notice that when we use *would* in a question, we often use *would* in the answer, too.

C

MAKING OFFERS

6 A: **Would you like to come** in?
B: Yes, please. Thank you.

7 A: **Would you like** some tea?
B: I'**d love** some, thanks.

8 A: **Would you like** me **to help** you?
B: That **would be** great, thanks.

We use questions with *would you like* to offer something politely, as in **6 – 8**.

To respond to offers with *would you like*, we may use the responses listed in Chart 6.4 C, as in **6**.

We may also respond to these offers with **I'd love** . . . or **that would be** + an adjective, as in **7 – 8**.

MAKING INVITATIONS

9 A: **Would you like to have** lunch on Friday?
B: I'm sorry. I'**d love to**, but I have to work.

We often use *would you like to* when we make an invitation, as in **9**.

To say no politely, we often use *I'd love to, but* . . . and give a reason. (A response just with *no* may seem impolite.)

GO ONLINE

23 | Using *I'd Like* and *I'd Like To* Complete each conversation with *I'd like* or *I'd like to*. Then practice with a partner.   `6.6 A`

WHAT DO YOU WANT?

1. A: What do you want to do tonight?

   B: _I'd like to_____ go to that new restaurant.

2. A: How can I help you?

   B: _____ two pounds of fish.

3. A: Can I help you?

   B: _____ try on these pants.

4. A: Can I get something for you?

   B: _____ a smaller size, please.

5. A: Good morning. Law Offices.

   B: _____ speak to Mr. Chavez.

6. A: Mr. Chavez is out of the office right now.

   B: _____ leave a message.

7. A: Can I help you find something?

   B: _____ this sweater in red, please.

8. A: Do you need something?

   B: _____ see that paper again.

9. A: Do you want to go to Café Royale?

   B: I think _____ try a new place this week.

10. A: _____ have one of those robot vacuum cleaners.

    B: I wonder how well they work.

> **FYI**
>
> We can also talk about offers with *want*. However, *would like* is more polite.
>
> A: What do you want to do tonight?
> B: I **want to go** to that new restaurant.

24 | Using *Would Like* + Noun Phrase + *To*- Infinitive Write ten sentences using information from this chart and your own ideas.   `6.6 A`

I'd like	movie theaters my friend radio stations textbook writers the administration the cafeteria the management the new student the teacher	to begin . . . to bring . . . to explain . . . to help . . . to make . . . to offer . . . to open . . . to play . . . to prepare . . . to show . . .

I'd like the administration to explain the new schedule.

Talk about It Share some of the sentences you wrote above with a partner. Do you want any of the same things?

A: I'd like the administration to explain the new schedule.
B: Me too! I don't understand it.

25 | Talking about Desires with *Would Like* Complete the questions using the verbs in parentheses and *would like*. Write your answer. **6.6 B**

1. A: What city _____ *would you like to visit* _____? (visit)

   B: _____

2. A: What famous person from history _____
   to? (talk)

   B: _____

3. A: What famous living person _____? (meet)

   B: _____

4. A: What moment in your life _____? (repeat)

   B: _____

5. A: Where _____ on vacation? (go)

   B: _____

6. A: What _____ for dinner tonight? (eat)

   B: _____

7. A: What superpower[13] _____? (have)

   B: _____

8. A: Where _____ in ten years? (be)

   B: _____

9. A: What other languages _____? (learn)

   B: _____

10. A: What special talent[14] _____? (have)

    B: _____

> **FYI**
>
> Sometimes *would like* expresses a wish. This may be something possible or impossible.
>
> **Possible**
> I'd like to visit Beijing.
>
> **Impossible**
> I'd like to talk to Napoleon.

Talk about It Ask a partner the questions above. After your partner answers, ask for more information.

A: What city would you like to visit?
B: I think I'd like to go to Beijing someday.
A: Why?

26 | Making Offers with *Would You Like* Complete these conversations with *would you like to*, *would you like*, or *would you like me to*. Then practice with a partner. **6.6 C**

AT A RESTAURANT

1. A: _____ *Would you like to* _____ look at the menu?

   B: Please.

2. A: _____ a salad?

   B: No, just the sandwich.

3. A: _____ bring you some water?

   B: That would be great.

4. A: _____ some dessert?

   B: No, thanks. I'm stuffed[15].

[13] **superpower:** an imaginary ability, such as being very strong, flying, or becoming invisible

[14] **talent:** a natural ability to do something well
[15] **stuffed:** full (informal)

5. A: _____ take these plates?

   B: Yes, please. We're all finished.

6. A: _____ sit near the window?

   B: Yes, perfect.

7. A: _____ anything else?

   B: Just the check, thanks.

8. A: _____ a table or a booth[16]?

   B: A booth, if there's one open.

Talk about It Work with a partner. Take turns asking the questions in Activity 26 again. Give your own responses.

A: Would you like to look at the menu?
B: No, thanks. I'll just have coffee.

27 | Identifying Offers and Desires Listen and complete these conversations. Add a period or a question mark. Then practice with a partner. `6.6 A–C`

AT A CLOTHING STORE

1. Clerk: Can I help you?

   Customer: Yes. _I'd like to_____ see this in blue.

2. Clerk: _____ keep the hangers

   Customer: Sure.

3. Clerk: _____ a different color

   Customer: No, I think I'll look for something else.

4. Customer: _____ try this on

   Clerk: OK. You can go on into the fitting room.

5. Clerk: Can I help you with anything else?

   Customer: _____ look at some accessories—

   maybe a belt or some jewelry

6. Customer: I don't really like these sleeves.

   Clerk: _____ look for a different style for you

7. Clerk: _____ hold this for you

   Customer: That would be great, thanks.

8. Clerk: _____ help you find something else

   Customer: No, thanks. I'm fine for now.

Think about It Label each sentence you completed above as *D* (desire) or *O* (offer). Then compare with your classmates.

"'I'd like to see this in blue' is a desire."

---

[16]**booth:** a table with benches in a restaurant

28 | Offering Help Write two offers of help for each picture. Remember: Besides *would like*, we can also use *can*, *could*, *may*, and *'ll* to make offers. See Chart 6.4 for more information. 6.6 C

Talk about It With a partner, choose a role for each picture above. One of you is a person in a picture, and the other is offering help. Role-play a conversation. Don't look at the offers you wrote.

A: *Can I help you with the door?*
B: *Yes, please!*
A: *No problem.*

29 | Making Invitations Work with a partner. One person invites the other to do something from the list on the left. The other person accepts. Then change roles. (Use the information in the boxes to begin and accept.) 6.6 C

1. have dinner with me

   A: *Are you doing anything tonight?*
   B: *No, not really.*
   A: *Would you like to have dinner with me?*
   B: *That sounds great!*

2. work in my group
3. sit next to me
4. watch a movie with me
5. come to a football game
6. join my group for lunch
7. study together after school
8. go to the park with me

BEGINNING AN INVITATION	
Are you busy later today?	Are you doing anything tonight?
Are you free on Saturday?	Do you have plans this weekend?

ACCEPTING AN INVITATION	
I'd love to.	That would be great.
Sure. What time?	Yeah. That sounds like fun.

Talk about It Role-play several of the invitations above again. This time, turn down the invitations by saying, "I'm sorry. I'd love to, but . . ." and giving an excuse.

6.7 Preferences with *Would Rather* and *(Would) Prefer*

A

WOULD RATHER VS. *WOULD PREFER*

1 A: Do you want to go out tonight?
B: No, I'd rather stay home.

2 A: Would you like some coffee?
B: I'd rather not have caffeine at this hour.

3 A: Do you know when you want to meet?
B: Well, I'd prefer a morning this week if that works for you.

4 A: Would you like coffee or tea?
B: I'd prefer coffee. Thanks.

When we prefer one situation to another, we often use *would rather (not)* + the **base form of a main verb**, as in **1 – 2**.

When we prefer one thing to another, we can use *would prefer* + a **noun phrase**, as in **3 – 4**.

> Notice: It is common to contract *would* as *'d*, especially in everyday conversation.

For information on using *prefer* + a gerund or to- infinitive, see Unit 7, pages 230 and 236.

B

GENERAL PREFERENCES: *WOULD RATHER* AND *PREFER*

5 Todd would rather wear jeans **than** dress up.

6 I would rather watch basketball **than** watch baseball any day.

7 Tina prefers raspberries **to** strawberries.
(NOT: ~~Tina would prefer raspberries to strawberries.~~)

8 A: Do you like tea?
B: Not really. I prefer coffee **to** tea.
(NOT: ~~I would prefer coffee to tea.~~)

When we prefer something in general, we can use *would rather*, as in **5 – 6**. We rarely use *would prefer* in this way. Instead, we use *prefer* + a **plural count noun** or **noncount noun**, as in **7 – 8**.

When we state two choices, we use:
- *would rather* A **than** B, as in **5 – 6**
- *prefer* A **to** B, as in **7 – 8**

C

ASKING QUESTIONS ABOUT PREFERENCES

9 A: Would you rather live in a cold place **or** a warm place?
B: I'd rather live in a warm place.

10 A: Would you prefer white **or** wheat bread?
B: Wheat, please.

11 A: Do you prefer warm weather **or** cool weather?
B: I prefer warm weather.

We can ask about preferences using *would rather*, *would prefer*, and *prefer*. We often use **or** to offer a choice in these questions, as in **9 – 11**.

---

30 | Using *I'd Rather* and *I'd Prefer* Underline the uses of *I'd rather* and circle the uses of *I'd prefer* in the responses on the right. Then match each sentence on the left with a response. **6.7 A**

1. Would you like to have a picnic? _g_
2. Do you want to have dinner at 9 tonight? ____
3. Let's get pizza for lunch. ____
4. I'd like to go to the beach today. ____
5. What do you think of your phone? ____
6. Do you want to go shopping? ____
7. Do you want to go to a baseball game tonight? ____
8. Do you like this book? ____

a. I don't know. I think I'd rather stay home.
b. Yes, but I'd prefer one with more activities.
c. Can we do something else? I'd rather not spend money.
d. It's OK but I'd prefer a larger screen.
e. I'd rather not*. I have a sunburn.
f. Actually, I'd prefer an earlier time, if that's OK.
g. I'd rather not eat outside. It's kind of cold.
h. I'd prefer Chinese food, if you don't mind.

Talk about It Work with a partner. Take turns reading the sentences on the left above. Give a new response. Try to use *I'd rather* or *I'd prefer*.

* I'd rather not can be a polite way to say no to a suggestion.

31 | Stating Preferences Complete this survey with *to* or *than*. Then check (✓) *True* or *False*. `6.7 B`

Survey: What Is Your Work Style?

		TRUE	FALSE
1. I would rather work with others _____*than*_____ work alone.		☐	☐
2. I prefer a quiet workplace _____ a noisy one.		☐	☐
3. I'd rather work indoors _____ outdoors.		☐	☐
4. I'd rather wear casual clothes _____ dress up.		☐	☐
5. I prefer a neat desk _____ a messy one.		☐	☐
6. I'd rather work with computers _____ talk to people.		☐	☐
7. I'd rather write _____ work with numbers.		☐	☐
8. I prefer busy days at work _____ slow days.		☐	☐

Write about It Compare your answers to the survey above with a partner. Then write about any differences between you and your partner.

I prefer busy days at work but Maria prefers slow days.

32 | Questions about General Preferences Complete these questions with *would you rather* or *do you prefer*. Add two questions of your own. `6.7 C`

Moving? Take Our Housing Survey

1. _____*Would you rather*_____ live in an apartment or a house?
2. _____ downtown or the suburbs[17]?
3. _____ live on a busy street or a quiet street?
4. _____ live in a single-story home or a home with two floors?
5. _____ carpeting or wood floors?
6. _____ electric appliances or gas appliances?
7. _____ have a yard or a swimming pool?
8. _____ modern homes or older homes?
9. _____
10. _____

FYI

When two choices repeat the same information, we often omit the repeated words.

Would you rather **live in a cold place** or (live in) **a warm place**?

Do you prefer **busy days at work** or **slow days** (at work)?

Talk about It Ask and answer the questions above with a partner.

A: Would you rather live in an apartment or a house?
B: I think I'd rather live in an apartment.
A: Really? Why?
B: I don't want to take care of a yard.

[17] **suburbs:** parts of a city away from downtown, usually with a lot of houses and not many businesses

6.8 Advice with *Should*, *Ought To*, and *Had Better*

A

1 You **should try** the new café. It's fantastic.

2 It's nice to see you. We **ought to visit** more often.

3 You**'d better hurry**. You're going to miss the meeting.

We make suggestions or give advice with **should**, **ought to**, and **had better**, as in **1 – 3**.

Notice: We usually shorten *had better* to *'d better*, as in **3**, especially in speaking.

B

SHOULD

4 You **should call** your mother. She's lonely.

5 You **shouldn't drink** so much soda. It's bad for you.

6 **Should I apply** for this scholarship?

7 What **should I take** for a sore throat?

OUGHT TO

8 You **ought to try** these strawberries. They're fantastic.

We use *should (not)* to give advice or to say that something is a good idea, as in **4 – 5**. We also use *should* to ask for advice, as in **6 – 7**.

Ought to is similar to *should*, but we use it much less often, as in **8**. Notice:

| **ought to** | + | the base form of a verb |

WARNING! We do not usually use *ought to* in negative statements or questions.

C

ADVERBS FOR SOFTENING ADVICE

9 You **should probably call** him tomorrow.

10 You **probably ought to read** the instructions.

11 **Maybe** you **should take** the other class.

12 **Perhaps** you **should call** a lawyer.

We sometimes use the adverbs **probably**, **maybe**, and **perhaps** to soften advice we give. Notice:

• We can use **probably** after *should*, as in **9**.

• We can use **probably** before *ought to*, as in **10**.

• We can use **maybe** and **perhaps** at the beginning of a sentence, as in **11 – 12**.

Perhaps is less common and sounds more formal.

D

HAD BETTER

13 Mother to son: You **had better be** home by 11.

(= If you aren't home by 11, you're going to get in trouble.)

14 They**'d better finish** the roof soon. It's going to rain next week.

15 I**'d better not stay** any longer. I'm going to be late!

We use *had better (not)* to give strong advice, as in **13 – 15**.

We often use *had better* to emphasize that something needs to happen soon. It often suggests that if the person doesn't follow the advice, something bad will happen.

WARNING! *Had better* does not refer to the past, even though it uses *had* (the past of *have*).

 GO ONLINE

---

33 | Noticing Advice Underline the advice in this conversation with *should*, *ought to*, and *had better*. **6.8 A**

VISITING A FRIEND

1. A: I'm so glad you're finally coming to see me! Be sure to bring some jeans and good walking shoes.

   B: OK. Are we going hiking or something?

   A: Yes, on Friday. But <u>you should also bring some nice clothes</u>. I made reservations at a really good restaurant for Saturday night.

2. B: Do I need to bring bedding[18]?

   A: No, don't worry about that. My roommate is gone for the weekend. You should probably bring an extra pillow, though. I think she took hers with her.

3. B: So what else are we doing?

   A: Well, it's up to you. Do you want to go shopping? Or would you rather do something like go to a museum? We've got a great science museum.

   B: Both of those sound good to me.

   A: Well, we won't have time for it all . . . you really ought to visit more often!

[18] **bedding:** sheets, blankets, and pillows

4. B: Maybe I should come again in the summer.

   A: That's a great idea! Come in July. I have two weeks off, and it'll be much warmer and drier. Oh, that reminds me: you'd better bring an umbrella. We've been getting a lot of rain lately.

5. B: I'll do that. Listen, I'd better start packing. I'll call you when I land, OK?

   A: Great! Can't wait to see you!

Think about It Is there any other advice in the conversation in Activity 33 that DOESN'T use a modal form?

34 | Using *Should* and *Shouldn't* for Advice Read this advice. Complete the sentences with *should* or *shouldn't* and an appropriate verb. `6.8 B`

Living with Your Roommates: Tips for Getting Along

1. If you have concerns[19], you _____ *should talk* _____ to your roommates about them. Communication is important.

2. Talk about what "clean" means. Different people have different ideas about cleanliness. You and your roommates _____ this issue to prevent[20] misunderstandings.

3. Make a cleanup schedule, and put it where everyone will see it every day. You _____ the schedule regularly so that one person isn't always doing the same job.

4. Check with your roommates before you put up pictures or decorations. One roommate _____ these decisions alone. Everyone needs to agree.

5. You _____ dirty dishes in the sink where they can attract[21] insects and other pests. You _____ always _____ your dishes right away.

6. You don't need to tell your roommates about everything you do, but you _____ them if you're going to be gone so they don't worry.

7. Respect each other's property. You _____ your roommates' food or borrow your roommates' clothes without permission.

8. Deal with problems right away. If you aren't happy about something, you _____ your roommates immediately. Otherwise, the problems will probably become worse.

Write about It Write three more tips for roommates like the ones above. Then share them with your classmates.

---

[19] **concerns:** worries or problems
[20] **prevent:** to stop something from happening
[21] **attract:** to make someone or something come somewhere

35 | Asking Questions with *Should* Use *should*, a subject, and a verb from the box to ask for advice about each situation. Then practice with a partner. 6.8 B

ask
bring
call
come
get
invite
look for
take
talk to
wait

1. A: Can you please go to the supermarket for me?

   B: What _____ *should I get* _____?

2. A: Now, don't stay out too late, OK?

   B: Well, what time _____ home?

3. A: You really need to get another job.

   B: I know, but what kind of job _____?

4. A: I think you need to get some advice.

   B: Who _____?

5. A: You sound terrible. There's some cough syrup in the cabinet.

   B: Good idea. How much _____?

6. A: Could you please call Andrea for me?

   B: _____ her cell?

7. A: Could you bring some chairs in from the other room?

   B: Sure. How many _____?

8. A: The company has really been doing well lately.

   B: Oh yeah? _____ the owner for a raise?

9. A: The new neighbors seem nice.

   B: Yeah, they do. _____ them over for dinner?

10. A: I wonder why the teacher isn't here yet.

    B: No idea. How long _____ for him?

Talk about It Work with a partner. Choose a place from this box. Ask for and give advice for that place.

classroom	doctor's office	mall	school office	train station

Classroom
A: Where should I sit?
B: You should sit in front.

36 | Using Adverbs with *Should* and *Ought To* Rewrite each sentence in the correct order. 6.8 C

HOW TO MAKE FRIENDS

1. with other people / you / probably / ought to / more time / spend

   You probably ought to spend more time with other people.

2. should / a club / probably / you / join

3. perhaps / join / a study group / should / you

4. you / to / more people / perhaps / introduce yourself / should

5. should / you / be / a little friendlier / maybe

6. volunteer somewhere/you/ought to/perhaps

7. a little more often/should/smile/maybe/you

8. you/ought to/go/maybe/to more social[22] events

Think about It The adverbs in the advice in Activity 36 make it softer. Why and when would we want our advice to be softer?

Write about It Write three more pieces of advice about making friends. Then share them with your classmates.

37 | Using *Had Better* Listen and complete these conversations. Then practice with a partner. **6.8 D**

SHORT ON TIME

1. A: They're waiting for me outside.

   B: _You'd better go._

2. A: The door says "Private."

   B: OK. _____ here, then. I'm sure she'll

   come out pretty soon.

3. A: _____. I've got a lot to do this afternoon.

   B: OK. It was nice seeing you again!

4. A: _____. I think my boss is coming back.

   B: OK. Call me later.

5. A: They're going to run out of those jeans at that price.

   B: You're right. _____ early tomorrow.

6. A: Why isn't Jack here yet?

   B: I don't know. But _____ a good excuse.

7. A: What's he yelling about?

   B: I don't know. But _____ in there. He'll yell at you, too.

8. A: I'm going to the SuperStore.

   B: _____. They close in a half an hour.

9. A: The car is all fixed now.

   B: _____ about that. It took long enough.

10. A: _____! We're leaving in a couple of minutes.

    B: I'm coming. I'm coming.

> **PRONUNCIATION**
>
> It is often difficult to hear the **'d** in sentences with **had better**.
>
> We say: "You better go."
>
> We write: You**'d better** go.

Write about It Write four conversations using the sentences in this box. Practice them with a partner.

I'd better get going.	We'd better stay here.	You'd better be careful.	You'd better hurry.

A: Do you know what time it is?
B: It's 3:00.
A: Oh! I'd better get going.
B: OK. See you later.

---

[22] **social:** connected to doing things with other people

6.9 Suggestions with *May* / *Might* / *Could* and Other Expressions

A

COULD, MIGHT, AND MAY **1** You **could wait** until tomorrow. **2 Maybe** you **could try** again tomorrow. **3** You **might want to think about** that a little more. **4** You **may want to try** that again.	We often use **could** (or **maybe** . . . **could**) to make suggestions, as in **1 – 2**. We also sometimes use the phrase **might** / **may want to** to make polite suggestions, as in **3 – 4**. In this case, *might* and *may* have a meaning similar to "maybe."

B

WHY DON'T / LET'S / HOW ABOUT / WHAT ABOUT **5** A: **Why don't** you **wear** the blue tie? B: Really? Do you think it looks OK? **6** A: **Why doesn't** Bob **wash** dishes while we make dessert? B: OK. What can I do?	We also use other non-modal expressions to make suggestions. We can use **why don't** / **doesn't** to make suggestions, as in **5 – 6**.
7 A: So, where should we go for dinner? B: **Let's try** the new Thai place. **8** A: I'm pretty hungry. B: OK. **Let's go out** right now.	We use **let's** to suggest an activity for you and another person, as in **7 – 8**. *Let's is a short form of let us. We rarely use the full form.*
9 A: What should I make for lunch? B: **How about a tuna sandwich?** **10** A: Who should I call? B: **What about Martin?** I think he can help you. **11** A: **How about taking a walk with me?** B: That sounds good. **12** A: I don't know where to take my aunt. B: **What about taking her to the History Museum?**	We use **how about** and **what about** to make suggestions—often to respond to a request for a suggestion. They are followed by: • a **noun phrase**, as in **9 – 10** • the **-ing form of a verb**, as in **11 – 12**

GO ONLINE

38 | **Making Suggestions with *Could* and *Might/May Want To*** Read these instructions from a teacher to students. Imagine that you have a friend who is not doing well in class. Change the instructions to polite suggestions. Rewrite each sentence with *could*, *might want to*, or *may want to*. 6.9 A

Having Trouble?
Here's How to Improve Your Grades

1. Form a study group.   *You might want to form a study group.*
2. Do fewer extracurricular activities[23].
3. Take better notes in class.
4. Do the practice problems at the end of the chapter, even if the teacher didn't assign them.
5. Do the reading early, so you have time to reread.
6. Proofread and rewrite your essays before you turn them in.
7. Look for online help.
8. Get a tutor.

FYI

Sometimes we make suggestions with **might** (without *want to*):

You **might try** the asparagus. I hear it's delicious.

---

[23] **extracurricular activities:** school activities that are not part of the regular class schedule

Write about It Write two suggestions for succeeding in your English class. Share them with your classmates.

39 | Making Suggestions with *Why Don't* Complete these conversations with suggestions, using your own ideas. Then practice with a partner. `6.9 B`

1. A: I need **some new boots**.

   B: Why don't _you try Robert's? They're having a sale._

   A: Sounds good. Let's go!

2. A: I'm so **tired**.

   B: Why don't _____

   A: I probably should.

3. A: Khalid has **a headache**.

   B: Why doesn't _____

   A: That's a good idea. I think I'll suggest that to him.

4. A: I need **a new phone**.

   B: Why don't _____

   A: Good idea.

5. A: I can't hear **the TV very well**.

   B: Why don't _____

   A: Could you do it for me, please?

6. A: Sara doesn't have **anything to do tonight**.

   B: Why doesn't _____

   A: OK, I'll invite her.

7. A: My **computer** isn't working.

   B: Why don't _____

   A: Yeah. I'll probably do that.

8. A: I can't find **my phone**!

   B: Why don't _____

   A: OK. I'll try that.

I need a new phone.

My computer isn't working.

Talk about It Replace the **bold** words in each conversation above with your own ideas. Make new conversations with a partner.

A: I need **a new computer**.
B: Why don't we go to OfficeWorld? I need some printer ink.
A: Sounds good. Let's go!

40 | Making Suggestions with *How About/What About* and *Let's* Complete each conversation with a suggestion, using your own ideas. Then practice with a partner. `6.9 B`

1. A: I don't know which classes to take next semester.

   B: How about _____?

2. A: I don't know what to make for dinner.

   B: What about _____?

3. A: My cousin is coming to visit. Where should I take her?

   B: What about _____?

4. A: What should we do tonight?

   B: I don't know. Let's _____.

5. A: Who should we invite to the concert?

   B: How about _____?

6. A: I'm so hungry.

   B: Let's _____.

Talk about It Work with a partner. Choose one of the conversations in Activity 40 (or a similar idea), and continue the conversation. Partner A, reject Partner B's first suggestion. Then present your conversation to another pair.

A: I don't know which classes to take next semester.
B: How about calculus?
A: I don't think I need any more math classes.
B: Then maybe you could take a business class.
A: That's a good idea. I'll do that.

41 | Giving Advice and Making Suggestions Write three suggestions for each person's problem. Use *should, had better, may/might want to, why don't,* and *what/how about*. `6.9 A–B`

PROBLEMS

1. I can't get to sleep at night. When I lie down in bed, I just can't stop thinking about things. It takes me hours to fall asleep.

   You should try some breathing exercises. Or you might want to play some soft music.

2. I have a co-worker who keeps talking to me while I'm working. It's very annoying. I try not to be very friendly with him, but he doesn't get the hint[24].

3. I'm having trouble getting my homework done because I'm addicted to the Internet. I turn on my computer to study, and pretty soon I'm watching videos and chatting with friends.

4. I'm always losing things. I leave my sweater in the classroom all the time, last week I lost my car keys, and now I can't find my wallet!

5. I have a friend who only calls me when she has a problem. I don't hear from her for weeks and weeks, and then she'll call and ask for help with something.

Write about It Write about a problem that you or someone you know has. Exchange papers with a partner, and write two suggestions or pieces of advice for each other.

[24]**hint:** something that you say, but not in a direct way

A

MUST (NOT)

1 Schools **must pay** taxes on that income. It is required by law.

2 The government **must cut** spending by 17 percent, or the city will be in trouble.

3 Employees **must not park** in the customer lot.

4 You **mustn't worry** about it.

We use **must**—mostly in writing—to say that something is necessary or is required, as in **1 – 2**.

We use **must not** to say something is not allowed or to strongly advise against something, as in **3 – 4**. We can contract *must not*, as in **4**, but it is not common.

WARNING! Using *must* in this way sounds very formal. We rarely use *must* with this meaning in spoken English.

B

HAVE TO

5 You **have to choose** one of these colors.

6 Everyone **has to help** with the laundry.

7 **Do** you **have to cook** tonight?

8 Why **does** she **have to leave** so early?

9 You **don't have to carry** those books. I'll take them later if you want.

Have to / has to also expresses necessity or requirement, as in **5 – 9**. It is much more common than *must* in speaking.

Have to is a **phrasal modal**. Unlike simple modals, *have to / has to* must agree with the subject.

We use *do / does* to form questions and negatives with **have to**, as in **7 – 9**.

HAD TO

10 A: **Did** he **have to work** late yesterday?
(NOT: ~~Must he work late yesterday?~~)
B: No, he didn't. But he **had to work** late on Tuesday.

We use **had to** and **didn't have to** to talk about things that were or were not necessary in the past, as in **10**.

C

DON'T HAVE TO VS. MUST NOT

11a He **doesn't have to park** the car. I'll be right back.
(This is not necessary. It's a choice.)

11b You **must not park** in a fire lane. (This is not allowed.)

The negative form of **have to**, as in **11a**, means "not necessary." This is not the same meaning as **must not**. **Must not** means something is not allowed or not advisable, as in **11b**.

D

HAVE GOT TO

12 People are not completing their work on time, and that **has got to change**.

13 I've **got to pick up** my brother after school.

14 I **don't have to be** at work until 10.
(NOT: ~~I don't have got to . . .~~)

We also use **have / 've got to** to say that something is necessary, as in **12 – 13**. It is very common in speaking.

We don't use *have got to* in questions or negative sentences. Instead, we use a form of *have to*.

42 | Using *Must* and *Must Not* Read about the problems in the staff break room. Write a list of rules. Use *must* and *must not.* 6.10 A

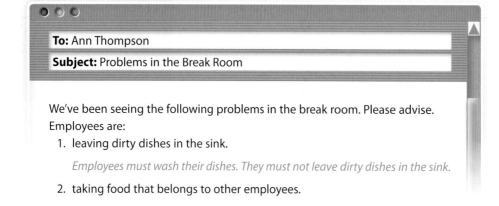

To: Ann Thompson

Subject: Problems in the Break Room

We've been seeing the following problems in the break room. Please advise. Employees are:

1. leaving dirty dishes in the sink.

Employees must wash their dishes. They must not leave dirty dishes in the sink.

2. taking food that belongs to other employees.

Employees are (*continued*):

3. leaving old lunches in the refrigerator.
4. not cleaning up spills in the microwave.
5. leaving crumbs on the table.
6. finishing the coffee and not making a new pot.
7. not returning to work on time.
8. leaving the lights and the television on when no one is in the room.

43 | Using *Have To/Don't Have To* Use *have to/not have to* to talk to a partner about rules for driving. Use these phrases. Do you and your partner agree on the rules? `6.10 B`

DRIVING

1. follow the rules of the road

   A: Everyone has to follow the rules of the road.
   B: Well, police officers don't always have to follow them.

2. wear a seat belt in the back seat
3. use your headlights in the daytime
4. go 15 miles per hour near schools
5. stop at all four-way intersections[25]
6. stop for ambulances
7. register[26] your car every year
8. learn to drive from a professional driving instructor

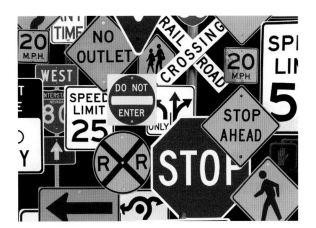

44 | Using *Have To* and *Had To* Complete these air travel conversations with positive and negative forms of *have to* or *had to* + a subject if necessary. Then practice with a partner. `6.10 B`

AIRPORT AND AIRPLANE CONVERSATIONS

1. Passenger 1: ___Do I have to_____ check this bag?

   Passenger 2: I'm not sure. It looks pretty big. It _____ fit under the seat if you want to take it on the plane.

   Passenger 1: Well, I _____ check it last time I flew; they let me put it in an overhead compartment.

2. Passenger: Where _____ check in?

   Clerk: You already have your boarding pass. You _____ check in. Just go straight to the gate.

3. Passenger: Why _____ pay for lunch? I _____ pay on this airline last year.

   Flight attendant: Maybe you were on a longer flight? We offer a free meal on flights over six hours long. I can bring you some peanuts. You _____ pay for those.

---

[25]**intersections:** places where two or more roads meet and cross each other

[26]**register:** to put a name on an official list

4. Passenger 1: Hey, what happened?

Passenger 2: My plane was late. I _____ run all the way across the airport to make my connection. I sure hope my bag doesn't get lost.

Passenger 1: Well, the airline _____ pay for your bag if they lose it.

Passenger 2: I'd rather have my bag!

45 | Using *Have To/Don't Have To* and *Must Not* Write sentences about air travel with *have to, don't have to*, and *must not*. Use these phrases. `6.10 B–C`

AIRLINE RULES

1. bring knives onto the airplane

   Passengers must not bring knives onto the airplane.

2. turn off your phone during takeoff

3. get out of your seat when the seat belt light is on

4. get a boarding pass

5. carry identification

6. pay for coffee or tea

7. buy a ticket for a baby

8. follow the pilot's instructions

Think about It Look at the sentences you wrote above that use *have to*. In which sentences could you change *have to* to *must*? Why?

Write about It Write four more sentences about air travel like the ones above. Use *must, must not, have to*, and *don't have to*.

46 | Using Modals of Obligation Write four sentences about each profession. Use *have to/don't have to* and *must/must not*. Then compare ideas with your classmates. `6.10 B–C`

JOB REQUIREMENTS

1. doctors

2. teachers

3. accountants

4. professional athletes

5. chefs

6. firefighters

7. computer programmers

8. administrative assistants

Doctors have to go to school for a long time.
Doctors must have a license.

47 | Pronunciation Note: *Got To* Listen to the note. Then do Activity 48.

In speaking, we often pronounce **got to** as "gotta." However, we don't write "gotta."

1 I **have got to** go.	*can sound like*	"I've **gotta** go."
2 She **has got to** try harder.	*can sound like*	"She's **gotta** try harder."
3 He **has got to** understand.	*can sound like*	"He's **gotta** understand."

It is also sometimes difficult to hear the **'ve** in sentences with **have got to**.

4 I **have got to** go.	*can sound like*	"I **gotta** go."

48 | Using *Have Got To* Look at Mika's calendar. Talk to a partner about what she *has got to/doesn't have to* do. Pay attention to the pronunciation of *got to*. `6.10 C–D`

	Sunday	Monday	Tuesday	Wednesday	Thursday	Friday	Saturday
morning		work 8–12	take Tim to doctor	work 8–12	do homework	clean house	garden
evening	do laundry	go to accounting class		go to accounting class		have dinner with the Wangs	

"On Sunday evening, Mika's got to do laundry."   *"She doesn't have to do anything on Tuesday evening."*

Talk about It Complete the calendar for yourself. Tell a partner what you've got to do this week. Pay attention to the pronunciation of *got to*.

	Sunday	Monday	Tuesday	Wednesday	Thursday	Friday	Saturday
morning							
evening							

Write about It Write three sentences about the schedule you made above and three sentences about your partner's schedule. Use *have/has got to* and *don't/doesn't have to*.

49 | Error Correction Correct any errors in these sentences. (Some sentences may not have any errors.)

1. Everyone must to work hard so we can finish on time.

   Everyone must work hard so we can finish on time.

2. I've got get home early today.
3. We must not pay for the concert. It's free.
4. Do the parents must come to the ceremony[27]?
5. He doesn't got to make dinner. I'll do it.
6. She hasn't to come to work early this week. The office is opening late.
7. You don't have to copy a friend's software. It's against the law.
8. Last year, we must pay an entrance fee[28], but it's not required anymore.

---

[27] **ceremony:** a formal event, such as a graduation   [28] **fee:** the money you pay to do something

6.11 Using Modals and Related Forms in Speaking

A

ASKING FOR PERMISSION TO SPEAK OR INTERRUPT

1 I'm sorry. **Can I say** something?

2 Can I tell you something?

3 Excuse me. **Could I ask** you a question?

4 I'm sorry. **May I interrupt** for a moment?

5 May I speak to you for a minute?

We often use the modals **can** and **could** as a polite way of interrupting someone or beginning to speak, as in **1 – 3**.

We also use **may** in a similar way, as in **4 – 5**. However, *may* is more formal and less common.

INTRODUCING RELATED IDEAS

6 A: I don't know how I'm going to finish all the papers we have to write this semester.
B: Yes, and **how about** the class project?
A: I know! It's a lot of work.

We can use the expressions **how about** and **what about** to introduce a related idea to a conversation, as in **6**.

B

MAKING A POLITE REQUEST

7 A: **Can I ask you** to speak a little louder?
B: Sure. Can you hear me now?

8 A: **Could I ask you** to close the window?
B: Of course.

9 A: **May I ask you** to be a little quieter?
B: Oh, sorry!

To make a request more polite, as in **7 – 9**, we sometimes use:

Can Could May	I ask	+	you	+	to- infinitive

We often make requests like these in formal situations and to ask for something difficult or uncomfortable.

C

USING REDUCED FORMS IN SPEAKING

10	would you		"wouldja"
11	could you		"couldja"
12	should you		"shouldja"
13	have got to	*sounds like*	"ve gotta"
14	has got to		"sgotta"
15	have to		"hafta"
16	has to		"hasta"

We often use reduced forms with modals in speaking, as in **10 – 16**.

WARNING! We do not write reduced forms.
(NOT: ~~I hafta complete my application by April 1.~~)
(NOT: ~~Wouldja please submit your reference by April 1.~~)

GO ONLINE

50 | Asking for Permission to Speak Listen to these conversations and complete the requests. Then practice with a partner. **6.11 A**

1. A: Excuse me, Professor. _Can I ask you_ _____ something?

   B: Yes, of course. What is it?

2. A: Mrs. Taylor?

   B: Yes?

   A: _____ after class?

3. A: . . . and at that point it looked as if the people were going to—

   B: I'm sorry. _____

   A: Sure. What is it?

4. A: Um. _____ something?

   B: Uh-huh.

5. A: So then I told her that I didn't really think that was a good idea, and—

   B: I'm sorry. _____ for a second?

6. A: That was the most boring book I've ever read.

   B: Are you kidding? I loved it! I thought it was really funny.

   A: No way! How about the part when—

   C: Wait. _____

   A: What?

7. A: Excuse me. _____ for a moment?

   B: Of course. Come on in.

8. A: I was telling my friend that he—

   B: Excuse me. I'm sorry. _____

51 | Having a Group Discussion Work in a group. As a group, choose one of these topics to discuss. As you are talking, use the expressions in the box to add new ideas or interrupt. `6.11 A`

1. a local sports team
2. a current news event
3. a famous person
4. a movie or TV show
5. what you're studying right now

> How about/What about . . . ?
> Can I say something?
> Could I ask a question?
> May I speak for a minute?

A: The Panthers played really well last weekend. They got a goal right away.
B: Yeah, and how about when they scored again? Just after halftime.
C: Can I ask you something?
A: Sure.

52 | Asking for a Favor Write a request for a favor for each situation. Use *can*, *could*, or *may* and a *to*- infinitive. Then compare ideas with a partner. `6.11 B`

1. Your professor is speaking very fast.

   I'm sorry. Can I ask you to speak more slowly?

2. You are leaving a restaurant. You drop your keys and they land under someone else's table.
3. You are trying to study in the library and someone is humming.
4. You meet an author and you want him to sign your book.
5. You are trying to hear a lecture, and someone near you is making a lot of noise.
6. You are at a movie and someone sits down in front of you. She is wearing a large hat.
7. Someone calls you when you are very busy.
8. You want to eat lunch at a table in the cafeteria. Someone has spread books and papers all over the table.
9. You want something at the market that is on a high shelf. There's a tall person standing next to you.
10. You forgot your glasses and can't see from the back of the classroom. All of the seats in front are taken.

53 | Listening for Reduced Modals Listen to these conversations and write the missing words, including the subject and the full form of the modal + verb. Then practice with a partner. Use reduced forms. `6.11 C`

1. A: _Could you bring_____ me the flashlight?

   I can't see what I'm doing.

   B: Sure.

2. A: _____ at 6:00.

   B: OK.

3. A: _____ earlier tomorrow.

   B: OK. I'll tell him.

4. A: _____ these to Sarah?

   I think she needs them.

   B: No problem.

5. A: When _____ back to

   the doctor?

   B: In about two months.

6. A: _____ you something.

   B: Yeah? What is it?

7. A: _____ about that

   already.

   B: How? I didn't tell her.

8. A: Why do _____ this?

   B: The boss wants us to.

6.12 Contrasting Modals in Speaking and Writing

The uses of the modals described in this unit are more common in speaking than in writing.

A

In everyday conversation, we often choose more informal modals or similar expressions, as in **1a – 4a**.

MORE INFORMAL
1a I **want to inquire** about the receptionist job.
2a **Can** you please **send** me the form?
3a **Can** you **help** me?
4a Please **call** me at 401-555-0134.

When we do use the modals from this unit in writing, we often choose a more polite form, as in **1b – 4b**.

MORE POLITE
1b I **would like to inquire** about the receptionist job.
2b **Could** you please **send** me the form?
3b I **would appreciate** your help.
4b **Could** you please **call** me at 401-555-0134?

B

USING *MAY* FOR PERMISSION IN WRITING

5 Passengers **may use** the bike rack on the back of the bus.

6 Passengers **may not bring** bicycles onto the bus.

We rarely use ***may*** for permission in speaking. When we do, it usually sounds very formal and unnatural. However, we do use *may* in writing to give and refuse permission, as in **5 – 6**.

---

54 | Making Requests in Writing Rewrite these sentences so that they are appropriate for more formal writing. `6.12 A`

WRITTEN CORRESPONDENCE

1. Please let us use your letter in our advertising.

   Would you please let us use your letter in our advertising?

2. I want to meet with you about a possible salary increase.

3. Can I return this item?

4. I want to ask about any internship possibilities.

5. Please reply as soon as possible.

6. Will you call me at your earliest convenience?

7. Can you look at the enclosed documents?

8. I want to receive the information as soon as possible.

9. Let me know if you have any questions.

10. Will you send me your contact information?

Write about It Choose one of these situations, and write a short email to your professor making a request. Make sure to explain clearly who you are, exactly what you want, and why. Thank him or her.

| a letter of recommendation | extra-credit homework | more time to complete an assignment |

55 | Using *May/May Not* Use these phrases to write about what students *may* and *may not* do at your school or in your class. Share your sentences with a partner. **6.12 B**

School Rules

1. smoke on campus
2. take food into the library
3. bring coffee into the classroom
4. use cell phones during class
5. wear a hat in the classroom
6. speak without raising their hands
7. miss more than five classes
8. contact their instructors at home

1. Students may not smoke on the central campus.

Write about It What rules would you add to the ones above? Write two more rules for your school. These can be rules that exist or that you think should exist. Then share your ideas with your classmates.

WRAP-UP Demonstrate Your Knowledge

A | SURVEY Ask five classmates these questions and write down their answers. Ask them for the reasons for their answers. (You can ask follow-up questions.)

1. Do you prefer ice cream or cake?
2. Would you rather have an ordinary home in an exotic place or an extraordinary home in an ordinary place?
3. Would you like to travel to outer space?
4. Would you rather be unusual or completely average?
5. Do you prefer early mornings or late nights?
6. Would you like to know your future?
7. Do you prefer classical music or pop music?
8. Would you like to be really famous?
9. Would you rather win $1 million or get your dream job?
10. Would you like to be able to read minds[29]?

Compare answers with a partner. Are there similarities in the answers you got?

[29] **read minds:** to know what other people are thinking

B | BROCHURE Create a short guide to your city. Think about what you would recommend to a visitor. Tell him or her where to go, what to bring, and how to act. Then create your guide. Include both pictures and text if possible. Then present your guide to your classmates.

"Hong Kong is a great city to visit. It's a very international city—a lot like London or New York. You usually have to get a visa to travel to Hong Kong, but that's pretty easy to do. You shouldn't visit during the summer because there are often cyclones. I think the best time to visit is between October and December. When you arrive, you should get . . . "

Tips for Traveling in Hong Kong

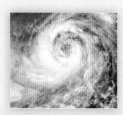

You shouldn't visit Hong Kong during the summer. There are often cyclones. The best time to visit is between October and December.

You should get an Octopus Card after you arrive. This is a quick and easy way to pay for the public transport system.

C | PERSONAL REFLECTION Compare your childhood to adulthood. Think about these questions. Then explain your experience (orally or in writing) to your classmates.

1. What chores did/do you do?
2. What was/is your bedtime?
3. Who prepared/prepares your food?

4. Who was/is in charge of your schedule?
5. Who earned/earns money to support you?
6. Who made/makes the decisions for you?

When I was a kid, I was always in a hurry to grow up. Life seemed easier then. I didn't have to worry about a lot. I had to do some chores—like cleaning my room and taking out the garbage. But my parents took care of me. . . .

D | ROLE-PLAY Work with a partner. Write a conversation for each picture. Use the modals from this unit. Include five or six lines in each conversation.

1.

2.

3.

4.

5.

6.

With your partner, practice your favorite conversation in Activity D. Perform your conversation for the class without reading it. As you listen to other students' role-plays, write down the modals you hear and their uses. For example: *can–permission, should–advice, would you–request.*

6.13 Summary of Modals I

MODALS	USES	EXAMPLES
can	Permission	Can I bring my bicycle onto the bus? I'm sorry. You can't bring your coffee into class.
	Offers	Can I help you with that box? It looks heavy.
	Requests	Can I have a napkin? I spilled something here.
could	Permission	Excuse me. Could I ask you a question?
	Offers	Could I give you a ride somewhere? I could open that package for you.
	Requests	Could you go to the store for me? I don't have time today.
	Suggestions	Maybe you could ask a friend for help.
had better ('d better)	Strong Advice Warning	You had better hurry! Everyone is leaving soon. You'd better not try that again. It's dangerous.
have to (phrasal modal)	Obligation / Lack of Necessity	He has to take one more test. Then he's finished for the year. He gave me the tickets. I didn't have to pay for anything. I couldn't go out last night because I had to work.
may	Permission	May I use your phone? I left mine in the car.
	Offers	May I help you with that?
	Suggestions	You may want to ask your teacher for help. You may not want to take that class—it's very difficult.
might	Suggestions	You might want to wear a coat. It's going to get cold tonight. You might not want to sit there. The seat is wet.
must	Obligation / Prohibition	Employees must wash their hands before returning to work. Employees must not wear jeans or sandals.
ought to	Advice	You ought to try this game. It's really fun.
will ('ll)	Offers	I'll bring you a sandwich.
	Requests	Will you take these downstairs for me?
would ('d)	Offers	Would you like some fruit?
	Desires	I'd love some ice cream. Thank you.
	Requests	Would you move a little to the left? Would you mind repeating that?
	Preferences	Would you prefer a sandwich or a salad? I'd prefer a salad.
		Would you rather eat later? No, I'd rather eat now.

7 Gerunds and *To-* Infinitives

By failing to prepare,
you are preparing to fail.

—BENJAMIN FRANKLIN, WRITER,
   SCIENTIST, AND STATESMAN
   (1706–1790)

Talk about It What does the quotation above mean? Do you agree or disagree?

WARM-UP

A | Read these statements and check (✓) *True* or *False* for you. Then compare answers with a partner. How are you the same or different?

WHAT ARE YOUR LIKES AND DISLIKES?

	TRUE	FALSE
1. I enjoy shopping.	☐	☐
2. I don't mind getting up early in the morning.	☐	☐
3. I love to watch old movies.	☐	☐
4. I like to sing.	☐	☐
5. I hate being late.	☐	☐
6. I'm not interested in traveling.	☐	☐
7. I don't like to exercise.	☐	☐
8. I can't stand to eat vegetables.	☐	☐

B | The green phrases in the statements above are gerunds. The blue phrases are *to*- infinitives. Based on the examples, are these statements true or false? Check (✓) your answers.

	TRUE	FALSE
1. A gerund can be one *-ing* word or a group of words with an *-ing* word.	☐	☐
2. A *to*- infinitive includes *to* + the base form of a verb.	☐	☐
3. Both a gerund and a *to*- infinitive can follow the main verb in a sentence.	☐	☐
4. A gerund can follow a preposition (e.g., *by, in, of*).	☐	☐
5. A *to*- infinitive can follow a preposition.	☐	☐

C | Look back at the quotation on page 228. Identify any gerunds or *to*- infinitives.

7.1 Verb + Gerund

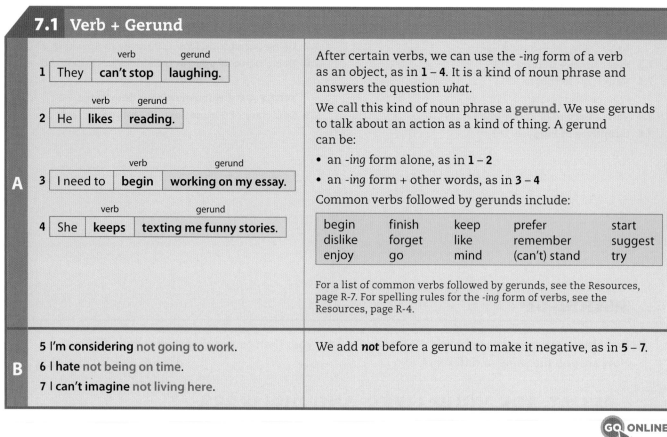

A

	verb	gerund
1	They	can't stop	laughing.

	verb	gerund
2	He	likes	reading.

	verb	gerund
3	I need to	begin	working on my essay.

	verb	gerund
4	She	keeps	texting me funny stories.

After certain verbs, we can use the *-ing* form of a verb as an object, as in **1 – 4**. It is a kind of noun phrase and answers the question *what*.

We call this kind of noun phrase a **gerund**. We use gerunds to talk about an action as a kind of thing. A gerund can be:

- an *-ing* form alone, as in **1 – 2**
- an *-ing* form + other words, as in **3 – 4**

Common verbs followed by gerunds include:

begin	finish	keep	prefer	start
dislike	forget	like	remember	suggest
enjoy	go	mind	(can't) stand	try

For a list of common verbs followed by gerunds, see the Resources, page R-7. For spelling rules for the *-ing* form of verbs, see the Resources, page R-4.

B

5 I'm **considering** not going to work.

6 I **hate** not being on time.

7 I **can't imagine** not living here.

We add **not** before a gerund to make it negative, as in **5 – 7**.

1 | Using a Verb + Gerund in Conversation Complete these conversations with the *-ing* form of the verb in parentheses. Then practice with a partner. `7.1 A`

1. A: I really enjoyed _____*meeting*_____ you. (meet)

   B: Me too.

2. A: Are you busy?

   B: No, we just finished _____. (eat)

3. A: Should I get a new computer? My old one is so slow.

   B: You know, I'd suggest _____. I think there might be

   a sale soon. (wait)

4. A: Do you have that book I lent you?

   B: I don't remember _____ a book from you. (borrow)

5. A: Amanda looks awfully worried these days. What's going on?

   B: I don't know, but I think she's going to quit her job.

   A: But I thought she liked _____ there. (work)

6. A: Why are you in such a hurry?

   B: What do you mean? You know I can't stand _____ late. (be)

7. A: Shhh. Stop _____! (talk)

   B: What's the matter?

   A: I just heard a strange noise.

8. A: Would you like me to drive now?

   B: Not yet. I can keep _____ for a while. (go)

> **PRONUNCIATION**
>
> In everyday conversation, you may hear some English speakers pronounce *-ing* as *-**in'***.
>
> Just quit **thinking** about it.
> (may sound like "thinkin'")
>
> She keeps **saying** the same thing.
> (may sound like "sayin'")

9. A: I'm going to buy a magazine.

   B: Well, don't be long. They're going to begin _____ the airplane

   in a few minutes. (board[1])

10. A: When are you going to start _____ an apartment? (look for)

    B: Next week.

11. A: Does anyone know the answer to the question? Khalid? What do you think?

    B: Would you mind _____ the question? (repeat)

12. A: Would you ever want an office job?

    B: Never! I really dislike _____ all day. (sit)

Think about It Circle the gerunds in Activity 1. Then write each gerund under the correct group in this chart.

A gerund can be an *-ing* form alone.	A gerund can be an *-ing* form + other words.
	meeting you

Think about It Look at the examples in the chart above. What kinds of other words can follow an *-ing* form?

2 | Asking Questions with a Verb + Gerund Complete these questions with the *-ing* form of the verb in parentheses. `7.1 A`

Personal Questions

1. Do you enjoy _____*cooking*_____? (cook)

2. Did you like _____ to school as a child? (go)

3. When did you begin _____ English? (study)

4. Did you start _____ any sports as a child? (play)

5. What is one thing you can remember _____ angry about? (get)

6. What do you usually do after you finish _____ dinner? (eat)

7. What do you suggest _____ for a headache? (take)

8. Is there anything you can't stand _____? (do)

Talk about It Ask a partner the questions above. Then tell the class one thing you learned about your partner.

"Ben doesn't enjoy cooking."

[1] **board:** to get on a bus, train, ship, plane, etc.

3 | Usage Note: *Go* + Gerund Read the note. Then do Activity 4.

> We often use *go* + a **gerund** for types of fun activities and recreation.
>
> | | | |
> |---|---|---|
> | **go** camping | **go** jogging | **go** shopping |
> | **go** exploring | **go** riding | **go** swimming |
> | **go** hiking | **go** running | **go** walking |

4 | Using *Go* + Gerund Complete the questions below with a word or phrase from the box. Use the *-ing* form of the **bold** verb. (Many different questions are possible.) `7.1 A`

> | | | | |
> |---|---|---|---|
> | **camp** (in the woods) | **hike** (in the mountains) | **shop** (for clothes) | **swim** (in the ocean) |
> | **explore** (in your city) | **jog** (in the morning) | **shop** (for food) | **walk** (with friends) |

YOUR HABITS AND YOUR TOWN

1. How often do you go _____ ?
2. Where do you usually go _____ ?
3. When did you last go _____ ?
4. Where did you last go _____ ?
5. Where can you go _____ ?
6. Do you enjoy going _____ ?
7. Do you ever go _____ ?
8. Would you like to go _____ someday?

Talk about It Ask a partner the questions you wrote above. Then tell the class one thing you learned about your partner.

"Maria never goes jogging."

5 | Using *Not* + Gerund Complete these sentences with the *-ing* form of the verb in parentheses. Use *not* where appropriate to make the sentences true. `7.1 B`

PEOPLE'S PREFERENCES

1. Most children love _____ candy. (eat)
2. Most children dislike _____ to bed early. (go)
3. Most children start _____ around age 1. (walk)
4. Most students like _____ a midterm test. (have)
5. Most students prefer _____ lots of homework every night. (do)
6. Many people prefer _____ alone. (travel)
7. Most people dislike _____ on holidays. (work)
8. Most doctors recommend _____. (exercise)
9. Some doctors recommend _____ after 8 p.m. (eat)

Write about It Write six sentences about what you *love, dislike, prefer,* or *recommend*.

I dislike going to bed early.

6 | Error Correction Correct any errors in these sentences. (Some sentences may not have any errors.)

1. She didn't remember she meets me.
2. I finished study at 8 and went out.
3. I like learned languages a lot.
4. We continued walk for a while.
5. I do not like be alone.
6. My grandfather continued worked until he was 80.
7. Many children start learn a second language when they are very young.
8. He speaks English well because he began studied at a young age.
9. I hope you don't mind to answer this question.
10. You can't avoid to make mistakes when you speak a second language.

7.2 Preposition + Gerund

A	**PREPOSITION + GERUND** **1** He left **without** saying anything. **2** You can improve your grades **by** studying more. **3** You can learn a lot **from** traveling.	We sometimes use the **prepositions without**, **by**, and **from** + a **gerund** to answer the question *how*, as in **1 – 3**.
B	**ADJECTIVE + PREPOSITION + GERUND** **4** I'm **tired of** watching this. **5** Aren't you **sick of** working on this? **6** I'm **shy about** giving orders.	Certain adjectives go together with specific prepositions. We often use a gerund after these **adjectives** + **prepositions**, as in **4 – 6**. For a list of common adjectives + prepositions followed by gerunds, see the Resources, page R-8.
C	**VERB + PREPOSITION + GERUND** **7** I don't **feel like** cooking tonight. **8** She's **thinking about** quitting her job. **9** We **look forward to** seeing them.	Certain verbs go together with specific prepositions. We often use a gerund after these **verbs** + **prepositions**, as in **7 – 9**. For a list of common verbs + prepositions followed by gerunds, see the Resources, page R-8.

 ONLINE

7 | Using a Preposition + Gerund Match the first part of each sentence on the left with a preposition + gerund on the right. (More than one answer may be possible.) `7.2 A`

EDUCATION

1. You won't do well on tests __d__
2. You can't learn a foreign language ____
3. You will learn a lot ____
4. You won't make your teacher happy ____
5. You can make your teacher happy ____

    a. by coming to class on time.
    b. by skipping class.
    c. without practicing.
    d. without studying.
    e. from taking notes in class.

HEALTH

6. You probably won't lose weight ____
7. Your skin can turn orange ____
8. You can get lung cancer[2] ____
9. You can damage your skin ____
10. You can lose weight easily ____

    f. by eating less.
    g. from eating too many carrots.
    h. from smoking cigarettes.
    i. without exercising.
    j. by sitting in the sun.

[2] **cancer:** a serious disease

Write about It Think of a different way to complete the first part of each sentence in Activity 7. Use *without, by,* or *from* + a gerund.

You won't do well on tests by not studying.

8 | Using an Adjective + Preposition + Gerund
Write ten meaningful questions using ideas from this chart. Use each gerund in the right column only once. (Many different questions are possible.) **7.2 B**

	Adjective + preposition		Gerund		
Are you	afraid of capable of good at	interested in nervous about tired of	becoming a doctor? being a student? doing puzzles? giving speeches?	getting hurt? listening? teaching?	being a chef in a restaurant? running a business? saying something stupid?

Talk about It Ask a partner the questions you wrote above.

A: Are you interested in becoming a doctor?
B: Do you mean a medical doctor? No, not really.

9 | Using a Verb + Preposition + Gerund
Complete each set of sentences with a verb + preposition from the box. **7.2 C**

1. It's getting late. We should _____*think about*_____ going to bed.

2. Elderly people often _____ falling down.

3. We should probably _____ going swimming. It's too cold.

4. Students often _____ having too much homework.

| complain about |
| forget about |
| think about |
| worry about |

5. Lots of young people _____ becoming an actor or musician.

6. Did you ever _____ doing something that you didn't do?

7. Most people don't _____ working when they are sick.

| admit to |
| dream of |
| feel like |

8. What do you _____ doing next year?

9. Are you going to _____ getting better grades?

10. Some parents don't _____ using physical punishment[3].

11. You should _____ being late to class.

| apologize for |
| believe in |
| plan on |
| work on |

12. My friends and I _____ doing scary things, but we never actually do them.

13. What can you _____ starting a fire?

14. It's dark outside, but I'm going to _____ looking for my lost watch.

| keep on |
| talk about |
| use for |

Write about It Write sentences about yourself using four of the verbs + prepositions above with gerunds.

I sometimes think about changing schools.

[3] **physical punishment:** hitting someone because he or she did something bad

10 | Using a Preposition + Gerund in Conversation Underline the gerunds. What comes before each gerund? Circle the form and check (✓) your answers. Then practice with a partner. `7.2 A–C`

	PREPOSITION ALONE	ADJECTIVE + PREPOSITION	VERB + PREPOSITION
1. A: What's the matter? B: Nothing really. I'm just (tired of) <u>watching this</u>.	☐	✓	☐
2. A: Are you doing anything special for the holiday? B: Yeah. I'm thinking of having some friends over.	☐	☐	☐
3. A: What are you planning on doing tomorrow? B: I'm probably just going to stay home.	☐	☐	☐
4. A: I need to leave early tomorrow. B: OK, but don't go without saying goodbye.	☐	☐	☐
5. A: Did you call David back? B: No. I don't feel like talking to him right now.	☐	☐	☐
6. A: You're really good at making presentations. B: You think so? A: Yeah.	☐	☐	☐
7. A: Are you still looking for an apartment? B: Yes, but I don't have much hope of finding one.	☐	☐	☐
8. A: I'm excited about working together. B: Me too.	☐	☐	☐
9. A: Are you going home soon? B: No, I'm going to keep on studying for a while.	☐	☐	☐

11 | Stating Ideas with Gerunds Complete these sentences with your own ideas. Use gerunds. `7.2 B–C`

ALL ABOUT ME

1. I'm good at _____ .

2. I'm afraid of _____ .

3. I sometimes worry about _____ .

4. I'm not capable of _____ .

5. I dream of _____ .

6. As a child, I sometimes complained about _____
_____ .

7. I often feel like _____ .

8. I think people should apologize for _____
_____ .

> **WARNING!**
>
> Be careful not to confuse a verb + the preposition to (which is followed by a gerund) with a to- infinitive (to + the base form of a verb).
>
> I **look forward to seeing** you. (NOT: ~~I look forward to see you.~~)
> I **want to see** you later.

Talk about It Compare your ideas above with your classmates. Make a list of all your different ideas.

I'm good at . . . organizing things
playing soccer
spending money

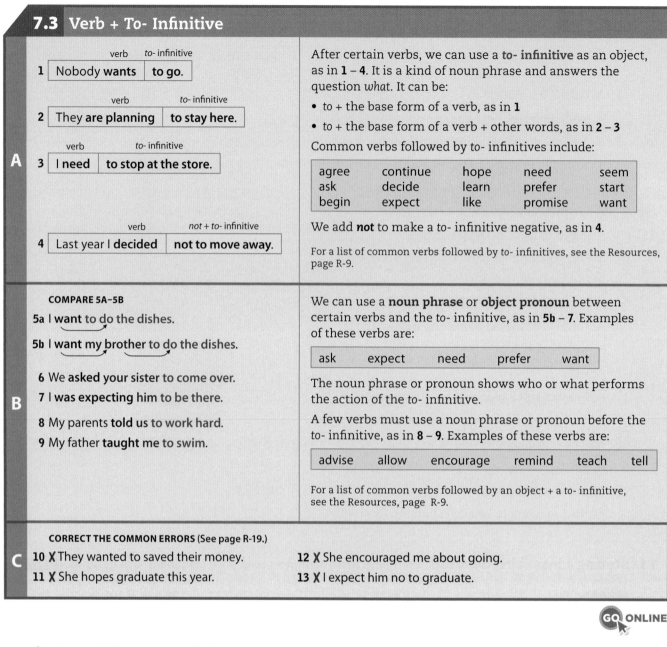

7.3 Verb + To- Infinitive

A

1 | verb / to- infinitive
Nobody **wants** | to go.

2 | verb / to- infinitive
They **are planning** | to stay here.

3 | verb / to- infinitive
I **need** | to stop at the store.

4 | verb / not + to- infinitive
Last year I **decided** | not to move away.

After certain verbs, we can use a **to- infinitive** as an object, as in **1 – 4**. It is a kind of noun phrase and answers the question *what*. It can be:

- to + the base form of a verb, as in **1**
- to + the base form of a verb + other words, as in **2 – 3**

Common verbs followed by *to-* infinitives include:

agree	continue	hope	need	seem
ask	decide	learn	prefer	start
begin	expect	like	promise	want

We add **not** to make a *to-* infinitive negative, as in **4**.

For a list of common verbs followed by *to-* infinitives, see the Resources, page R-9.

B

COMPARE 5A–5B

5a I **want** to do the dishes.

5b I **want** my brother to do the dishes.

6 We **asked** your sister to come over.

7 I **was expecting** him to be there.

8 My parents **told** us to work hard.

9 My father **taught** me to swim.

We can use a **noun phrase** or **object pronoun** between certain verbs and the *to-* infinitive, as in **5b – 7**. Examples of these verbs are:

ask	expect	need	prefer	want

The noun phrase or pronoun shows who or what performs the action of the *to-* infinitive.

A few verbs must use a noun phrase or pronoun before the *to-* infinitive, as in **8 – 9**. Examples of these verbs are:

advise	allow	encourage	remind	teach	tell

For a list of common verbs followed by an object + a *to-* infinitive, see the Resources, page R-9.

C

CORRECT THE COMMON ERRORS (See page R-19.)

10 ✗ They wanted to saved their money.

11 ✗ She hopes graduate this year.

12 ✗ She encouraged me about going.

13 ✗ I expect him no to graduate.

 GO ONLINE

12 | Using Verbs + *To-* Infinitives in Conversation Complete each conversation with the *to-* infinitive form of a verb from the box. Then practice with a partner. 7.3 A

1. A: Do you want _____ *to do* _____ something tonight?

   B: Sure. Let's eat out somewhere.

2. A: Is Hassan still sick?

   B: Yes, but I think he's starting _____ a little better.

3. A: Can I start the meeting?

   B: Go ahead. Everyone seems _____ here.

4. A: What's the matter?

   B: I can't continue _____ with Mika. She's driving me crazy.

5. A: I'll see you later.

   B: Yes, I hope _____ you soon.

be
do
feel
see
work

6. A: How did you learn _____ a car?

   B: My father taught me.

7. A: Are you ready?

   B: For what?

   A: Come on. You agreed _____ me with my homework.

   B: OK. OK.

8. A: I thought you were going to a movie.

   B: I decided _____.

9. A: What did you get Anna for her birthday?

   B: Do you promise _____ her?

   A: Of course.

10. A: Are you leaving soon?

    B: No, I expect _____ here for another hour.

be
drive
(not) go
help
(not) tell

🔊 13 | Pronunciation Note: *To* Listen to the note. Then do Activities 14 and 15.

> With a *to-* infinitive, we usually pronounce **to** like /tə/ or sometimes just /t/. It can be difficult to hear.
>
> **1** She wants **to learn to speak** Chinese.   *sounds like*   "She wants /tə/ learn /t/ speak Chinese."
>
> When **to** is the last word in a sentence, speakers pronounce its full sound. It sounds like /tu/.
>
> **2** A: Did you pay the rent?
>   B: Oh, no. I forgot **to**.

🔊 14 | Pronouncing *To-* Infinitives Listen to each question and write the verb + *to-* infinitive you hear. Then practice saying the questions. `7.3 A`

YOUR SCHEDULE

1. Where do you _____ *expect to be* _____ at this time tomorrow?

2. Where do you _____ tomorrow?

3. What do you _____ tonight?

4. Who do you _____ tomorrow?

5. What do you _____ in the morning?

6. Where do you _____ the afternoon tomorrow?

7. When do you _____ tomorrow?

8. When do you _____ a vacation?

9. What do you _____?

10. How many times a day do you _____?

Write about It Write answers to the questions above. Use complete sentences.

1. I expect to be at home at this time tomorrow.

15 | Listening for a Verb (+ Noun Phrase) + _To_- Infinitive Listen and check (✓) the sentence you hear. `7.3 B`

1. ☐ a. I don't want to do the dishes.
   ☑ b. I don't want him to do the dishes.

2. ☐ a. She doesn't want to go.
   ☐ b. She doesn't want them to go.

3. ☐ a. They didn't ask to help.
   ☐ b. They didn't ask us to help.

4. ☐ a. My brother doesn't need to be there.
   ☐ b. My brother doesn't need me to be there.

5. ☐ a. I expect to call her at noon.
   ☐ b. I expect her to call at noon.

6. ☐ a. Do you want to go with them?
   ☐ b. Do you want me to go with them?

7. ☐ a. Did she ask to come over?
   ☐ b. Did she ask him to come over?

8. ☐ a. Do you want to go somewhere?
   ☐ b. Do you want her to go somewhere?

9. ☐ a. Do you want to stay?
   ☐ b. Do you want me to stay?

10. ☐ a. When do they expect to get there?
    ☐ b. When do they expect you to get there?

Talk about It Work with a partner. Read a sentence in each pair above. Ask your partner to say "sentence A" or "sentence B."

16 | Using a Verb (+ Noun Phrase) + _To_- Infinitive Use each quotation to write a new sentence. Some sentences will need a noun phrase before the _to_- infinitive, and some will not. `7.3 B`

REPORTING STATEMENTS

1. Toshi: "I don't expect my brother to help."

   Toshi doesn't expect _his brother to help_____.

2. Emma: "I expect to be there by 7."

   Emma expects _____.

3. Kate: "I want John to read something."

   Kate wants _____.

4. Carlos: "I really want to see that movie."

   Carlos _____.

5. Sam: "I need someone to give me a ride to school."

   Sam _____.

6. Mary: "I advised David to get there early."

   _____

7. Isabel: "I told my brother to do his homework."

   _____

8. Rob: "I encouraged Amanda to take the job."

   _____

9. Sarah: "I taught my sister to ride a bike."

   _____

10. Matt: "I really don't want to leave."

    _____

17 | Using a Verb + Noun Phrase + *To*- Infinitive Write six meaningful questions using ideas from the chart. (Many different questions are possible.) 7.3 B

EXPECTATIONS

		advise		
		allow		
What do	parents	ask	their children	
What should	children	encourage	their parents	to do?
	teachers	expect	their students	
	students	need	their teachers	
		tell		
		want		

What do children need their parents to do?

Talk about It Ask a partner the questions you wrote above.

A: *What do children need their parents to do?*
B: *They need their parents to keep them safe.*

18 | Error Correction Correct any errors in these sentences. (Some sentences may not have any errors.)

1. We hoped getting there early.
2. I helped they to move to a new apartment.
3. He doesn't want lose his job.
4. They invited her about going.
5. They expected he to do well in school.
6. I never offered him to help.
7. My parents gave us lots of advice. For example, they told to work very hard.
8. We must encourage to be good students and listen carefully.

7.4 Verb + Gerund or *To*- Infinitive

VERB + GERUND	VERB + GERUND OR *TO*- INFINITIVE	VERB + *TO*- INFINITIVE
After some verbs, we can only use a gerund, as in **1**.	With a small group of verbs*, we can use either a gerund or a *to*-infinitive, as in **2a – 2b**.	After some verbs, we can only use a *to*- infinitive, as in **3**.
1 I enjoy playing the guitar. (NOT: ~~I enjoy to play the guitar.~~)	**2a I hate leaving.** **2b I hate to leave.**	**3 I agreed to go with him.** (NOT: ~~I agreed going with him.~~)

A

appreciate • avoid • consider
discuss • dislike • enjoy
finish • go • imagine
keep • mind • miss
practice • quit • suggest

advise • begin • continue
hate • like • love
prefer • (can't) stand • start

agree • ask • choose
decide • expect • fail
get • hope • need • offer
plan • promise • refuse
say • seem • want

For a list of common verbs followed by gerunds or *to*- infinitives, see the Resources, page R-9.

* With some verbs (such as *forget, remember, stop,* and *try*), there is a difference in meaning when you use a gerund or a *to*- infinitive. See the Resources, page R-9, for examples.

◄)) **19 | Listening for a Verb + Gerund or *To*- Infinitive** Listen and complete these conversations. Then practice with a partner. 7.4 A

1. A: Why didn't you ask me for help?

   B: You know I _____ *hate to ask* _____ for help.

2. A: What do you _____ tomorrow?

   B: Nothing special.

3. A: How do you like that book?

   B: I don't know. I just _____ it.

4. A: Why do you _____ your brother?

   B: Because I'm worried about him.

5. A: Why can't I go out tonight?

   B: Because you _____ your homework.

6. A: Let's have dinner here tonight.

   B: Are you sure? I don't mind going out.

   A: No, really. It's no problem. I _____.

Why didn't you ask me for help?

7. A: Are you ready to leave?

   B: Give me 20 more minutes.

   A: I _____ this but we are going to be late.

8. A: Why did you turn the TV off?

   B: Because I _____ reality TV shows. They're terrible.

Think about It In which of the conversations above could you use either a gerund or a *to*- infinitive?

20 | Gerund or *To*- Infinitive? Complete these conversations with the gerund or *to*- infinitive form of the verb in parentheses. (More than one answer may be possible.) Then practice with a partner. 7.4 A

1. A: I hope you feel better tomorrow.

   B: Me too. I hate _____ *being* _____ sick. (be)

2. A: How was your trip?

   B: I can't begin _____ it. (describe)

3. A: How's John doing?

   B: Better. He even started _____ a bit. (eat)

4. A: Where are you going?

   B: I just want _____ some fresh air. (get)

5. A: Where's Anna?

   B: She didn't plan _____ with me. (come)

6. A: Would you mind _____ me a soda from the fridge? (get)

   B: Sure.

7. A: I'm worried about that test tomorrow.

   B: I know. I don't even like _____ it. (think about)

8. A: I hate my job.

   B: Well, maybe you should consider _____ a new one. (look for)

> **F Y I**
>
> We usually avoid using two *-ing* forms right next to each other (one as a progressive main verb and one as a gerund). This is especially true after verbs like *begin*, *continue*, and *start*.
>
> **I'm starting keeping** a journal. (awkward)
>
> **I'm starting to keep** a journal. (better)

9. A: Are we having lunch with James?

   B: Yeah. He suggested _____ at his office. (meet)

10. A: Can I help you?

    B: Sure. I'd love _____ some help. (have)

11. A: How's your car?

    B: It seems _____ OK. (be)

12. A: I don't think we should continue _____ on this. (work)

    B: I don't either.

Think about It In which of the conversations in Activity 20 could you use either a gerund or a *to-* infinitive?

21 | Changing Forms Circle the gerunds and underline the *to-* infinitives in these sentences. Then rewrite the sentence using the other form when possible. **7.4 A**

About Me

1. I decided to start running and being more active outdoors.

   I decided to start to run and be more active outdoors.

2. I like to ride my bike and play football.

3. I don't enjoy watching horror films because I don't like to feel scared.

4. I can't imagine having the same job my whole life.

5. I started to study English when I was a child.

6. In the next ten years, I hope to become a doctor.

7. I'm a very competitive[4] person and I hate to lose to someone else.

8. I miss seeing my family and eating my mother's cooking.

9. I can't stand to make bad decisions.

10. I don't mind working hard when I want to accomplish something.

11. I am a morning person. I love to exercise early in the morning and eat a big breakfast.

12. I started playing tennis when I was very young, and I hope to keep playing throughout my life.

F Y I

When we use a series of *to-* infinitives, it is not necessary to repeat the word *to*.

I like **to ride my bike** and (to) **play football**.

Think about It Sentences 1 and 12 above contain both *to-* infinitives and gerunds. What do you notice about how they are used together?

Talk about It Take turns reading the sentences above aloud with a partner. Say if any of the sentences are true for you.

Write about It Think of a different way to complete each sentence above with a gerund or *to-* infinitive. Write about yourself and say what you decided, like, don't enjoy, etc.

   I decided to stop eating fast food.   *I like to read and go for long walks.*

---

[4]**competitive:** wanting to win or be better than other people

7.5 Infinitives of Purpose

A

1 I exercise **to stay healthy**. **2** I just called **to ask a question**. **3** A: Why did you bring your computer? B: **To show you some pictures.** **4** We left at 5 **in order to get there on time**. **5** We need to wait another month **in order to be absolutely certain**.	We sometimes use a **to- infinitive** as a kind of adverb. It answers the question *for what purpose* or *why*, as in **1 – 5**. We sometimes use the words **in order** before the **to- infinitive**, as in **4 – 5**.

22 | Identifying Infinitives of Purpose Underline the infinitive of purpose in each question. Then answer the questions. `7.5 A`

Survey Questions

1. What do you like to do <u>to relax</u>?

   I like to read a good book to relax.

2. What do you like to do to challenge yourself?
3. What do you need to do to get good grades in school?
4. What can you do to improve your English?
5. What should you keep doing in order to stay healthy?
6. What do you have to do to be successful in life?
7. What do you need to do to find a good job?
8. What skills do you need to run your own business?
9. What do children need in order to have a happy childhood?
10. What changes would you need to make to spend more time with your family?

Talk about It Choose one of the questions above and interview your classmates. Then report their answers to the class.

"I asked the question, 'What do you like to do to relax?' Most people said they like to watch TV to relax, and a few people like to listen to music."

23 | Choosing Infinitives of Purpose Complete each sentence below with an idea from the box. `7.5 A`

to borrow some books	to cut the meat	to get some bread	to ride a bicycle
to buy a book	to earn money	to get to work	to wash the dishes

WHAT IS THE PURPOSE?

1. He put on an apron *to wash the dishes* _____.
2. He went to the library _____.
3. She went to a bookstore _____.
4. She used a sharp knife _____.

apron

242

5. She put on a helmet _____.

6. He takes a bus _____.

7. She goes to work _____.

8. He went to the grocery store _____.

helmet

Write about It Think of different ways to complete the sentences in Activity 23 with infinitives of purpose.

He put on an apron to cook dinner.   *She put on a helmet to go skiing.*

24 | Using Infinitives of Purpose Write as many answers as you can for each question. Try to use infinitives of purpose. `7.5 A`

1. Why do you use the Internet?

To email my friends. To shop . . .

2. Why do you study English?
3. Why do people exercise?
4. Why do people travel?
5. Why do people work?
6. Why do people eat?

Why do you use the Internet?

Talk about It Compare your ideas above with your classmates. Make a list of all your different ideas.

7.6 Gerunds and To- Infinitives as Subjects

GERUND AS SUBJECT

	gerund	verb	
1	Staying healthy	is	important.

	gerund	verb	
2	Being good parents	isn't	easy.

	gerund	verb	
3	Cooking a good meal	takes	time.

	gerund	verb	
4	Not getting enough sleep	can make	you sick.

We can use a **gerund** as the subject of a sentence, as in **1 – 4**. Notice that we use a singular verb when the subject is a gerund.

Remember: We use *not* to make a gerund negative, as in **4**.

TO- INFINITIVE AS SUBJECT

	to- infinitive	verb	
5	To learn a new language	isn't	easy.

IT + BE + ADJECTIVE + TO- INFINITIVE

6	It isn't	easy	to learn a new language.

(= To learn a new language isn't easy.)

7	It's	nice	to be here.

(= To be here is nice.)

It is uncommon and very formal to use a **to-infinitive** as the subject of a sentence, as in **5**.

Instead, we sometimes begin a sentence with *it* and use an adjective + a to- infinitive, as in **6 – 7**. *It* is a placeholder for the subject.

Common adjectives followed by a *to-* infinitive are:

bad	easy	hard	impossible
difficult	good	important	possible

GO ONLINE

25 | Identifying Gerund Subjects Underline the gerund subject in each sentence. Circle the verb. Then check (✓) *Agree* or *Disagree*. `7.6 A`

HEALTH	AGREE	DISAGREE
1. Learning a new language is good for your brain.	☐	☐
2. Riding a bike is good exercise.	☐	☐
3. Exercising makes you strong.	☐	☐
4. Eating fish makes you smart.	☐	☐
5. Smoking is bad for your health.	☐	☐
6. Drinking a glass of warm milk helps you fall asleep.	☐	☐
7. Sitting too close to your computer screen will ruin[5] your eyes.	☐	☐
8. Swimming is good for your body.	☐	☐
9. Feeling a lot of stress isn't good for you.	☐	☐
10. Eating a lot of carrots improves your eyesight.	☐	☐

Talk about It Take turns reading the sentences above aloud with a partner. See if your partner agrees or disagrees and why.

A: *Learning a new language is good for your brain.*
B: *I agree with that.*   OR   B: *I'm not sure. Sometimes it gives me a headache.*

Write about It Think of a different subject for each sentence above, and write new sentences.

Doing puzzles is good for your brain.

26 | Using Adjectives + *To-* Infinitives Choose adjectives from the boxes to complete the questions. Use each adjective only once. (More than one adjective may be possible.) `7.6 B`

WHAT'S YOUR OPINION?

1. Why is it _____ to be a good parent?

2. Is it ever _____ to cry at work or school?

3. Is it _____ to vote?

4. Is it _____ to travel alone?

5. Is it _____ to spend a lot of money when you travel?

dangerous
difficult
important
necessary
OK

6. Why is it _____ to get a good education?

7. Is it _____ to skip classes?

8. When is it _____ to dress up?

9. Why is it _____ to divide by zero?

10. Is it _____ to learn English?

bad
easy
important
impossible
necessary

Talk about It Ask a partner the questions above.

A: *Why is it difficult to be a good parent?*
B: *I don't know. I guess because a child needs a parent for everything. . . .*

[5] **ruin:** to damage something so that it no longer is good

27 | Using *It* with *To*- Infinitives Rewrite each sentence using *it* + *be* + an adjective + a *to*- infinitive. `7.6 B`

1. Skiing can be dangerous.

   It can be dangerous to ski.

2. Having a day off is nice.
3. Eating sweet things is OK sometimes.
4. Learning a new language isn't easy.
5. Getting some exercise every day is important.
6. Traveling is exciting.
7. Sitting all day is bad for your health.
8. Finding a good job isn't hard.
9. Getting up early can be difficult.
10. Knowing another language is helpful.

Write about It Think of a different *to*- infinitive for each sentence above, and write new sentences.

It can be dangerous to drive on the highway.

7.7 Using Gerunds and *To*- Infinitives in Speaking

A	**PRONOUNCING *WANT* + *TO*- INFINITIVE**	The verb ***want*** + *to*- infinitive is very common in conversation, as in **1 – 3**. We often pronounce *want to* as "wanna."
	1 What do you **want to do?** (sounds like "wanna do")	
	2 I **want to go.** (sounds like "wanna go")	
	3 He didn't **want to talk about it.** (sounds like "wanna talk")	**WARNING!** We do not use "wanna" in writing.

B	**MAKING A REQUEST WITH *WOULD YOU MIND***	In speaking, we often use *would you mind* + a **gerund** to make a polite request, as in **4 – 6**.
	4 A: Would you mind **taking this for me?** B: No problem. (= No, I wouldn't mind.)	
	5 A: Would you mind **giving me a ride?** B: No, not at all. (= No, I wouldn't mind.)	Notice: We often use a negative response to agree to a request with *would you mind*. Some examples are:
	6 A: Would you mind **coming over here?** B: OK.	No problem. No, of course not. No, not at all. No, that's fine.

GO ONLINE

---

28 | Pronouncing *Want* + *To*- Infinitive Listen and write the missing words. Then practice with a partner. Practice the pronunciation of *want to* as "wanna." `7.7 A`

1. A: What do you _____ after class?

   B: Nothing special.

2. A: Do you _____ for a cup of coffee?

   B: Sure.

3. A: Tell me about yourself.

   B: What do you _____?

   A: Well, where did you grow up?

   B: In Turkey.

4. A: I don't _____ anything tonight.

   B: I don't either.

5. A: Where do you _____ today?

   B: Doesn't matter to me.

6. A: Let's see a movie tonight.

   B: Not tonight. I really just _____ home.

7. A: Where's Amanda?

   B: She didn't _____.

8. A: Is your brother coming with us?

   B: No, he doesn't _____ right now.

9. A: Do you _____ with us?

   B: Sure. I'd love to.

10. A: Do you _____ me later?

   B: Sure. What time?

Talk about It Work with a partner. Choose three of the sentences you completed in Activity 28. Write new conversations with them. Then present one conversation to the class.

A: What do you want to do after class?
B: I don't know. Maybe we should see a movie.

29 | Using *Would You Mind* + Gerund Rewrite each conversation. Use *would you mind* + a gerund in the request. Remember that a negative response means you agree. 7.7 B

MAKING REQUESTS

1. A: Could you open the door for me, please?

   B: Sure.

2. A: Would you please turn the TV down?

   B: OK.

3. A: Can you give me a ride to work tomorrow?

   B: Of course. What time?

4. A: Could you go to the store for me?

   B: Sure. What do you need?

5. A: Could you bring me another glass of water, please?

   B: Yes, I'll be right back with it.

6. A: Could you pass me the salt, please?

   B: Sure.

7. A: Could you wait for just a minute?

   B: OK, but I don't want to be late.

8. A: Could you take our picture?

   B: Sure. I'd be happy to.

REQUEST WITH WOULD YOU MIND

1. A: *Would you mind opening the door for me, please?*

   B: *No, of course not.*

2. A: _____

   _____

   B: _____

3. A: _____

   _____

   B: _____

4. A: _____

   _____

   B: _____

5. A: _____

   _____

   B: _____

6. A: _____

   _____

   B: _____

7. A: _____

   _____

   B: _____

8. A: _____

   _____

   B: _____

Talk about It Where would you hear each request above? Discuss your ideas with your classmates.

7.8 Using Gerunds and To- Infinitives in Writing

A

USING THE SAME FORM IN LISTS

1 Group decision making involves three steps:
- writing the discussion questions
- brainstorming alternatives
- evaluating alternatives

2 A good introduction has several functions:
- to get the attention of the audience
- to state the purpose of the presentation
- to describe the presenter's qualifications

We sometimes use **gerunds** and **to- infinitives** when we write lists of items, as in **1 – 2**.

Notice that the items in each list have the same grammatical form. We don't mix grammatical forms in a list.

GRAMMAR TERM: When we use the same grammatical form in this way, we call it **parallelism**.

B

USING THE SAME FORM IN A SERIES OF IDEAS

3 Eating well, exercising, and not worrying are good for your health.

4 In the next few years, I hope to finish my education, get a job, and maybe start a family.
(= to finish my education, to get a job, and maybe to start a family)

When we write a series of ideas, we make them parallel—they use the same grammatical form.

- Sentence **3** has three subjects: *eating well, exercising, and not worrying*. The writer uses the same grammatical form for each one.
- Sentence **4** has three objects of the verb *hope*. Remember: When we use a series of to- infinitives, it is not necessary to repeat the word *to*.

30 | Listing Ideas Add another idea to each list. Use the same form as the other ideas in the list. (Make them parallel.) `7.8 A`

THREE THINGS

1. Parents have many important responsibilities:
   - keeping their children safe
   - modeling[6] good behavior
   - _____

2. You can use the Internet to do many useful things:
   - to look for a job
   - to read the news
   - _____

3. Three simple things can help you stay healthy:
   - eating good food
   - getting enough sleep
   - _____

---

[6]**model:** to show or demonstrate

4. Children can learn several important things from playing sports:
   - to value[7] physical activity
   - to work together as a team
   - _____

5. The United Nations has several important functions:
   - to keep peace in the world
   - to help solve economic problems
   - _____

31 | Using a Series of Ideas Complete these sentences with your own ideas. Use the same form as other ideas in the series. (Make them parallel.) 7.8 B

1. Lots of people go to local parks to have a picnic and _____*get some exercise*_____.
2. Skiing and _____ are popular cold-weather sports.
3. On a sunny day, most people enjoy being outside, _____, and _____.
4. Parents should encourage their children to be polite, _____, and _____.
5. Parents can teach their children good behavior without yelling at them or _____.
6. Before you get on an airplane, it's necessary to go through security and _____.
7. People join clubs to have fun and _____.
8. On a vacation, many people enjoy visiting new places, _____, and _____.
9. Lots of people dream of making a lot of money and _____.
10. You can learn a lot from reading, _____, and _____.

WRAP-UP Demonstrate Your Knowledge

A | DISCUSSION Work with a partner. Find something both of you can't stand doing, dislike doing, enjoy doing, etc. Then report your answers to the class.

are good at	are interested in	can't stand	dislike	enjoy	hate	like	want

"Both of us can't stand getting up early in the morning."
"Both of us enjoy . . ."
"Both of us hate . . ."

[7] **value:** to think that something is important

B | SURVEY Ask your classmates questions to find the information below. Use the verb and the correct form of the phrase in parentheses. When someone answers yes, write the person's name in the box.

A: Do you like to play football?
B: No, I don't.

A: Do you like to play football?
C: Yes, I do.

FIND SOMEONE WHO . . .

1. like (play football)	4. worry about (find a job)	7. plan (study tomorrow)
Name: _____	Name: _____	Name: _____
2. plan on (go to school next year)	5. enjoy (cook)	8. expect (take a trip soon)
Name: _____	Name: _____	Name: _____
3. like (play board games)	6. is good at (play the piano)	9. want (work in the medical field)
Name: _____	Name: _____	Name: _____

C | WRITING What is one of your future goals? How do you plan to reach that goal? Answer these questions in a short piece of writing.

Becoming a teacher of young children is one of my future goals. I plan to reach this goal by studying hard and getting good grades. I hope to go to graduate school to get a master's degree in education. I am also interested in . . .

7.9 Summary of Gerunds and To- Infinitives

GERUNDS

VERB + GERUND	I just **started** writing. I can't **imagine** writing a computer program. I **finished** writing my paper last night.
PREPOSITION + GERUND	I got a blister **from** writing. I'm **tired of** writing these letters. I **feel like** writing her a message.
GERUND AS SUBJECT	Writing was never a great subject for me. Writing in a journal is a creative outlet. Writing is like a muscle. You need to exercise it.

TO- INFINITIVES

VERB + *TO*- INFINITIVE	Do you **promise** to write? I **need** to write a business plan.
VERB + OBJECT + *TO*- INFINITIVE	Do you **want me** to write this? I **told my brother** to write to you.
INFINITIVE OF PURPOSE	She wrote **to ask for money.** I need a computer **in order to write this report.**
***TO*- INFINITIVE AS SUBJECT**	**To write badly** is easy. (not typical) **To write in your own words** is important. (not typical)
***IT* + *BE* + ADJECTIVE + *TO*- INFINITIVE**	**It**'s easy to write badly. **It** is important to write in your own words.

Resources

I. Non-Action Verbs

agree	consist of	fear	include	mind	recognize	think
appear	contain	feel	involve	need	remember	understand
appreciate	cost	fit	know	owe	see	want
be	dislike	hate	like	own	seem	weigh
believe	doubt	have	look	possess	smell	wish
belong	envy	hear	love	prefer	suppose	
conclude	equal	imagine	mean	realize	taste	

Remember:

- A non-action verb describes a state (an unchanging condition).
- Non-action verbs are also called **stative verbs**.
- Some verbs have more than one meaning. They can function as a non-action verb in one context and an action verb in another.

II. Linking Verbs

appear	become	get*	look	seem	sound	turn*
be	feel	grow*	remain	smell	taste	

* with a meaning of *become*

Remember: A linking verb can have an adjective as a complement.

III. Irregular Verbs

BASE FORM	SIMPLE PAST	PAST PARTICIPLE
beat	beat	beaten
become	became	become
begin	began	begun
bend	bent	bent
bet	bet	bet
bite	bit	bitten
bleed	bled	bled
break	broke	broken
bring	brought	brought
build	built	built
buy	bought	bought
catch	caught	caught
choose	chose	chosen
come	came	come
cost	cost	cost
cut	cut	cut
dig	dug	dug
draw	drew	drawn
drink	drank	drunk
drive	drove	driven
eat	ate	eaten
fall	fell	fallen
feed	fed	fed
feel	felt	felt
fight	fought	fought
find	found	found
fly	flew	flown
forbid	forbade	forbidden
forget	forgot	forgotten
forgive	forgave	forgiven
freeze	froze	frozen
get	got	gotten
give	gave	given
go	went	gone
grow	grew	grown
hear	heard	heard
hide	hid	hidden
hit	hit	hit
hold	held	held
hurt	hurt	hurt
keep	kept	kept
know	knew	known
lay	laid	laid
lead	led	led
leave	left	left
lend	lent	lent
let	let	let

BASE FORM	SIMPLE PAST	PAST PARTICIPLE
lose	lost	lost
make	made	made
mean	meant	meant
meet	met	met
pay	paid	paid
put	put	put
quit	quit	quit
read	read	read
ride	rode	ridden
ring	rang	rung
rise	rose	risen
run	ran	run
say	said	said
see	saw	seen
sell	sold	sold
send	sent	sent
set	set	set
sew	sewed	sewn
shake	shook	shaken
shoot	shot	shot
show	showed	shown
shut	shut	shut
sing	sang	sung
sink	sank	sunk
sit	sat	sat
sleep	slept	slept
speak	spoke	spoken
speed	sped	sped
spend	spent	spent
spread	spread	spread
stand	stood	stood
steal	stole	stolen
swear	swore	sworn
sweep	swept	swept
swim	swam	swum
take	took	taken
teach	taught	taught
tear	tore	torn
tell	told	told
think	thought	thought
throw	threw	thrown
understand	understood	understood
wake	woke	woken
wear	wore	worn
win	won	won
write	wrote	written

IV. Spelling Rules for the -s/-es Form of Verbs

To form the third-person singular *(he/she/it)* for the simple present:

1 Add *-es* to verbs that end in *-sh, -ch, -ss, -s, -x,* or *-z.*

finish	finishes	touch	touches	pass	passes	relax	relaxes

2 For verbs ending in a consonant + *-y,* change the *-y* to *-i* and add *-es.*

study	studies	worry	worries	deny	denies	fly	flies

3 Three verbs have a special spelling:

go	goes	do	does	have	has

4 For all other verbs, add *-s.*

like	likes	buy	buys	see	sees	speak	speaks

V. Spelling Rules for the -ing Form of Verbs

1 The base form of the verb ends in a vowel + consonant sound + *-e:*	Drop the *-e* and add *-ing.* live–living **cause**–causing be**come**–becoming **take**–taking
2 The base form is one syllable, and it ends in one vowel + one consonant (except *-w, -x,* or *-y*):	Double the final consonant and add *-ing.* **put**–putting **win**–winning **drop**–dropping
3 The base form has more than one syllable, it ends in one vowel + one consonant (except *-w, -x,* or *-y*), and the last syllable is stressed:	Double the final consonant and add *-ing.* for·**get**–forgetting be·**gin**–beginning com·**mit**–committing
4 The base form ends in *-ie:*	Change the *-ie* to *-y* and add *-ing.* **die**–dying **tie**–tying **lie**–lying
5 For other verbs:	Add *-ing.* play–playing show–showing help–helping

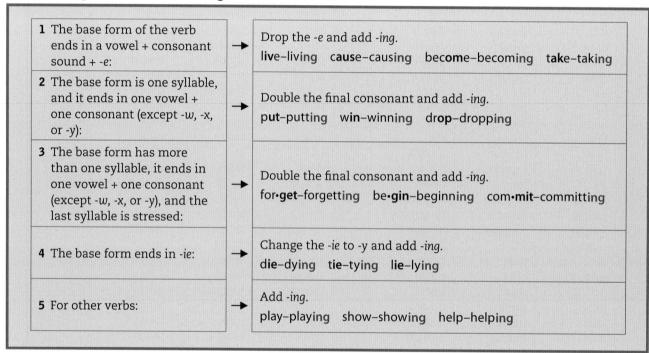

VI. Spelling Rules for the -ed Form of Verbs

SPELLING RULES	base form	simple past
When the base form of a regular verb ends in -e, **add -d**.	close refuse	closed refused
When the base form ends in a consonant + **-y, change the -y to -i and add -ed**.	stud**y** worr**y** identif**y**	stud**ied** worr**ied** identif**ied**
When the base form has one syllable and ends in a **c**onsonant + **v**owel + **c**onsonant (CVC), **double the final consonant and add -ed**. (Warning! Do not double a final w, x, or y: play / played, wax / waxed, row / rowed.)	plan jog drop	planned jogged dropped
When the base form of a two-syllable verb ends in a **c**onsonant + **v**owel + **c**onsonant (CVC) and the last syllable is stressed, **double the final consonant and add -ed**.	re•**fer** re•**gret**	referred regretted
For all other regular verbs, **add -ed**.	open destroy	opened destroyed

VII. Common Transitive Verbs

VERB + DIRECT OBJECT

Examples: *begin the day; believe everything; bring a sweater*

allow	close*	end*	include	love	raise	show	visit*
ask*	complete	enjoy	intend	make	read*	speak*	want
attempt	consider	expect	introduce	mean	receive	start*	wash*
begin*	create	feel*	invent	meet*	recognize	study*	watch*
believe*	cut*	find	involve	move*	refuse	surround	win*
bring	describe	follow*	keep*	need	remember*	take	write*
build	design	forgive	know*	pass*	save	teach	
buy	destroy	hear*	leave*	pay*	say	tell	
call*	develop	help*	lend	produce	see*	think*	
carry	discover	hold*	like	provide	send	throw	
cause	do	identify	lose*	put	serve	use	

* verbs that we can also use intransitively (without a direct object)

Remember: Transitive verbs need an object (a noun phrase or pronoun) to complete their meaning.

VERB + INDIRECT OBJECT + DIRECT OBJECT

Examples: *ask the teacher a question; bring your sister a sweater*

ask	forgive	lend*	pay	save	teach*
bring	give*	make	promise*	send*	tell*
buy	hand*	offer*	read*	serve*	throw*
find	leave*	owe*	refuse	show*	wish*

* The indirect object can come before or after the direct object.

VIII. Common Intransitive Verbs

Examples: *The movie begins at 8:00. She doesn't hear very well.*

agree	cough	freeze*	lie	remember*	stop*
appear	cut*	go	live	ring*	study*
arrive	decrease*	happen	look	rise	swim
begin*	die	hear*	lose*	see*	visit*
belong	disappear	help*	matter	shake*	wait
bleed	dream*	hide*	meet*	sit	walk*
break*	drown	hurt*	move*	sleep	wash*
burn*	end*	increase*	pass*	sneeze	watch*
call*	fall	laugh	rain	snow	win*
close*	follow*	leave*	read*	start*	work
come					

* verbs that we can also use transitively (with a direct object)

Remember: Intransitive verbs make sense without an object.

IX. Common Transitive Multi-Word Verbs

act out	clear out	finish off	keep out	pay off	set aside	think of
blow away	close down	finish up	laugh off	pick out	set down	think over
blow up	come across	flag down	lay aside	pick up	shake up	think up
break down	cover up	get across	lay down	pin down	shave off	throw away
break off	cut off	get along with	leave out	play back	shut down	throw down
bring out	cut out	get into	let down	point out	shut off	throw out
bring up	dig out	get off	let out	pour out	sign up	try on
call off	dig up	get on	lock up	put aside	slow down	turn back
call on	do away with	get over	look after	put away	sort out	turn down
call up	do over	give away	look down on	put down	stretch out	turn off
carry on	do without	give out	look forward to	put off	sweep away	use up
carry out	drop off	give up	look over	put on	take after	wake up
check into	dry off	hand in	look up	put up with	take back	wash off
check off	dry out	hand out	look up to	read back	take down	wash out
check out	eat up	heat up	make up	read over	take off	wear down
check over	empty out	help out	mix up	ring up	take on	wear out
cheer up	figure out	hold off	move out	round off	take out	work out
chop down	fill out	hold up	open up	run over	take over	write down
clean off	fill up	hunt down	pass over	save up	take up	write off
clean up	find out	jot down	pay back	see through	tell off	

Remember: Transitive multi-word verbs need an object (a noun phrase or pronoun) to complete their meaning.

Some multi-word verbs have more than one meaning. We can use them transitively in one context and intransitively in another.

Examples: They **broke down** the door to get inside. (transitive)

My car **broke down** on the bridge. (intransitive)

You can't **turn back** the clock. (transitive)

Let's **turn back** now. (intransitive)

X. Common Intransitive Multi-Word Verbs

back up	cry out	get up	keep out	pull up	sign off	start off
blow out	dig in	go off	melt away	quiet down	sit up	take off
break down	drive off	grow back	move in	rest up	slow down	turn over
calm down	eat out	grow up	move out	roll over	slow up	turn up
carry on	end up	hang on	pass by	run away	speak up	wake up
catch on	fade away	heat up	pass on	set off	speed up	wear down
catch up	fall over	hurry up	pass out	show off	split up	wear off
cool off	get back	join in	pull through	shut up	stand up	

Remember: An intransitive multi-word verb = a multi-word verb that can be used without an object.

Some multi-word verbs have more than one meaning. We can use them transitively in one context and intransitively in another.

Examples: You need to **cheer up**. (intransitive)

I tried everything, but I couldn't **cheer her up**. (transitive)

Don't **give up**! You can do it. (intransitive)

I **gave up soda** and lost five pounds. (transitive)

XI. Common Verbs Followed by Gerunds

VERB + GERUND

Examples: *appreciate having; avoid getting; denied knowing*

admit	continue*	enjoy	love*	prefer*	risk
advise	defend	finish	mean**	quit	start*
appreciate	delay	forget**	mention	recall	stop**
avoid	deny	hate*	mind	recommend	suggest
begin*	detest	imagine	miss	regret**	tolerate
can't help	discuss	involve	need**	remember**	try**
can't stand*	dislike	keep	postpone	resist	
consider	dread*	like*	practice	resume	

* can also be followed by a *to-* infinitive   ** can be followed by a *to-* infinitive but with a change in meaning

VERB + OBJECT + GERUND

Examples: *hear him talking; saw my friends leaving; found them sitting*

discover	feel	find	hear	notice	see	watch

XII. Common Verbs + Prepositions Followed by Gerunds

Examples: *argue about going; apologize for being; cope with losing; dream of becoming*

VERB + *ABOUT*	VERB + *AT*	VERB + *FOR*	VERB + *IN*	VERB + *INTO*
argue about care about complain about forget about talk about think about worry about	aim at work at	apologize for blame for care for forgive for thank for use for	believe in result in specialize in succeed in	look into

VERB + *LIKE*	VERB + *OF*	VERB + *ON*	VERB + *TO*	VERB + *WITH*
feel like	accuse of approve of dream of hear of think of	concentrate on depend on go on insist on keep on plan on work on	admit to confess to object to	cope with deal with

XIII. Common Adjectives + Prepositions Followed by Gerunds

Examples: *afraid of being; bad at making; excited about going*

ADJECTIVE + *OF* + GERUND	ADJECTIVE + *AT* + GERUND	ADJECTIVE + *ABOUT* + GERUND
afraid of aware of capable of fond of incapable of proud of tired of	bad at better at effective at good at great at successful at upset at	bad about concerned about enthusiastic about excited about happy about nervous about serious about sorry about worried about

ADJECTIVE + *FROM* + GERUND	ADJECTIVE + *IN* + GERUND	ADJECTIVE + *FOR* + GERUND
different from evident from exempt from free from obvious from safe from tired from	crucial in effective in important in interested in involved in useful in	available for crucial for famous for important for necessary for responsible for sorry for suitable for useful for

XIV. Common Verbs Followed by To- Infinitives

VERB + _TO_- INFINITIVE

Examples: *agree to go; asked to leave; decide to stay*

afford	can't stand*	desire	hope	plan	remember**	threaten
agree	claim	dread*	intend	prefer*	request	try**
aim	consent	fall	learn	prepare	say	volunteer
appear	continue*	forbid	like*	pretend	seek	vow
ask	dare	forget**	love*	proceed	seem	wait
attempt	decide	get	manage	promise	start*	want
beg	decline	hate*	mean**	prove	stop**	wish
begin*	demand	help	need**	refuse	struggle	
bother	deserve	hesitate	offer	regret**	tend	

* can also be followed by a gerund   ** can be followed by a gerund but with a change in meaning

VERB + OBJECT + _TO_- INFINITIVE

Examples: *advised me to go; reminded me to call; helped them to move*

advise**	beg*	encourage**	hate*	know**	permit**	teach**
allow**	believe**	expect*	help*	like*	persuade**	tell**
appoint**	challenge**	forbid**	imagine**	love*	prefer*	urge**
ask*	choose*	force**	instruct**	need*	promise*	want*
assume**	consider**	get*	judge**	order**	remind**	warn**

* object is optional   ** object is required

XV. Common Verbs Followed by Gerunds or To- Infinitives

Examples: *begin working / begin to understand; continue talking / continue to work*

begin	forget*	love	prefer	start
can't stand	hate	mean*	regret*	stop*
continue	like	need*	remember*	try*

* with a change in meaning

XVI. Examples of Differences in Meaning Between Gerunds and To- Infinitives

VERB	GERUND	_TO_- INFINITIVE
forget	I'll never **forget watching** her win the race. (= I'll never forget the time I watched her win the race.)	I **forgot to watch** the race on TV. (= The race was on TV but I didn't watch it.)
mean	Being an adult **means having** responsibilities. (= involves/necessitates responsibilities)	I **meant to call** but I didn't have time. (= intended/planned to call)
remember	I **remembered seeing** his picture in the newspaper. (= First I saw his picture; later I remembered it.)	I **remembered to call** him. (= First I remembered and then I called him.)
stop	She finally **stopped talking**. (= She was talking and then she stopped.)	She **stopped to talk** to me. (= She stopped first so she could talk to me.)
try	I **tried calling** but no one was at home. (= I made the phone call but no one answered.)	I **tried to call** but my phone wasn't working. (= I made the effort but I couldn't call.)

XVII. Common Noncount Nouns

advice	coffee*	flour	homework	medicine*	peace	snow
air	confidence	fruit*	information	milk	physics	soap
baggage	courage	fun	glass*	money	progress	spaghetti
beauty	economics	furniture	heat	music	rain	sugar
behavior*	electricity	gasoline	jewelry	news	research	traffic
blood	entertainment	grammar	knowledge	noise*	rice	truth*
bread	equipment	hair*	literature	organization*	safety	violence
cash	evidence	happiness	luck	oxygen	salt	water
chemistry	excitement	health	luggage	paint*	sand	weather
clothing	experience*	help	mathematics	patience	smoke	work*

* often has a count meaning or a noncount meaning

XVIII. Common Noun Suffixes

SUFFIX	EXAMPLES	SUFFIX	EXAMPLES	SUFFIX	EXAMPLES
-age	shortage storage	-er	painter singer	-ity	inequality purity
-ance -ence -ancy -ency	appearance existence vacancy frequency	-hood	brotherhood childhood neighborhood sisterhood	-ment	announcement development excitement resentment
-ant -ent	assistant consultant president student	-ian	comedian historian librarian	-ness	gentleness kindness loneliness sadness
-ation	examination organization	-ics	athletics physics	-ology	biology ecology psychology
-cracy	autocracy democracy	-ion	action connection	-or	actor conductor inventor
-ee	employee trainee	-ist	artist capitalist scientist	-ship	citizenship friendship

XIX. Common Noun + Noun Combinations

family	+	business / friend / history / life / member / room / support / values
government	+	agency / employee / official / policy / program / regulation / spending
police	+	car / chief / department / force / interview / officer / station
world	+	bank / championship / cup / economy / leader / record / trade / view / war
business	+	administration / community / leader / owner / people / plan / school / world
car	+	accident / company / crash / door / keys / radio / seat / wash / window
city	+	center / council / government / hall / limits / manager / official / police / street
health	+	benefits / care / insurance / officials / problems / professionals / services
labor	+	costs / day / force / market / movement / party / relations / statistics / union
TV	+	ad / camera / commercial / guide / movie / news / series / set / show / station

XX. Common Adjectives

These are the 100 most common adjectives in English in order of frequency.

other	little	human	full	current	serious	religious
new*	important	local	special	wrong*	ready	cold
good*	political	late	easy	private	simple	final
high	bad	hard*	clear	past	left	main
old*	white*	major	recent	foreign	physical	green
great	real	better	certain	fine	general	nice*
big*	best	economic	personal	common	environmental	huge
American	right*	strong	open	poor	financial	popular
small	social	possible	red	natural	blue	traditional
large	only	whole*	difficult*	significant	democratic	cultural
national	public	free	available	similar	dark	
young	sure*	military	likely	hot	various	
different*	low	true*	short	dead*	entire	
black*	early	federal	single	central	close	
long*	able*	international	medical	happy*	legal	

* common in conversation

XXI. Common Adjective Suffixes

SUFFIX	MEANING	EXAMPLE
-able -ible -ble	possible to	acceptable noticeable divisible
-al	connected with	environmental experimental
-ant -ent	having a particular quality	different
-centric	concerned with or interested in	egocentric
-ed	having a particular state or quality	bored patterned
-ese	from a place	Chinese Japanese
-free	without the thing mentioned	fat-free tax-free
-ful	having a particular quality	helpful useful
-ial	typical of	dictatorial
-ical	connected with	economical physical

SUFFIX	MEANING	EXAMPLE
-ing	producing a particular state or effect	exciting interesting
-ish	describing nationality or language	English Spanish
-ive	having a particular quality	attractive effective
-less	not having something	fearless hopeless
-like	similar to	childlike
-looking	having the appearance	good-looking odd-looking
-most	the furthest	southernmost topmost
-ous	having a particular quality	dangerous religious
-proof	to protect against the thing mentioned	soundproof waterproof
-y	having the quality of the thing mentioned	fatty rainy thirsty

Taken from *Oxford American Dictionary for learners of English*

XXII. Common Adverbs of Degree

absolutely	entirely	highly	quite	slightly	too*
almost	exactly*	more	rather	so	totally
awfully	extremely	nearly	real*	somewhat	utterly
completely	fairly	perfectly	really*	terribly	very*
definitely	fully	pretty*	relatively	thoroughly	

* common in conversation

COMMON ERRORS CORRECTIONS

1.2 Simple Present Statements (page 7)

CORRECTION

14 ✗ She don't have time for this.

✓ She doesn't have time for this.

15 ✗ He email his family a lot.

✓ He emails his family a lot.

16 ✗ She is a housewife and have three children.

✓ She is a housewife and has three children.

17 ✗ It make me happy.

✓ It makes me happy.

EXPLANATION

I / You / We / They	don't have . . . email . . . have . . . make . . .

He / She / It	doesn't have . . . emails . . . has . . . makes . . .

D

1.5 Using Time Expressions with the Simple Present (page 20)

CORRECTION

16 ✗ He walks to school usually every morning.

✓ He usually walks to school every morning.

17 ✗ They always are busy.

✓ They are always busy.

EXPLANATION

Notice the correct order of words:

subject	adverb of frequency	verb

subject	verb be	adverb of frequency

18 ✗ They always don't leave a tip.

✓ They don't always leave a tip.

✓ They never leave a tip.

Notice the correct order of words:

subject	helping verb	adverb of frequency	verb

There are two ways to correct this sentence:

They don't always leave a tip means "Sometimes they *do* leave a tip, but sometimes (about 10 to 50 percent of the time) they *don't* leave a tip."

They never leave a tip means "They leave a tip 0 percent of the time."

19 ✗ John don't never visit us.

✓ John never visits us.

We don't use *not* with a negative adverb (*hardly ever, rarely, seldom, almost never, never*).

D

1.8 Comparing the Simple Present and Present Progressive (page 29)

C

CORRECTION	EXPLANATION
7 ✗ I'm usually **going** to school on Monday. ✓ I usually **go** to school on Monday.	We usually describe present habits with simple present verbs (**go**), not present progressive verbs ('*m going*).
8 ✗ He **cooks** dinner right now. ✓ He **is cooking** dinner right now.	We describe things in progress now with present progressive verbs (**is cooking**), not simple present verbs (*cooks*).
9 ✗ You're always **make** fun of me. ✓ You always **make** fun of me.	For the simple present, we don't use a form of *be* ('*re*) with the main verb. We just use the main verb (**make**).
10 ✗ They **watching** TV every evening. ✓ They **watch** TV every evening.	For the simple present of most verbs, we use *they* + base form (**watch**), not the -*ing* form (*watching*).

2.2 Simple Past Statements with Regular and Irregular Verbs (page 47)

C

CORRECTION	EXPLANATION
12 ✗ He **attend**, but he **fail**. ✓ He **attended**, but he **failed**.	For the simple past of regular verbs, we add -**d** or -**ed** to the base form.
13 ✗ He **teached** me everything. ✓ He **taught** me everything.	*Teach* is an irregular verb. The simple past form is **taught**.
14 ✗ I sat and **think** for a while. ✓ I sat and **thought** for a while.	The simple past form of the verb *think* is **thought**.
15 ✗ My grandfather **dead** five years ago. ✓ My grandfather **died** five years ago.	The word *dead* is an adjective. The verb form is *die*. The simple past form is **died**.

2.3 Simple Past Negative Statements and Questions (page 52)

D

CORRECTION	EXPLANATION
12 ✗ They **don't go** shopping last weekend. ✓ They **didn't go** shopping last weekend.	We use **didn't** (not *don't*) + base form for simple past negative statements. (We use *don't* for simple present negative statements.)
13 ✗ I **no hear** the news last night. ✓ I **didn't hear** the news last night.	For simple past negative statements, we use *did* + *not* (**didn't**) + base form.
14 ✗ Who **go** with you? ✓ Who **went** with you?	When the *wh-* word is the subject, we use: ┌─────────────┐ ┌──────────────────────────┐ │ *wh-* word │ + │ past form of main verb │ └─────────────┘ └──────────────────────────┘
15 ✗ When you get there? ✓ When **did** you get there?	For *wh-* questions, we use: ┌─────────────┐ ┌──────┐ ┌─────────┐ ┌───────────┐ │ *wh-* word │ + │ *did* │ + │ subject │ + │ base form │ └─────────────┘ └──────┘ └─────────┘ └───────────┘

2.4 Simple Past of the Verb *Be* (page 56)

D

CORRECTION	EXPLANATION
17 ✗ I absent yesterday. ✓ I **was** absent yesterday.	*Absent* is an adjective. We use: `subject` + `verb be` + `adjective`

18 ✗ It was rain yesterday.
✓ It **was rainy** yesterday.
✓ It **rained** yesterday.
	Rain is a regular verb; *rainy* is an adjective. We use:
	
	`it` + `verb be` + `adjective (rainy)`
	
	or
	
	`it` + `verb (rained)`

19 ✗ Was you late again? ✓ **Were** you late again?	`Was` `I / he / she / it . . . ?` `Were` `you / we / they . . . ?`
20 ✗ Where you were last night? ✓ **Where were you** last night?	Notice the correct order of words: `wh- word` + `verb be` + `subject . . . ?`

2.6 Time Clauses with the Simple Past (page 62)

C

CORRECTION	EXPLANATION
8 ✗ After left the class, something happened. ✓ After (**I, we, everyone, the teacher,** etc.) left the class, something happened.	A clause needs a **subject** and a verb.
9 ✗ I meet her last week when I start the class. ✓ I **met** her last week when I **started** the class.	We don't use present verb forms (*meet, start*) with the time expression *last week*. The simple past forms are **met** and **started**.

10 ✗ I left, before she got there.
✓ I left before she got there.
✓ **Before she got there,** I left.
	We use a comma (,) at the end of a time clause when it comes before (not after) the main clause.
	
	no comma
	`main clause` `time clause`
	
	comma
	`time clause` `,` `main clause`

11 ✗ He gave me advice when I need it. ✓ He **gave** me advice when I **needed** it. ✓ He **gives** me advice when I **need** it.	When the main clause and the time clause refer to the same time frame, we use similar verb forms (*gave / needed*; *gives / need*).

3.5 Subject-Verb Agreement (page 95)

D

CORRECTION	EXPLANATION
11 ✗ My family help me a lot. ✓ My family **helps** me a lot. 12 ✗ My husband miss us when he is away. ✓ My husband **misses** us when he is away. 13 ✗ That person don't know my name. ✓ That person **doesn't** know my name.	The words *family*, *husband*, and *person* are singular count nouns. We use them with singular (not plural) verbs.
14 ✗ Some people in my class is never on time. ✓ Some people in my class **are** never on time.	The word *people* (a plural count noun) is the subject of the sentence. We use a plural verb (**are**) with a plural count noun.

3.6 Noun Suffixes (page 98)

C

CORRECTION	EXPLANATION
6 ✗ My happy did not continue very long. ✓ My **happiness** did not continue very long. 7 ✗ I think his lazy hurt him. ✓ I think his **laziness** hurt him. 8 ✗ The most important thing is appreciate for my parents. ✓ The most important thing is **appreciation** for my parents. 9 ✗ My parents taught me that educate is important. ✓ My parents taught me that **education** is important.	When a word functions as a noun, it's important to use the noun form of the word. adjective + suffix = noun happy + -ness = happiness lazy + -ness = laziness verb + suffix = noun appreciate + -ion = appreciation educate + -ion = education

3.9 Using No Article (Ø) (page 107)

C

CORRECTION	EXPLANATION
8 ✗ He gave me sandwich for breakfast. ✓ He gave me **sandwiches** for breakfast. ✓ He gave me **a sandwich** for breakfast.	We can use no article (Ø) before a plural count noun (*sandwiches*). We can use *a*, *an*, or *the* before a singular count noun (*sandwich*).
9 ✗ Tokyo and Kyoto are some cities in Japan. ✓ Tokyo and Kyoto are cities in Japan. 10 ✗ I learned that the friends are very important. ✓ I learned that friends are very important.	We don't use *some* or *the* when we are talking about something in general. We use no article (Ø) instead.

4.2 Subject Pronouns vs. Object Pronouns; *One and Ones* (page 123)

C

CORRECTION	EXPLANATION
10 ✗ Her father gave she a new computer. ✓ Her father gave **her** a new computer. **11** ✗ Tom talked to Lisa and I. ✓ Tom talked to Lisa and **me**.	<table><tr><td>Subject Pronouns</td><td>I / you / he / she / it / we / you / they</td></tr><tr><td>Object Pronouns</td><td>me / you / him / her / it / us / you / them</td></tr></table>
12 ✗ He saved some of his money and spent some of them. ✓ He saved some of his money and spent some of **it**. **13** ✗ We bought a lot of gifts for our friends. I hope they like it. ✓ We bought a lot of gifts for our friends. I hope they like **them**.	*Money* = a noncount noun; we use **it** to refer back to a noncount noun. *Gifts* = a plural count noun; we use **them** to refer back to a plural count noun.

4.3 Reflexive Pronouns (page 127)

C

CORRECTION	EXPLANATION
13 ✗ This society must help it self. ✓ This society must help **itself**. **14** ✗ We always make tortillas ourself. ✓ We always make tortillas **ourselves**.	The reflexive pronouns are: <table><tr><td>myself</td><td>yourself</td><td>himself</td><td>herself</td><td>itself</td></tr><tr><td>ourselves</td><td>yourselves</td><td>themselves</td><td></td><td></td></tr></table>
15 ✗ I can make a better future for me here. ✓ I can make a better future for **myself** here.	When the subject and the object are the same person, we use a reflexive pronoun (**myself**), not an object pronoun (*me*).
16 ✗ We made a plan for spending ourself money. ✓ We made a plan for spending **our** money. ✓ We made a plan for spending **the** money **ourselves**.	Before a noun (*money*), we can use a possessive determiner (**our**, *my*, *your*, etc.), not a reflexive pronoun (*ourself*). We sometimes use a reflexive pronoun at the end of a clause to give emphasis (*spending the money* **ourselves**).

4.4 Each Other and One Another (page 130)

CORRECTION	EXPLANATION
6 ✗ They had a problem each other. ✓ They had a problem with each other.	We use: `had a problem with` + `noun / pronoun`
7 ✗ They didn't like one anothers. ✓ They didn't like one another. ✓ They didn't like each other. ✓ They didn't like one another's spouses.	*One another* does not have a plural form.
8 ✗ My parents have a great relationship. They truly love themselves. ✓ They truly love each other.	**They truly love themselves** = "My mother loves herself and my father loves himself." **They truly love each other** = "My mother loves my father and my father loves my mother."

C

4.5 Indefinite Pronouns (page 133)

CORRECTION	EXPLANATION
11 ✗ I didn't see nothing. ✓ I didn't see anything. ✓ I saw nothing.	We don't normally use *nobody*, *no one*, or *nothing* in a sentence with *not*.
12 ✗ I thought everythings were free in the U.S. ✓ I thought everything was free in the U.S. ✓ I thought all things were free in the U.S. **13** ✗ Everyone want to come. ✓ Everyone wants to come. ✓ Everyone wanted to come.	Indefinite pronouns are always singular. We use a singular verb (**was**, **wants**) with them.
14 ✗ I don't want to see somebody. ✓ I don't want to see anybody. ✓ I want to see somebody.	We don't usually use *somebody*, *someone*, or *something* after *not*.

C

4.11 Measure Words (page 148)

B

CORRECTION	EXPLANATION
8 ✗ I would like two **cup** of coffee, please. ✓ I would like two **cups** of coffee, please. **9** ✗ He drank two **bottle** of milks! ✓ He drank two **bottles** of milk! **10** ✗ Can you get me three boxes of **cracker**? ✓ Can you get me three boxes of **crackers**?	We use *two* + a **plural** measure word (*cups*) + *of* + a noncount noun (*coffee / milk*) or plural count noun (*crackers*).
11 ✗ My teacher gave us bunch of **test**. ✓ My teacher gave us **a** bunch of **tests**.	We use **a** / *an* / *one* + a singular measure word (*bunch*) + *of* + a plural count noun (*tests*) or noncount noun.

5.6 Time Clauses with the Future (page 179)

C

CORRECTION	EXPLANATION
10 ✗ I'm going to start looking for a job after I **will finish** school. ✓ I'm going to start looking for a job after I **finish** school. **11** ✗ She's going to take some time off before she **is going to start** her new job. ✓ She's going to take some time off before she **starts** her new job.	We sometimes use a time clause in a sentence about the future. We use a **present form** in the time clause even though we are talking about the future.

7.3 Verb + *To-* Infinitive (page 236)

C

CORRECTION	EXPLANATION
10 ✗ They wanted to **saved** their money. ✓ They wanted to **save** their money. **11** ✗ She hopes graduate this year. ✓ She hopes **to** graduate this year.	A *to-* infinitive = *to* + the **base form** of a verb (**save**), not *to* + the simple past form (*saved*).
12 ✗ She encouraged me **about going**. ✓ She encouraged me **to go**.	We use: | *encourage*	+	object pronoun (*me*) or noun phrase	+	*to-* infinitive	
13 ✗ I expect him **no** to graduate. ✓ I expect him **not** to graduate.	To make a *to-* infinitive negative, we use **not** + *to-* infinitive.

Index

U

Underlining for titles of books, movies, etc., 83

V

Verb forms
  future, 162–169, 174–187
  modals, 169–227
  past progressive, 65–75
  present progressive, 23–30, 35–41
  simple past, 44–64, 69–75
  simple present, 4–23, 29–30
Verbs. *See also* Verb forms
  action, 30
  base form of, 7, 33
  with both active and non-active
      meaning, 30
  + gerunds, 230, R-7
  + gerunds or *to-* infinitives, 239, R-9
  helping (*See* Helping verbs)
  -ing form of, 23
  intransitive, R-6
    common, R-6
    multi-word, R-7
  irregular, R-3 (*See also* Irregular
      verbs)
  linking (*See* Linking verbs)
  modals (*See* Modals)
  multi-word, 39
  non-action, 4, 30, 178, R-2
  + prepositions + followed by
      gerunds, R-8
  regular (*See* Regular verbs)
  spelling rules
    for *-ed* form of, 50, R-5
    for *-ing* form of, 24, R-4
    for *-s/-es*, 8, 87, R-4
  + *to-* infinitives, 236, R-9
  transitive, R-5
    common, R-5
    multi-word, R-6

W

Warnings with *had better,* 211, 227
Was/were, 56, 65, 75
When, 65
  in past time clauses, 65
While in past time clauses, 65
Wh- questions. *See under* Questions
Will
  vs. *be going to*, 162, 163, 164, 165, 168
  as future form, 169–174, 179–187
      (*See also* Future forms)
  for offers, 197, 227
  for predictions, 169, 187
  for promises, 169
  for requests, 201, 227

Would
  for desires, offers, and invitations,
      204, 227
    would like/would you like, 204, 227
  for requests, 201, 227
    would you mind, 201
  would prefer/would rather for
      preference, 209, 227
Writing
  cohesion in, 155
  connecting ideas in, 71
  descriptions in, 38
  first-person accounts in, 155
  future forms in, 184
  gerunds and *to-* infinitives in, 247
  imperatives in, 38
  instructions in, 38, 105
  modals in, 224
  parallelism in, 247
  past forms in, 71
  plural nouns in, 87
  present forms in, 8
  pronouns and determiners in, 155
  sentence variety in, 71, 98
  summaries, 38
  using first, second, and third person
      in, 155

Y

Yes/no questions. *See under* Questions
You as subject of imperatives, 33

Z

Zero article, 107

ELEMENTS *of* SUCCESS
Online Practice

How to Register for Elements of Success Online Practice

Follow these steps to register for *Elements of Success Online Practice*:

1. Go to www.elementsofsuccessonline.com and click

2. Read and agree to the terms of use.

3. Enter the Access Code that came with your Student Book. Your code is written on the inside back cover of your book.

4. Enter your personal information (first and last name, email address, and password).

5. Click the Elements of Success 2 Student Book.

> It is very important to select the Elements of Success 2 book. Please click the **GREEN** Elements of Success 2 cover.

   If you don't know which book to select, **STOP**. Continue when you know the book cover to click.

6. Enter your class ID to join your class, and click NEXT. Your class ID is on the line below, or your teacher will give it to you on a different piece of paper.

   _____

   You don't need a class ID code. If you do not have a class ID code, click Skip. To enter this code later, choose Join a Class from your Home page.

7. Once you're done, click Activities to begin using *Elements of Success Online Practice*.

Next time you want to use *Elements of Success Online Practice*, just go to www.elementsofsuccessonline.com and log in with your email address and password.